KU-527-207

WORKING WITH ,
Aggressive
YOUTH

Also from the Boys Town Press

Teaching Social Skills to Youth, 2nd Ed.

Teaching Social Skills to Youth with Mental Health Disorders

Skills for Families, Skills for Life, 2nd Ed.

Great Days Ahead: Parenting Children Who Have ADHD with Hope and Confidence

The Well-Managed Classroom

Safe and Healthy Secondary Schools

Tools for Teaching Social Skills in School

More Tools for Teaching Social Skills in School

Common Sense Parenting®, 3rd Ed.

Help! There's a Toddler in the House!

Common Sense Parenting of Toddlers and Preschoolers

Common Sense Parenting Learn-at-Home DVD Kit

Common Sense Parenting DVDs:

    Building Relationships

    Teaching Children Self-Control

    Correcting Misbehavior

    Preventing Problem Behavior

    Teaching Kids to Make Good Decisions

    Helping Kids Succeed in School

Parenting to Build Character in Your Teen

Adolescence and Other Temporary Mental Disorders (DVD)

Changing Children's Behavior by Changing the People,
    Places and Activities in Their Lives

Good Night, Sweet Dreams, I Love You: Now Get into Bed and Go to Sleep

Competing with Character®

There Are No Simple Rules for Dating My Daughter

Who's Raising Your Child?

No Room for Bullies

Dealing with Your Kids' 7 Biggest Troubles

Practical Tools for Foster Parents

For Adolescents

Guys, Let's Keep It Real

Little Sisters, Listen Up

Boundaries: A Guide for Teens

A Good Friend

Who's in the Mirror?

What's Right for Me?

**For a Boys Town Press catalog, visit BoysTownPress.org
or call 1-800-282-6657.**

Boys Town National Hotline
1-800-448-3000
A crisis, resource and referral number for kids and parents.

WITHDRAWN FROM STOCK

WORKING WITH
Aggressive
YOUTH

Positive Strategies to Teach Self-Control and Prevent Violence

LIMERICK
0069 2514
COUNTY LIBRARY

Daniel L. Daly, Ph.D.
with Michael N. Sterba, M.H.D.

BOYS TOWN
Press

Boys Town, Nebraska

Working with Aggressive Youth

Published by the Boys Town Press
14100 Crawford St.
Boys Town, NE 68010

Copyright © 2011 Father Flanagan's Boys' Home

ISBN: 978-1-934490-15-0

All rights reserved under International and Pan-American Copyright Conventions. Permission is granted to make hard copies of the skill sheets on the included CD-ROM for professional purposes. No other part of this book may be reproduced, stored in a retrieval system, or transmitted in any form or by any means, electronic, mechanical, photocopying, recording or otherwise, without express written permission of the publisher, except for brief quotations or critical reviews. For information address the Boys Town Press, 14100 Crawford St., Boys Town, NE 68010 or btpress@BoysTown.org.

Boys Town Press is the publishing division of Boys Town, a national organization serving children and families.

Publisher's Cataloging in Publication

Daly, Daniel L.

Working with aggressive youth : positive strategies to teach self-control and prevent violence / Daniel L. Daly ; with Michael N. Sterba. -- Boys Town, Neb. : Boys Town Press, c2011.

p. ; cm.

ISBN: 978-1-934490-15-0
Includes bibliographical references and index.

1. Behavior therapy for teenagers. 2. Behavior therapy for children. 3. Aggressiveness in adolescence--Treatment. 4. Aggressiveness in children--Treatment. 5. Child psycopathology--Treatment. 6. Adolescent psychopathology--Treatment. 7. Adolescent psychotherapy. 8. Child psychotherapy. 9. Social skills in children--Study and teaching. 10. Social skills in adolescence--Study and teaching. I. Sterba, Michael. II. Title.

RJ506.V56 D35 2011
618.92/89142--dc22   1108

10 9 8 7 6 5 4 3 2 1

Dedication

To the five men, all Roman Catholic priests, who have provided the leadership and guidance over Boys Town's ninety-four years of existence: Father Edward J. Flanagan, who founded Boys Town and became the progenitor of all the ideas that have lead us to this point; Monsignor Nicholas Wegner, who continued Father Flanagan's youth-service goals and mission and who, through his financial genius, helped Boys Town become a financially sustainable organization; Monsignor Robert Hupp, who had the wisdom and foresight to bring a more science-based approach to Boys Town following the cultural changes of the late 1960s and early 1970s; Father Val J. Peter, who took Boys Town from being a potent and extremely important organization that effected policy in the center of the country in Nebraska to one that not only effected national policy but also serves children in multiple locations throughout the country; and Father Steven Boes, who took the Boys Town concept and grew it asymptotically in his first five years from serving more than eight thousand children to more than twenty-four thousand today. Without the planning and foresight of these five men, hundreds of thousands of children would not have been helped and Boys Town would not be the vibrant, cutting-edge organization it is today.

Finally, to the children and families Boys Town serves whose desire to live better, fuller lives and find a spirituality that Father Flanagan believed should exist in all human interactions: You have been a constant stimulus for this organization to grow and improve so we can walk with you on your journey to healing and hope.

Acknowledgments

This book would not have been possible without the dedicated and ongoing efforts of many people. We surveyed and interviewed the following Boys Town content experts: Dr. Pat Friman, Dr. Ron Thompson, Dr. Jon Huefner, Dr. Tom Riemers, Lisa Batenhorst, Peg Reit, Amy Simpson, Deb Orduna, Julie Almquist, Kim Haugen, Gary Feller, Lana Temple-Plotz, Chris O'Brien, Paula Jones, Cathy DeSalvo, and Tanya Wright. These people gave us our broad-based focus on how we are dealing with aggressive youth in our schools, Behavioral Health Clinic, Treatment Family Homes[SM], IRTC[SM], and In-Home Family Services[SM] across the country. Thank you for your time and expertise.

We would also like to thank the staff at the Boys Town Press[SM] and others involved in the production of Boys Town products and materials for their dedication, commitment, and support.

The stimulus for this book came from Laura Tatten who wanted the most current version of Boys Town's expertise in dealing with aggressive and violent youth. She felt the parents and caretakers in our communities needed our latest version.

Table of Contents

Introduction

An **EIGHT-YEAR-OLD BOY** *snatches a basketball away from a classmate during recess. When a teacher asks him to give the ball back, the boy glares at the teacher, turns his body and the ball away, and yells, "I want it! It's mine! Leave me alone, you idiot!" He sits on the ground clutching the ball and glowers at his teacher and classmate.*

A **GROUP OF THIRTEEN-YEAR-OLD GIRLS** *are gathered in a circle at the lobby of a theater talking and laughing about the movie they just saw. Another girl from the neighborhood approaches the group and says, "That movie was great! Did you guys like it?" One of the girls in the group frowns, rolls her eyes, and shakes her head "No" to the others. No one in the group looks at the girl or responds to her question; they all start talking and laughing to each other again while slowly walking away.*

A **TEN-YEAR-OLD BOY** *at a long-term residential program loses his privileges because of poor grades and school misconduct. After dinner, the boy asks to go play basketball outside. When staff tell him "No," that he has extra study time to get caught up with homework, the boy starts crying and shouts, "If I can't go, I'm gonna kick your a–!" When the staff member asks the boy to calm down, he knocks over a lamp, picks it up, and hurls it at the staff member.*

A **FIFTEEN-YEAR-OLD GIRL** *visits a social networking site on the Internet and posts insulting and vulgar comments about another female classmate. Later, the girl persuades other kids from school to help her create an online group dedicated to calling the female classmate names and spreading nasty rumors about her. Over time, as the ruthless name-calling and gossip continue to appear on the Internet and in text* *messages, the classmate becomes despondent and depressed and tries to hurt herself.*

A **FOURTEEN-YEAR-OLD BOY** *threatens to shoot and kill another student who harassed and physically assaulted the boy the previous day. A teacher is tipped off about the boy's threats by other students and the police are called. They search the boy's locker and backpack and confiscate a loaded handgun. The student is arrested and transported to a juvenile detention facility.*

It's troubling to witness incidents and read stories like these and see youngsters turning to aggressive and violent acts as ways to deal with and solve their problems. But these kinds of cruel behaviors and offensive actions are occurring every day in homes, neighborhoods, schools, and cities all over the United States. Understanding and dealing with aggression and violence in children and adolescents is a difficult and complex issue. Yet, it is a problem that must be addressed and corrected if youngsters are to learn to peacefully coexist with others in society and ultimately lead happy and successful lives.

Many current trends are being blamed for today's occurrences of youth aggression and violence. Some people cite the soaring divorce rate and single-parent homes; others say youth have become desensitized to aggression and violence by what they see in the movies, on television, and in video games. The glamorization of brutal behavior that dominates certain music lyrics and videos also is seen as a culprit. Still others argue that the availability of weapons like knives and guns, or the use and abuse of drugs and alcohol have led to horrific incidents of aggressive and violent acts by children and teens.

Separately, none of these factors is probably the root cause of aggression and violence. However, it is possible that a compilation of these factors strongly influences youth who already have a propensity to use aggression as a way of coping with life's obstacles. A youth's aggressive and violent tendencies can be fueled and validated by all these influences. In other words, these kids may be getting the message that it's okay to lash out in mean, hurtful, and destructive ways.

Biology (neurotransmitters and genetics) and psychosocial processes (thoughts and feelings) often have a direct impact on a youngster's aggression problem, and they can play a crucial role in a child's treatment. However, Boys Town also believes that most youth who choose aggression and violence have learned or been taught, often unwittingly, to use these kinds of abusive behaviors by others in their environment (parents, other adults,

2

caregivers, siblings, friends, etc.). They learn that aggression and violence are options for solving problems from seeing others who are influential in their lives frequently use these behaviors. Most of these same aggressive and violent youngsters haven't had the opportunity to learn more positive ways of coping with and solving disagreements they have with others. These kids just don't know any other way to handle the difficult, frustrating, or upsetting situations that inevitably arise.

Boys Town knows these kids well. Our professionally trained staff have worked with and helped thousands of aggressive and violent youth in a variety of settings. As a result, Boys Town has designed and developed some excellent strategies that can help reduce aggression. These strategies are at the heart of the Boys Town Model^{SM}, a model that teaches children and adolescents self-control and is extremely effective with aggressive youngsters.

Many youth have long histories of using aggressive behavior. Aggressive kids have learned that bullying and intimidating others or viciously lashing out when things aren't going their way is an effective method of getting what they want. Over time, these behaviors become deeply ingrained in the way these youth interact with others.

Boys Town believes that one very important component in helping children and teens overcome their aggression problems is teaching prosocial skills and behaviors that can take the place of the aggressive behaviors that have been used in the past. In addition, these same youngsters may have a certain biological condition that requires medication, or have faulty psychosocial processes that need to be corrected. Possibly expanding treatment to include all three areas not only can reduce aggression but also allow youngsters to get their needs met in a more socially acceptable manner.

Boys Town knows kids can change. We've seen it happen time and again with youngsters whom others have given up on. Throughout Boys Town's long history, many youth – including aggressive and violent kids – have learned to cope with and respond to anger, frustration, disappointment, and other unpleasant feelings in new, appropriate ways that enable them to lead happy, productive lives.

The goal of this book is to better equip caregivers with interventions, treatment options, and Treatment Plans for teaching aggressive youth how to replace unhealthy, antisocial, and destructive ways of behaving with ways that are healthy, socially acceptable, and safe. It provides a clear picture of aggression, and offers some practical, effective short- and long-term ideas and strategies for defusing aggression in youth. This approach can be used by any adult – teachers, school counselors, social workers, probation officers, psychologists, foster parents, child-care staff and administrators, and other youth care professionals – responsible for shaping children's lives.

What Is in This Book?

There are three parts to this book. In the first part, Chapters 1 and 2 define what aggression is (and what it is not) and introduce and discuss two different types of aggression and how to identify each one. In addition, there is an exploration of some of the most respected and current theories about why kids become aggressive, along with the importance of understanding these reasons. Some of Boys Town's own studies will be introduced to provide insight into aggression in youth.

The second part of this book includes Chapters 3 through 8. These chapters contain a description and explanation of how to deal with aggressive behavior through the approach and proven teaching methods developed at Boys Town and incorporated into the Boys Town Model℠. There will be an explanation of each teaching method and how it helps to bring about change in a child's behavior. These methods meet a wide range of needs, from teaching skills before they will be used to correcting misbehavior to praising positive behavior. Also presented is research data that show that kids – including aggressive kids – who receive treatment that is based on the Boys Town Model get better.

Chapters 9 through 12 form the third part of this book. Here, there is a discussion of treatment planning and the various treatment strategies that can be utilized to help children and adolescents reduce aggressive behaviors. Sample Treatment Plans from a variety of settings will be presented to help caregivers see how intervention strategies can be developed for aggressive youth and used in different environments. Also, there is a social skills chart that can be used as an easy reference guide for caregivers as they teach new, prosocial skills to replace old, aggressive behaviors. This chart not only lists skills, but also shows which skills work best with specific types of aggressive behaviors.

We hope you find this book useful in your work with children and adolescents. Aggression in youngsters is an extremely troubling and complex issue in today's society, especially for those caring adults who take on this problem every day. Helping a child overcome his or her aggressive behaviors requires patience, vigilance, knowledge, and experience. Our desire is to provide some sound and useful strategies for developing clear and effective treatment interventions that can help you lead troubled youth back to the path of success.

"Our young people are our greatest asset. Give them a chance and they will make a good account of themselves."

– Father Edward J. Flanagan, Founder of Boys Town

An Overview of Aggression

Aggression, like a chameleon, often takes on a different appearance to different people. A child's behavior that one person considers harmless may be seen as a sign of serious problems by someone else. That is why it is imperative that caregivers adopt a standard definition for aggression as they learn new ways of dealing with children and youth who display aggressive behaviors. An accurate definition and a solid understanding of what aggression is (and what it is not) are absolutely necessary before effective Treatment Plans can be developed.

Aggression takes different forms and is defined as "...intentional behaviors that may cause psychological or physical harm to others. Aggression includes physical (e.g., hitting, pushing, or scratching), verbal (name-calling, teasing, or threatening), and relational (isolating a peer on purpose or passing negative or untruthful rumors) behaviors. A relatively new form of aggression is cyberbullying...," where kids use electronic means (the Internet, emails, text messages, phones, etc.) to attack peers (Horne, Raczynski, & Orpinas, 2008). In addition, aggression can take the form of overt and covert behaviors (Patterson, Shaw, Snyder, & Yoerger, 2005). This is a good definition of aggression because it goes to the heart of the most negative aspect of aggressive behavior – hurting others.

Obviously, many behaviors can fall within this definition: arguing, fighting, taking something from someone, calling others names, pushing and shoving, hitting, kicking, showing disrespect, and making fun of others. And all kids engage in these and other negative behaviors as part of normal development. Aggression becomes a serious problem, however, when a pattern of such behaviors develops and a youngster routinely uses aggressive behaviors to get his or her needs met, or when the intensity or severity of these behaviors increases. Then, caregivers must act quickly to prevent these behaviors from getting worse or becoming ingrained in a youth's personality.

Aggression is a complex and difficult problem. There are no easy answers that can make aggressive and violent behavior magically disappear from a youngster's life. Helping youngsters overcome their aggression problem requires hard work, tenacity, and creativity from caregivers.

The earlier adults recognize that children are turning to aggression and intervene, the more likely it is that these youth can learn positive ways to interact with others and get what they want. The hope for aggressive children lies in the ability of caregivers to recognize and acknowledge that youth are developing aggressive habits, and to take action in a positive, effective manner. Steering kids away from aggression and back to a path that can lead them to success at home, in school, on the job, and in life, is the only option.

Aggression doesn't occur in a vacuum; many factors can affect how a child behaves in different situations (e.g., the child's relationship with a person he or she is interacting with, how badly a child wants something, a problem at home or school that a caregiver is unaware of, how a youngster slept the previous night, etc.). Some days there are no signs of aggressive behavior and you see only a charming, loving child. Many days, you might deal with less-severe or covert forms of aggression. On other days – more than you care to experience – aggressive behaviors might dominate the child's personality. Understanding and effectively dealing with the day-to-day occurrences of less-severe aggressive behaviors like noncompliance, teasing, whining, and scolding before they escalate to hitting, kicking, vandalism, and in extreme cases, serious physical assault, is one of the important ways of helping children learn self-control skills and other positive alternative behaviors.

In recent years, it seems that the most severe forms of aggressive behaviors – assault, rape, murder – are occurring with greater frequency. However, not all aggressive kids commit these types of vicious and extreme acts of violence. Aggression comes in many different shapes and sizes. The majority of aggressive youth engage in much more subtle forms of aggressive behavior. For example, a daughter might whine and complain every time her parents ask her to clean up her messy room in order to get out of doing the task. Or a male student might glare at a teacher while she is criticizing his poorly done assignment, hoping to intimidate her so she won't have him redo it.

These types of lower-level aggressive behaviors are harder to detect and many times are overlooked and ignored. The danger here is that, left unattended, these behaviors are reinforced and can actually escalate over time. Recognizing and treating aggression at its lowest levels can prevent kids from resorting to more severe forms of aggression, including physical assault and other acts of violent behavior.

This chapter will discuss the five levels of severity in aggression – from subtle and covert behaviors to overt, violent acts – and provide some examples of behaviors at each level.

There also will be a detailed explanation of proactive and reactive aggression. Understanding and identifying the behaviors that make up these two distinctly different types of aggression enables caregivers to develop appropriate intervention strategies. And, there will be a discussion of bullying, a common and frustrating problem for kids of all ages.

Anger and assertiveness are often mistaken for aggression. To give parents and caregivers a clearer picture of aggression, a short discussion, along with examples, is included to help clarify this misconception. Key issues in the development of aggression and violence in youth will be explored so that you can have a richer, comprehensive picture of aggression.

To begin, let's take a look at the prevalence of aggression among today's young people.

Scope of the Problem

Unfortunately, aggressive and violent behavior is all too common among today's youngsters, and a major problem for society. The U.S. Office of the Surgeon General states that "public health studies show that youth violence is an ongoing, startling pervasive problem" (U.S. Department of Health and Human Services, 2001), and that "there is considerable evidence that youth involvement in serious forms of violent behavior is quite stable over time and remains a serious national problem" (U.S. Department of Health and Human Services, 2007).

A good way to assess and measure the youth aggression and violence problem is to look at data from organizations dedicated to gathering information about its magnitude, causes, and prevention. These organizations provide valuable statistics and other data for those who work to develop effective prevention and intervention strategies. The following information – the most recent data available is from 2007 – helps to define the scope of the nation's youth aggression and violence problem:

> More than one in three high school students reported being in a physical fight (Centers for Disease Control and Prevention, 2009).

> The National Center for Education Statistics reports that thirty-two percent of students ages twelve to eighteen reported having been bullied at school during the school year and four percent reported having been cyber-bullied. Twenty-one percent of students ages twelve to eighteen said they had experienced bullying that consisted of being made fun of; eighteen percent reported being the subject of rumors; eleven percent said that they were pushed, shoved, tripped, or spit on; six percent said they were threatened with harm; five percent said they were excluded from activities on purpose; and four percent said that someone tried to make them do things they did not want to do and that their property was destroyed on purpose (Dinkes, Kemp, & Baum, 2009).

> More than 668,000 young people ages ten to twenty-four were treated in emergency departments for injuries sustained in violence (Centers for Disease Control and Prevention, 2009).

> According to the Office of Juvenile Justice and Delinquency Prevention (OJJDP), juveniles accounted for sixteen percent of all violent crime arrests (e.g., aggravated assault, robbery, gang, fights, or rape) and twenty-six percent of all property crime arrests (Puzzanchera, 2009).

These data clearly show that far too many youngsters are involved in acts of delinquency that include aggressive and violent behavior. Turning to anger, aggression, and violence as a way of coping with life's challenges can deal a devastating blow to a child's efforts to become a productive and valued member of society. Children who learn and adopt these behaviors have trouble making and keeping friends, and their relationships with parents and siblings can be damaged or destroyed. Adults label them as "troublemakers" or "dangerous" or "delinquents," and eventually, well-intentioned people (teachers, coaches, counselors, youth group leaders) who want to help, stop trying as frustration and despair set in. Instead, they turn their attention to kids who want to learn and grow. Ultimately, children who choose aggression and violence fail in school, on the playground, in the neighborhood, and at home.

Left unchecked, these harmful behaviors become more polished and carry over into adulthood where they can result in more insidious aggressive acts. Spousal and child abuse, drug and alcohol abuse and dependency, robbery, and assaultive criminal activity become the norm, destroying the prospects of having a good job, a happy marriage, and a loving family.

Five Levels of Severity in Aggression

Aggression can develop along a continuum and vary in degrees. The behaviors along this continuum are diverse and become drastically more harsh as youth move from lower-level behaviors like noncompliance and yelling to higher levels like assault and murder. However, the common factor that binds all these aggressive behaviors together is the end result: Kids get their way or get their needs met.

Knowledge of the wide variety of behaviors that make up aggression enables caregivers to assess the seriousness of a child's problem. This is the first – and perhaps the most important – step in developing appropriate and effective treatment strategies for troubled youngsters.

By studying the extensive research of others and through many years of experience working with thousands of aggressive and violent children and adolescents, Boys Town has identified five levels of aggression. *(See Figure 1.)*

These five levels range in extremes from covert and low-level behaviors like noncompliance, ignoring or excluding others, alliance building, crying, whining, and teasing (Level I – noncompliance and/or making threatening statements or gestures) to the highest level, which involves overt acts of violence like physical assault, rape, and murder (Level V – using violence toward people, with the potential for causing serious injury or death). Movement along the continuum – from Level I to Level V – is characterized by an increase in the intensity and severity of the aggressive behaviors being displayed. For instance, the behaviors included in Level III (harming or killing animals) are more serious and severe than those that make up Level II (causing property damage).

(Keep in mind that Figure 1 contains examples of just a few of the behaviors in each level and is not an all-inclusive list – or a strict hierarchy – of aggressive and violent behavior. These examples are offered as a general description of the kinds of aggressive and violent behaviors that characterize each level.)

This same type of continuum also applies to the aggressive behaviors within each level. For example, Level I (noncompliance and/or making threatening statements or gestures) behaviors like yelling or cursing – although extremely inappropriate – are not as serious or severe as making verbal threats to others or self.

....

Figure 1

Five Levels of Severity in Aggression

LEVEL I – *Noncompliance and/or Making Threatening Statements or Gestures*

A youngster regularly responds with subtle forms of aggression and/or verbal and nonverbal threats.

Examples (Noncompliance):

- Youth repeatedly refuses to do what a parent, teacher, or other authority figure asks

- Whining and crying

- Sarcastic responses – youth responds with a voice tone that conveys the message, "Don't bug me"

- Criticism – youth responds with verbal or nonverbal negative criticism of another person's behavior or characteristics

- Teasing

- Ignoring or excluding others

- Alliance building

Examples (Threats):

- Using demanding statements ("Make me something to eat!")

- Repetitive verbal or nonverbal behavior that is intended to annoy (e.g., repeatedly pounding a fist on a table)

- Staring and glaring

- Clenching a fist or both fists

- Cursing and yelling

- Malicious gossip or rumor spreading

- Ultimatums ("If I can't go to the movie, I'm gonna kick your a--!")

- Invading someone's personal space

- Physically aggressive posturing (towering over a person in a threatening manner)

- Verbally threatening another person or self

- Cyber-bullying

LEVEL II – *Causing Property Damage*

A youngster frequently responds with actions that damage property.

Examples:

- Throwing objects

- Punching or kicking stationary objects (punching or kicking a hole through a wall)

- Vandalism

- Stealing

- Fire-setting

- Arson

....

LEVEL III – *Harming or Killing Animals*

A youngster frequently is cruel to animals, or tortures or kills them.

Examples:

- Hitting or kicking an animal
- Poisoning an animal
- Stabbing or shooting an animal
- Torturing an animal
- Setting an animal on fire

LEVEL IV – *Physically Harming Others or Self*

A youngster consistently responds with a behavior that physically hurts others or self, but does not produce long-lasting or permanent physical or psychological damage.

Examples:

- Poking a finger in someone's chest
- Pushing or shoving
- Pushing, throwing, or kicking objects at others
- Wrestling
- Punching
- Fighting
- Attempting to hurt self (carving in own skin)

LEVEL V – *Using Violence toward People, with the Potential for Causing Serious Injury or Death*

A youngster responds with a behavior that physically hurts others or self and produces long-lasting or permanent physical or psychological damage.

Examples:

- Stalking
- Bomb threats
- Terrorism
- Aggravated assault
- Rape
- Suicide
- Murder

Some children and teens who advance to the highest level of aggressive behaviors – Level V – do so in a sequential fashion, moving from one behavior to the next within a level, and then from one level to the next. Other kids, however, might suddenly move from using Level I aggressive behaviors like whining and teasing to a Level V act like assault or rape or murder. With these kids, there can be few or no warning signs or clues that a youth is about to act in a highly aggressive or violent manner.

It is very important to remember that every child is different and each child's situation is unique. So – in the absence of any intervention – how slowly or quickly youth move from one level to the next (or from one aggressive behavior to the next within a level) is highly individualized and depends on many factors in a child's life. The five levels are simply guidelines, an assessment tool that helps you to more competently and accurately gauge the seriousness of a youth's aggression problem. This assessment will help you determine what course of action to take. The levels should not be used to label youngsters or to indicate that they are beyond help.

Many of you reading this book are probably caring for a youth (or a population of youngsters) who is displaying aggressive behaviors at the higher levels. This makes dealing with the youngster's severe behaviors more difficult and frustrating. Hang in there! There is hope; these youth can be helped. It is important for you to realize that the first step in reducing aggression in youngsters is developing the ability to accurately recognize and evaluate the seriousness of a child's aggression problem. This gives you a place to start – a baseline – that can help you as you initially develop a plan for effective treatment, and later assess whether intervention strategies are working or need adjustment.

What Aggression Is Not: Anger and Assertiveness

The five levels of severity in aggression provide a strong foundation for understanding what aggressive behavior is, and the wide range of behaviors that make up aggression. However, it is equally important for caregivers to recognize that there are certain behaviors and instances that may on the surface appear to be aggressive, but in reality are not. Anger and assertiveness fall into this category.

Knowing what aggression is not enables caregivers to distinguish between appropriate – even prosocial – behavior that should be praised and reinforced, and harmful, aggressive behavior that requires intervention. For example, a youth who "takes the bull by the horns" to accomplish a goal might be seen as being aggressive when, in fact, he or she is actually showing self-reliance, independence, and assertiveness. Knowledge of these differences will have a tremendous impact on how you deal with a youngster's behavior and the treatment strategies you develop and use with youth.

This section will discuss how anger and assertiveness are sometimes mistaken for aggression, and the factors that determine when anger and assertiveness cross over the line into aggression.

Aggression and Anger

JASON, *a ten-year-old boy, walks into his bedroom and finds his prized baseball card collection strewn about the floor. Several cards are ripped and others have been smudged with a permanent marker.*

Mary, Jason's three-year-old stepsister, is standing with her back to Jason, coloring on one of Jason's favorite posters. Jason yells at Mary to stop; she drops the marker and runs out of the room. Instead of chasing after her, Jason stomps downstairs sobbing, and loudly tells his stepmother what happened. After talking with his stepmother for a few minutes, Jason is able to calm down. They agree that the ruined cards and poster will be replaced.

THIRTEEN-YEAR-OLD *Tonya gets braces for her teeth. When she arrives at school the next day, she waits for someone to call her names or tell her how stupid and ugly she looks; she is ready to show everyone what happens if they "mess" with her. Few kids say anything. All the students know that Tonya might lash out at them, as she has many times in the past.*

At lunch, Tommy, a new student, sits across from Tonya at a table. On a dare from some of the boys he wants to impress, Tommy takes a piece of tin foil from his lunch sack, puts it on his teeth, and flashes a huge grin at Tonya.

Tonya shouts, "Stop it you a-----!" Suddenly, she picks up her lunch tray and throws it at Tommy, hitting him in the head. Then she climbs over the table and grabs Tommy's hair, trying to pull it out in clumps. Within seconds, both kids fall to the floor, where Tonya starts to punch, kick, and bite Tommy. It takes three teachers to pull Tonya off Tommy, who ends up with a cut on his cheek, a swollen eye, and a bite mark on his forearm that requires stitches. As a result of the melee, Tonya is expelled from school; the fight is the last straw in a long list of incidents where Tonya directed aggressive and violent behavior toward classmates and staff.

Anger is a feeling that all youngsters commonly experience during childhood and adolescence. Anger can be justified or unjustified. An example of justified anger would be a youngster who becomes angry when she finds out a friend lied to her. Unjustified anger is illustrated by a child who gets mad when told he can't have a piece of cake before dinner.

In the examples with Jason and Tonya, both kids were justified in feeling angry. Most youngsters would be mad if a special possession was destroyed or if someone teased and made fun of them. However, what sets these two youngsters apart is how they react and behave when they feel angry.

Jason's actions following his initial feelings of anger were appropriate, socially acceptable, and healthy ways for a ten-year-old to deal with what his sister did. The end result was that there were no serious aggressive behaviors, no one was hurt, and Jason was able to get his needs met by talking with his stepmother. Even though Jason was mad, he was still able to make a good decision to get an adult involved. In fact, Jason should receive a pat on the back from his stepmother for handling a potentially volatile situation in a constructive way. This would reinforce Jason's pro-social response and increase the likelihood that he will react the same way when he gets mad in the future.

On the other hand, Tonya's feelings of anger resulted in dangerous, antisocial, and violent behaviors. Her way of reacting to situations when she gets mad is to strike out in destructive and harmful ways. This results in many negative consequences, the most obvious being her expulsion from school. Other consequences might include alienation from friends and teachers, and relationship problems with siblings and parents at home. Obviously, Tonya's use of high-level aggressive and violent behaviors when she is angry warrants immediate professional intervention.

Many kids have learned how to control their anger or express it appropriately; others have not, and respond with aggressive behaviors. These are the kids who require intervention and help in learning new, more appropriate ways of handling situations where they become angry.

Whether anger is justified or not, youngsters must learn how to control their feelings and the behaviors they use to express them. Caregivers can help kids learn to do this is by teaching them not to get angry when things don't go their way or they don't get what they want and, when they do get angry, how to respond in more appropriate, healthier ways. When kids learn that they can control negative thoughts and feelings, they will be better able to control negative behaviors.

Aggression and Assertiveness

JANICE *is a fifteen-year-old student who earns excellent grades in all her classes. Her goal is to receive all "A's" during high school so she can earn a college scholarship. But, Janice's teachers and classmates don't like her very much because she's so obnoxious.*

Janice constantly bombards her teachers with mundane or irrelevant questions, or verbally challenges them on everything from simple class rules to grades she receives on assignments and tests. This always happens during class time and takes a lot of teaching time and attention away from the other students. Janice's teachers have asked her to come to them after class with questions and other issues, but Janice ignores their requests – she demands answers right then and there.

Janice's classmates are frustrated because she dominates the teacher's time. Once assignments and tests are handed back, Janice pesters other students about what grade they received, and constantly boasts about her high marks.

ELEVEN-YEAR-OLD MARK *just moved into a new house with his foster parents and is trying to make friends with other kids in the neighborhood. For the last two weeks, Paul, the neighborhood bully has been "hassling" Mark whenever they are together with a group of kids from the area. Paul teases Mark about his thick glasses and constantly puts Mark down in front of others by calling him a "nerd" and "loser."*

When Paul isn't around, Mark gets along with almost all of the neighborhood kids. But when Paul is present, many of the other kids laugh at Paul's remarks and join in the teasing.

Mark finally decides to do something about Paul's continual harassment. One day after school, Mark goes over to Paul's house and asks Paul to stop making fun of him. At first, Paul laughs at Mark's request and tells him to "get lost." Mark is nervous and intimidated, but he calmly tells Paul that if the teasing doesn't stop right away, he will get their parents involved. Paul, afraid of what his mother might do, reluctantly agrees to leave Mark alone.

Assertiveness is defined by Lange and Jakubowski (1976) as "... standing up for personal rights and expressing thoughts, feelings, and beliefs in *direct, honest,* and *appropriate* ways which do not violate another person's rights." This definition – which has remained constant over time – also applies to a situation where a person stands up for or defends another person (when an older youth teases a younger child, another youngster steps in and asks the older youth to stop).

An integral part of assertiveness is respect. More specifically, this involves respect for one's own needs and rights and for the needs and rights of others. Assertiveness is not simply a way to get what one wants – it is a two-way street where the needs and rights of everyone involved are important.

Given the examples with Janice and Mark, many caregivers would maintain that both kids are being assertive because they are getting their needs met without harming anyone. However, there are significant differences in how each youth goes about solving the problems they have with others.

On the surface, Janice appears to be acting assertively; she is standing up for her rights and expressing her thoughts, feelings, and beliefs in direct and honest ways. But, she is not doing so in the appropriate manner that her teachers requested. In addition, Janice is violating the rights of her classmates because she ignores their need for help, attention, and instruction from the teacher. In fact, much of her behavior could be considered low-level forms of aggression (noncompliance, teasing, demanding statements, etc.) that require correction from her teachers and parents.

On the other hand, Mark demonstrates assertive behavior in resolving his issues with Paul, the neighborhood bully. He stands up for his rights and needs in a direct, honest, and appropriate way while also respecting Paul's rights and needs. How? Instead of asking Paul in front of the other kids to stop making fun of him, Mark goes to Paul's house to meet with him alone. This allows Paul to save face and avoid any embarrassment in front of his peers. Mark also gives Paul an opportunity to change his behavior by talking about getting their parents involved instead of simply telling the parents. Mark's assertive approach contributes to a favorable outcome. Lange and Jakubowski (1976) state that "...a by-product of responsible assertion is that people often do get what they want. Why? Because most people become cooperative when they are approached in a way which is both respectful of self and respectful of others."

Many times a youngster's behavior may appear assertive when it is actually inappropriate, or in some cases, aggressive. Again, the key question in determining whether a youth's behavior is assertive involves appropriate behavior and respecting rights: Is the youngster standing up for his or her rights and needs (or the rights and needs of another person) in honest and appropriate ways that also respect the rights of others? If the answer is "Yes," then the child is being assertive. If the answer is "No," then intervention is required to help the youth learn more responsible and acceptable ways of getting his or her needs met.

Reactive Aggression and Proactive Aggression

DURING *the last three years, fourteen-year-old Travon has been arrested for shoplifting clothes and shoes at an athletic apparel store, vandalizing the house of a girl who refused to be his girlfriend, trespassing on school property, and stealing an expensive mountain bike from another youth at the local mall. At school, Travon is considered a troublemaker and a behavior problem; many of his afternoons are spent in after-school detention – if he shows up. He constantly makes excuses and tries to sweet-talk his way out of detention and other negative consequences. When that doesn't work, he often gets angry and challenges his teachers. As a result, many of Travon's teachers let him off the hook and dismiss any consequences because they don't want to deal with his temper tantrums.*

Big for his age, Travon is taller and stronger than his classmates. Most students are afraid of him, and he uses his physical superiority to intimidate others, which allows him to get what he wants. Travon teases his fellow classmates, threatens them, dominates them, laughs at them, and always seems to be fighting. The only friends he has are older boys who also are labeled as "troublemakers" and "bullies" by teachers and parents.

Travon uses these same aggressive behaviors at home to get out of doing chores, homework, or any activity he doesn't like. His parents are fed up with him, and their attempts to punish Travon for his negative behavior inevitably result in shouting matches. Travon ends up winning these arguments by escalating his yelling and screaming to cursing, verbal threats, and physically aggressive posturing; eventually his parents give up out of frustration. In the end, Travon escapes any consequences from his parents for his inappropriate actions at home or school.

TINA *is an eleven-year-old girl who recently was arrested for assaulting a teacher for the second time in ten months. In the latest incident, Tina was arguing with her teacher over a detention she got for being late to class following lunch. (This was the third time in three days that Tina had been late.) Tina initially began making excuses and blamed another student for her tardiness; she refused to accept the detention and ignored her teacher's requests to calm down. Eventually, Tina started to curse, shout, and verbally threaten her teacher. When the teacher asked Tina to leave the classroom and report to the office, Tina "lost it" and shoved the teacher over a chair, then started to hit and kick her. Tina even tried to choke the teacher. The teacher suffered a gash on the back of her head and had to make a trip to the emergency room for stitches.*

Other teachers describe Tina as "a bomb ready to explode." Most teachers ignore Tina's minor offenses for fear of having to deal with her explosive temper. Tina is an outcast at school and in her neighborhood. She overreacts to minor problems and is viewed as volatile and short-tempered. Other kids don't want to play with her because she might lash out at any time. Tina has been involved in many fights with both girls and boys in her neighborhood and at school. Usually, Tina doesn't start these fights, but she does escalate conflicts and doesn't try to avoid them.

Tina's parents are divorced and she lives with her mother. At home, Tina regularly punches and kicks her younger brother, two sisters, and mother.

In these examples, Travon and Tina share many common problems. Other kids don't like them and they have few, if any, friends. Teachers are frustrated with their constant outbursts and are growing weary of battling with them. And their relationships with their parents and siblings at home are in shambles. For both Travon and Tina, one common destructive element is the major source of their difficulties: They both have learned that using aggressive behaviors is the most effective way to get what they want, escape trouble and negative consequences, or avoid something they don't want to do.

Despite this similarity, Tina and Travon use aggression in different ways. In order to get his needs met, Travon bullies and hassles others. In other words, Travon **initiates** situations where he uses aggressive behaviors. Tina, on the other hand, **responds** with aggressive behaviors to the actions or behaviors of others. She loses control of her emotions and actions without thinking of the consequences and rapidly explodes in angry and hostile outbursts when an obstacle gets in her way.

Kenneth Dodge, a noted researcher on aggression in children, refers to these distinct types of aggressive behaviors as **proactive aggression** (Bobby) and **reactive aggression** (Tina). According to Murray-Close & Ostrov (2009), "…proactive aggression is defined as planned and goal-directed aggressive behaviors, reactive aggression consists of aggressive displays enacted in anger following perceived negative experiences such as provocation or frustration (Card & Little, 2006; Crick & Dodge, 1996; Dodge, 1991)."

Understanding and identifying which type of aggressive behavior a youth tends to use is an integral part of developing a strategy for teaching aggressive youth more appropriate responses to situations that frustrate, anger, or upset them. When caregivers understand the "what" and "why" of proactive and reactive aggressive behavior, they are better able to cope with and help very difficult and frustrating children and adolescents.

Catching aggression when it is at lower levels, and becoming adept at recognizing the type of aggressive behavior a youth displays also enables you to more accurately develop effective intervention strategies. This is important because, in many cases, using or choosing the wrong type of intervention may actually cause aggressive behavior to get worse.

The next two sections will take a closer look at reactive and proactive aggression and how to identify each one.

Reactive Aggression

Youngsters who use reactive aggression tend to become bothered and upset by the actions and reactions of others, and respond in an emotionally charged manner. Often, parents and caregivers refer to these kids as "having a short fuse" because they can quickly go from being calm to being very angry over even minor issues, like receiving a simple "No" answer or earning a small consequence for a negative behavior.

Some of these youngsters enjoy teasing other kids, but they don't like to be teased. They tend to misread situations and respond with quick and frequent temper outbursts. Other kids usually are afraid of them and view them as unpredictable.

Other reactive aggressive kids are explosive. They frequently have faulty thinking patterns and are quick to react to what they perceive as a hostile world. They are very sensitive to teasing and ridicule. When they can't avoid conflict, they often escalate it by using verbal and physical aggression.

Youngsters who use aggression reactively are unable to control their actions when they become angry, frustrated, and fearful. They are like the two-year-old child in a restaurant who becomes angry and throws a tantrum because she can't have something she wants. That may be a normal and common response for most two-year-olds, but it is socially unacceptable and inappropriate for an older child or adolescent.

Reactive aggressive kids tend to explode with high levels of aggressive and, at times, violent behavior. They don't typically move through the five levels of severity in aggression in a sequential or logical fashion, but usually proceed directly to more severe types of aggression like yelling, cursing, verbal threats, punching, or fighting.

Generally speaking, peers and classmates don't like these youngsters, and they can be a tremendous source of frustration for parents, caregivers, and teachers because no one knows when they might erupt. These kids can be outgoing and gregarious or quiet and passive, but their aggressive response to feelings of anger, frustration, or fear is the same: It's unpredictable – even to the youngster – and laden with emotion.

Proactive Aggression

Instead of responding aggressively to conflict with others (reactive aggression), kids who use proactive aggression tend to initiate aggressive acts. Caregivers often refer to them as "manipulators" or "bullies." Aggression in these youngsters is more thought out and serves a purpose: It helps them reach a goal.

Many of these youngsters are known for "starting trouble," and are seen by other kids as bullies. They constantly tease, shove, call people names, gossip and spread malicious rumors, etc., and often start fights for no apparent reason. Generally, they do poorly in school, both academically and socially.

Some youngsters who are proactive aggressive have learned to get their needs met by "setting up" others. They like to argue, threaten, and use other aggressive behaviors (relational, verbal, and physical) in order to get people to give in to their demands. They don't get along well with others and like to intimidate them.

Over time, proactive aggressive youth learn that they can get what they want by using aggressive behaviors. In fact, because their aggressive behavior is more cognitively oriented and calculating, these youth don't necessarily have to be angry or upset. With proactive aggression, hostile and inappropriate behavior is a harmful instrument for achieving goals, much like a construction worker uses a wrecking ball to destroy a building.

Children who use proactive aggression are apt to move through the five levels of severity in aggression in a more sequential, orderly manner. The tendency is to begin with lower-level aggressive behaviors and escalate to higher-level behaviors if a particular aggressive act is no longer achieving the desired results. For example, if a youngster finds that whining or complaining isn't enough to get out of doing chores at home, she will "turn up the heat" so to speak, resorting to more severe behaviors like yelling and cursing. Over time – without intervention – these kids might up the ante to the highest levels of aggression, like physically harming others or themselves (Level IV) or using violence toward people, with the potential for causing injury (Level V).

Proactive aggressive children and adolescents tend to use the aggressive behaviors that have worked in the past with a particular individual or in a particular situation. Once these kids learn what level of aggression helps them accomplish their goal, they frequently begin at that level in every subsequent interaction that involves conflict. For instance, a youth may begin an argument with a parent by immediately using verbal threats or throwing objects; during a conflict with a teacher or a coach, however, that same child might use lower-level aggressive behaviors like noncompliance, whining, or crying.

Younger proactive aggressive kids are not necessarily disliked by their peers and classmates. However, as these kids get older, other children begin to see them in a more negative light. Like reactive aggressive kids, the personalities of proactive aggressive youngsters can range from outgoing and sociable to quiet and passive. So, when attempting to distinguish proactive aggressive youth from reactive aggressive youth, the key question involves **intent:** Is the child deliberately using aggression as a tool to serve a purpose or meet a goal?

Dodge (1991) states: "All behaviors have aspects of reaction and proaction, in that one can make guesses regarding the precipitants as well as the functions of all behaviors." This is true for aggressive behavior. In extreme cases, it is much easier for parents and caregivers to distinguish between proactive and reactive aggression by looking at whether or not a child is angry and by determining the function of the aggressive behavior. On the other hand, the task of identification is more difficult with kids who are on the fringes. In either situation, it is important for parents and caregivers to accurately identify which type of aggression pattern a youngster is using so that responsible, effective intervention and treatment can be developed.

Bullying

AARON, *a sophomore, is feared by most of the students in his high school – and he likes it that way. Being taller and stronger than most of the other kids, Aaron is the only underclassman to make the varsity football team, and he will probably be a starting player. The*

LIMERICK
00692514
COUNTY LIBRARY

coaches praise Aaron, a linebacker on defense, for his ferocious play and brutal hits.

Aaron, however, doesn't leave this "football" behavior on the playing field. In school and in his neighborhood, Aaron uses his physical superiority to make others do what he wants. He thoroughly enjoys badgering and "shaking down" smaller kids for money or other possessions. For example, Aaron recently threatened to "kick the s— out" of a younger boy in his neighborhood if the boy didn't give his iPod to Aaron. The boy handed it over because he knew from past experience that Aaron wouldn't hesitate to follow through with his threat. The boy was terrified and didn't tell an adult what happened because Aaron threatened to hurt the boy if he told anyone.

For fun, Aaron often intimidates other kids into doing things that are degrading and humiliating. For example, during lunch period one day he tried to force another male student to drink a mixture of milk and urine. When the boy refused, Aaron grabbed the boy's hair, wrestled him to the floor, and poured the concoction into the boy's mouth. No one – including the victim – reported this to a teacher because they were afraid that Aaron would get them for "squealing."

In schools and neighborhoods around the world, wherever there are children, there are bullies. Kids like Aaron rule over and terrorize their victims mercilessly, and more often than not, get away with it. Why? Because victims of bullies and witnesses fear that the bully will "get" them if they tell an adult. So, victims go on suffering in silence as they are repeatedly hassled and tormented.

Bullying is defined by Olweus (1996) as "aggressive behavior or intentional 'harmdoing,' which is carried out repeatedly and over time in an interpersonal relationship characterized by an imbalance of power." Bullying "…often occurs without apparent provocation" and includes negative actions that "…can be carried out by physical contact, by words, or in other ways, such as making faces or mean gestures, and intentional exclusion from a group." Additionally, one of the goals of bullying is acquiring possessions – money, cigarettes, alcohol, and other things a bully values (Olweus, 1996). In sum, a bully consciously, deliberately, and repeatedly uses aggression to get what he or she wants from other youngsters who have difficulty defending themselves either physically or emotionally from the harassment. Bullying, therefore, is considered a form of proactive aggression.

Studies on bullying show that youth who are younger and weaker are victimized most often, and that the bully-victim relationship tends to last a long time unless there is some sort of intervention from parents or caretakers. Also, bullies and their victims usually are boys. However, there is a good deal of bullying that goes on among girls. One big difference between boy and girl bullies is that boys use physical force or tactics (pushing, kicking or tripping, punching, etc.) while girls tend to use more subtle, covert, and relational forms of harassment like "...slandering, spreading of rumors, intentional exclusion from the group, and manipulation of friendship relations" (Olweus, 1996). These subtle and covert forms of bullying, according to Olweus (1996), are "more difficult to detect for adults."

How can parents and caregivers determine if a child they live with or care for is a bully? What are some of the characteristics of bullying that parents and caregivers should be aware of that would help them identify a problem? Olweus's research (1996) provides some answers to these questions:

> ❯ Bullies engage in aggressive and violent acts **in order to get something.** So, much of their behavior originates from a strong desire to obtain things or items that they feel they need or want.

> ❯ Bullies have **a positive attitude toward aggression** and violence. They enjoy the physical and emotional pain they inflict on others and won't hesitate to use intimidating and harassing behaviors.

> ❯ A strong **need to control and dominate** others – kids and adults – drives a bully's behavior.

> ❯ Bullies **overgeneralize** aggressive behaviors and have few alternative skills to obtain status or attention.

> ❯ Bullies are **impulsive**. If they see something they want, they go after it without thinking about how their aggressive actions affect others or even the consequences to themselves.

> ❯ A bully has **little, if any, empathy** for his or her victims. Bullies simply don't care about the devastating impact their behavior can have on other people's lives.

> ❯ Contrary to popular belief, bullies **do not suffer from low self-esteem.** Surprisingly, the opposite is true: Bullies have little anxiety and are very secure in their identity.

> ❯ There is an **imbalance of power** between a bully and his or her victim. A typical victim is unable to defend himself or

herself either physically or emotionally from a bully's harassment.

> Bullies who engage in extremely violent acts (assault, rape, murder) have **easy access to a deadly weapon,** like a knife or a gun.

Whatever form bullying takes – from simple verbal harassment to cyber-bullying to physical violence – it creates a harmful situation for both the bully and the victim. Children and adolescents who learn to rely on the use of force to get what they want will fail in a society where positive, appropriate social interaction between people is a key to success. In extreme cases, this failure can include alienation, criminal activity and incarceration, and an absence of meaningful relationships. For the victim, there is the immediate fear, humiliation, and pain of being singled out for abuse, as well as possible long-lasting effects like loss of self-confidence or a feeling of inferiority. Some victims of bullies also tend to become or remain victims in other areas of their lives as they mature.

As with any form of aggression, bullying demands immediate intervention. In later chapters, we will discuss some treatment approaches and strategies for working with bullies and youth who use other forms of proactive aggression. For an in-depth discussion of bullying and how to effectively address bullying behaviors, see the Boys Town book, *No Room for Bullies* (Boys Town Press, 2005).

What We Know: A Summary of Aggression and Violence Studies

Aggression and violence have been well-studied by many researchers. The focus of their work has been wide and varied, involving the diverse issues that affect the development of aggressive and violent behavior during infancy, childhood, and adolescence. Rolf Loeber (1997) has put together a comprehensive piece that summarizes the body of excellent research in this area.

The information included in this section is intended to help round out and give you a fuller picture of aggression and violence in children and adolescents. A summary of the more pertinent and interesting information and findings is provided here:

> During infancy (birth to one year old), boys are more likely to show forms of anger than girls. However, neither sex yet displays aggressive behaviors, other than rage and frustration, which are typical for infants.

> Aggressive behaviors, typically in the form of temper tantrums directed at adults and other children, begin at age two or three. There is no noticeable difference between boys and girls at this age regarding the frequency of aggressive incidents.

> From ages three through six years, the difference in the level of aggressive behavior between boys and girls becomes more pronounced. Typically, males display higher levels of physically aggressive behavior than girls. Girls in this age range tend to use lower levels of aggressive behavior like crying, whining, excluding others from the group, gossiping, and so on.

> Most girls and many boys show an overall decrease in aggressive behaviors toward peers and adults and an increase in the use of interpersonal skills between the ages of six and twelve years. Only a small percentage of boys are unable to control their aggressive tendencies. However, both sexes frequently use aggressive behavior with siblings during this period. There also is the appearance of behaviors like cruelty toward others or animals. The emergence of these behaviors can signal the possible development of mental health problems such as Conduct Disorder or Oppositional Defiant Disorder, or more severe aggression problems.

A number of changes regarding aggression occur during adolescence and young adulthood. These include:

> Aggression tends to increase in severity and involves more hostile acts toward others that cause serious mental, emotional, or physical damage, or death. This can be attributed to three things: Youngsters are physically stronger; there is a higher use of deadly weapons in confrontations; and it is easy for youngsters to obtain deadly weapons.

> Peer groups have a strong influence on youngsters, and a group as a whole tends to use aggression or violence (e.g., hassling a younger child to give up a possession or causing property damage to a school).

> The lure of gangs becomes stronger. Youngsters who join gangs have greater access to deadly weapons and are more likely to engage in severe forms of aggressive and violent acts.

> Adult-child conflict increases during this period. Kids are getting physically stronger, and aggressive youth are more likely to hit or physically harm an adult.

> Conflicts between boys and girls increase. Girls have more conflicts with boys than boys have with girls. This creates more aggression between the sexes, and as dating begins, aggressive and violent acts like physical assault or rape are more likely to occur.

> Some youngsters become sexually active and some have children of their own. Youngsters who become parents may begin abusing their own children and/or partners.

> The age of onset for aggressive behaviors gradually increases with each level of aggression. More specifically, behaviors included in the lowest level of aggression (Level I) typically begin at about age three. Level II, Level III, and Level IV aggressive behaviors usually start to emerge around age ten, while behaviors at Level V – using violence toward people, with the potential for causing death – often begin at about age eleven.

> Physical aggression (hitting, kicking, punching, etc.) is more likely to occur early in life, but the prevalence of such behavior decreases during adolescence. However, the use of serious violence (aggravated assault, rape, suicide, murder, etc.) tends to increase during adolescence.

> Youngsters who begin to use aggressive behavior early in life are much more likely to engage in severe forms of aggression and violence later in life. Several researchers have found that most violent adults involved in their studies also were aggressive when they were young.

> Youngsters whose parents report that their children have difficult temperaments are more likely to develop aggression problems.

Research indicates that **biology and genes** influence the development of aggressive and violent behavior in children and adolescents. **Neurobiological factors** also play a role, but their exact role(s) is not yet fully understood (Lober & Pardini, 2008).

There are several **cognitive factors** that can promote aggression in children and adolescents, and hinder a youth's ability to maintain self-control during times of upset or crisis. These include:

> Low intelligence and academic problems.

> Difficulty paying and maintaining attention.

> Inability to generate solutions to problems or conflict in a nonaggressive manner.

> Misinterpreting or misreading social cues from others. Aggressive kids tend to think others are responding to them with an aggressive intent, when in fact that is not the case. This misinterpretation tends to elicit an aggressive response from the youngster.

> Exposure to a multitude of conflicts and aggression in the child's environment. This can lead to a preoccupation with aggression that increases the likelihood that a youth will use the antisocial behaviors he or she sees being used by others. In fact, overexposure to aggression and violence can dramatically influence a youngster's perception of the use of hostile behaviors; over time, he or she actually begins to view the use of these behaviors in a favorable light.

Family factors can influence and promote the development of aggression and violence in youngsters. Some of these include:

> Insecure attachment relationships between children and their mothers during infancy, which can lead to behavior problems.

> Parental disciplinary practices that include coercive interactions, physical punishment or unreasonably punitive discipline, and physical abuse.

> Single-parent homes, where children are more likely to develop aggressive and violent tendencies.

> Highly aggressive children are rejected by their peers as early as age six. As adolescents, these same kids do have friends, but the friends usually are other aggressive or deviant peers.

> Neighborhoods where aggression and violence are commonplace can significantly influence the development of aggressive and violent behaviors in kids. Further, this influence can lead children to adopt various levels of aggressive and violent behavior at an earlier age.

> Patterson (1990) found that girls who are highly aggressive also tend to be depressed.

Despite being well-researched, aggression and violence remain complicated issues. The information presented in this section is extremely valuable in helping caregivers quickly identify the signals that indicate that a child is learning or developing aggressive or violent tendencies. Caregivers must heed these warning signs and begin developing a plan to steer youth back to the road to success.

Summary

Just as a doctor must make an accurate diagnosis to heal a patient, you must be able to accurately diagnose a youngster's behavioral or emotional problems in order to develop an effective Treatment Plan. This is especially true with aggression. The more knowledge you have about what aggression is and what it is not, the more proficient you will be in identifying a youngster's level of aggression and the forms of aggression the child tends to use. Ultimately, this enhances the quality of treatment and increases the chances that a child will overcome his or her aggression problem.

CHAPTER 2

Why Are Kids Aggressive?

How does aggressive behavior become part of a youngster's life? When and where does aggression begin to develop in children and adolescents? Is it "nature" or "nurture?" The classic debate of whether biology (nature) or environment (nurture) has a greater impact on a child's development has dominated the landscape of this issue – and numerous other issues in the field of psychology – for many years. However, choosing one theory over the other as the end-all answer is both shortsighted and irresponsible. The only hope for gaining a solid foothold on understanding this complex problem and providing effective treatment is to adopt a multidimensional view. That involves taking into account the importance and value of various approaches to helping youth overcome their aggression problems, and not confining treatment possibilities to only one modality.

Researchers have identified the significant and relevant role that biology, environment, and cognitive and perceptual processes play in the development of aggression and violence. Grisso (1996) states: "Each of the three perspectives has different pieces of a map that lead to the destination we all seek." This means that just as there is no single cause for the development of aggression in youngsters, there also is no one definitive explanation or treatment approach (Borum & Verhaagen, 2006).

Boys Town subscribes to this philosophy. We believe that aggression and other antisocial behaviors are learned and evolve from the many influences in a youngster's environment (parents, siblings, friends, other adults

29

and family members), and from faulty cognitive and perceptual processes (thoughts and feelings). That is why the Boys Town Model emphasizes teaching troubled youngsters alternative appropriate behaviors to replace old, negative behaviors. In addition, Boys Town helps aggressive kids correct flawed cognitive and perceptual patterns and the impact that they have on behaviors. Finally, it is important to note that we believe that biological interventions (e.g., psychotropic medications) sometimes can be an important piece of the puzzle when developing effective and therapeutic Treatment Plans for aggressive youngsters.

The concepts for this treatment philosophy are deeply rooted in research and theories on the causes of aggression in children. To effectively work with youth in your care, it is important to understand why youngsters sometimes explode in antagonistic, aggressive, and even violent ways toward themselves and others. Caregivers who are familiar with the various theories on aggression and violence are more likely to provide effective treatment that can help youth change these negative behaviors. Effective treatment also stems from a good understanding of the origins of a youth's negative behavior and why and how it continues to be reinforced. This is especially important when teaching youth alternative ways to calmly and rationally deal with stressful or adverse situations. When you take the time to do your "homework" on these issues, you can more easily identify problems and possible solutions, which results in better care for the youth.

In order to provide some necessary insight on this issue, this chapter will focus on the findings of Gerald Patterson and Nicholas Long, two researchers whose extensive work has greatly influenced the strategies and teaching techniques Boys Town has refined for working with aggressive and violent youth. Both men have developed respected theories that seek to explain why youth respond to conflict in aggressive and violent ways, and how caregivers can effectively work with these youth. The two main theories we will be exploring are Patterson's Coercion Process and Long's Conflict Cycle. There also will be a brief discussion of the biological factors that can affect the development of aggressive behavior in children and adolescents.

The Coercion Process – Patterson

Coercion refers to the use of one or more aggressive behaviors or acts by a youth in response to the behavior of another person who generally is an authority figure (mother, father, teacher, foster parent, or other caregiver). The authority figure then responds to the youth's aggressive behavior in one of two ways, labeled by Patterson (1982) as **escape conditioning** or **negative synchronicity.** The end result of both types of responses is the same: The youth's aggressive behavior is reinforced. Over time, the youth is trained to use aggressive behavior whenever confronted with conflict because this behavior usually gets the youth what he or she wants. This cycle of reinforcing negative or aggressive youth behavior through counterproductive authority responses is called the **Coercion Process**.

Socially skilled youth have learned to use appropriate behaviors to resolve negative or unpleasant social situations. However, children who do not learn socially appropriate behaviors will develop coping mechanisms to overcome these deficiencies. Children who have not been taught appropriate social skills learn to use the response that works best for them in a given situation. Children are extremely tuned in to their social environment and learn to match their behavior to inadequate parental discipline and responses, lack of structure, poor problem-solving abilities, and what they see as "hassles" from adults.

The following sections explain the concepts of escape conditioning and negative synchronicity, and present examples of each.

Escape Conditioning

In this scenario, the authority figure gives in and submits to the youth's coercive attack or aggressive behavior. Thus, the unpleasant interaction abruptly ends and the authority figure escapes any further unpleasant or painful exchanges with the youth. Unfortunately, this only reinforces the youth's aggressive behavior by demonstrating that the authority figure will withdraw aversive behaviors if the child's behavior escalates beyond "tolerable" limits.

EXAMPLE – A mother scolds her son for staying out well past his curfew. The son responds by screaming at his mother, "Stop your d--- b-------. I don't know what the h--- your problem is!" The son shouts these verbally aggressive statements (coercion) at his mother so she will stop scolding him. The mother immediately ceases the scolding and walks away, avoiding any further conflict with the son. The son does not receive a consequence for staying out past his curfew, and has now learned that he can stop or escape his mother's scolding by becoming verbally aggressive.

Negative Synchronicity

In this situation, the authority figure immediately responds with aversive behavior when a youth engages in an aggressive behavior. The coercive youth, in turn, escalates the intensity of aggressive behavior until he or she "out-punishes" the authority figure. Eventually, the youth's aggressive behavior intensifies to the point where the authority figure con-cedes and ends the interaction. Again, the authority figure's response rein-forces the youth's aggressive behavior.

Patterson showed that members of clinic-referred families were often entrenched in this type of behavior-reaction cycle, and were roughly twice as likely as members of "normal" families to respond in this combative interaction style.

EXAMPLE – A father comes home after a long day's work and begins scolding his son for not taking out the trash. The son screams at his father, "You take that s--- out yourself!" The father angrily shouts back, "I run this house and if you know what's good for you, you'll do what I tell you! Go take that d--- trash out! Now!" The son increases the intensity and severity of his aggressive behavior by shouting back at his father, cursing, and kicking the leg of the kitchen table. In turn, the father threatens to "ground" the son. Upping the ante, the son responds by aggressively walking toward his father with clenched fists, angrily shouting, "I'll do what I want. If you don't like it, I'll kick your a--!" At this point, the father backs away and leaves the room, ending the hostile exchange. The son has learned that by escalating the intensity and sever-ity of his aggressive behaviors, he can avoid taking out the trash and eventually stop his father's aversive behaviors.

Patterson's research helps to explain many of the clinical problems, including children's aggressive and violent behavior, that caregivers see today in increasing numbers. Coercive children respond to authority fig-ures by trying to "out-punish" them. In some families, these aggressive behaviors are reinforced so often that the coercive child actually runs the family and controls the social setting. If these youth do not receive conse-quences for their aggressive behaviors, they continue to use them when-ever someone confronts them. These behaviors eventually spill over into interactions with others – family members, teachers, and other kids – whom the coercive child tries to out-punish or out-intimidate. The result often is a child who depends solely on negative, aggressive, or aversive behaviors to get his or her needs met or to interact with others.

The Conflict Cycle – Long

Long believes that a crisis has its root cause in an unresolved incident, and is the product of a youth's stress that is kept alive by the actions and the reactions of others. The incident arouses strong emotions in the youth and others who are involved, and even a minor disagreement can spiral into a major crisis.

When a youth's feelings are aroused by stress, the youth learns to behave in ways that shield him or her from painful feelings. Others (parents, teachers, peers) perceive the youth's behavior as negative, and they respond in a negative fashion toward the youth. This response produces additional stress and the youth again reacts in an inappropriate manner to protect himself or herself from further hurtful feelings. If unbroken, this spiraling action-reaction cycle dominates interactions the youth has with others. This process is called the Conflict Cycle.

The Conflict Cycle follows this pattern: The first step is a stressful event (e.g., frustration, failure, rejection) that triggers a troubled youth's irrational or negative beliefs ("Nothing good ever happens to me!"; "This teacher is out to get me!"). Negative thoughts determine and trigger negative feelings and anxieties, which drive the youth's aggressive behavior. The aggressive behaviors (yelling, screaming, threatening, sarcasm, refusing to speak) incite others, who not only pick up the youth's negative feelings but also frequently mirror the youth's negative behaviors. This aversive reaction increases the youth's stress, triggers more intense feelings, and drives more aggressive behavior. The youth's behavior leads the people around him or her to feel even more anger and frustration. This cycle continues until it escalates into a no-win power struggle. Wood and Long (1991) say: "Logic, caring, and compassion are lost, and the only goal is to win the power struggle."

In the end, the youth's irrational beliefs ("Nothing good ever happens to me!"; "That teacher is out to get me!") that started the Conflict Cycle sequence are reinforced, and the youth has no reason to change or alter the irrational beliefs and aggressive behaviors.

The following is an example of the Conflict Cycle. *(The cycle is illustrated in Figure 1.)*

EXAMPLE – A youth is absent from school and misses a math test. Because the youth doesn't have a legitimate written excuse for the absence the next day, the teacher tells her she must take the math exam after school or receive an "F." *(Event creating Stress – Cycle 1 Begins)*. The youth is frustrated because she does not want to stay after school and miss play practice *(Feelings/Anxieties)*. She makes several excuses, attempting to talk her way out of staying after school to take the test *(Negative Behavior)*. The teacher tells the student to be quiet, accept the situation, and start her current math assignment *(Others' Reactions creating More Stress – Cycle 2 Begins)*. Becoming agitated *(Feelings/Anxieties)*, the youth begins to yell at the teacher about being unfair *(Negative Behavior)*. The teacher responds by sarcastically saying, "You probably skipped school yesterday anyway. You're lucky I don't just give you an 'F.'" *(Others' Reactions*

Figure 1
Conflict Cycle

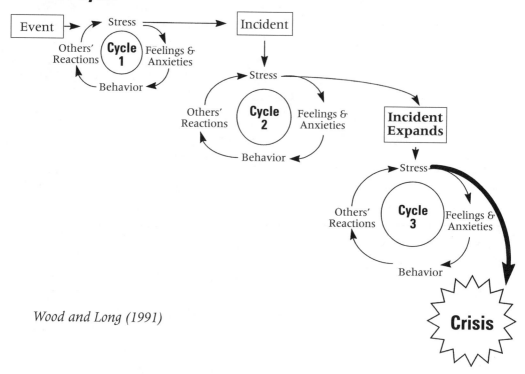

Wood and Long (1991)

creating More Stress – Cycle 3 Begins). Embarrassed in front of her classmates *(Feelings/Anxieties)*, the youth begins to scream and curse at the teacher *(Negative Behavior)*. The teacher angrily yells at the youth to report to the office, which will result in a call home *(Others' Reactions creating More Stress – Crisis)*. Now the youth is extremely angry and frustrated over the additional consequence. She knocks her books to the floor, throws a pen at the teacher, and tips over her desk before leaving the classroom and walking out of school.

Biology

As mentioned earlier, biology is another important and valuable perspective to consider, both when evaluating a child's aggression problem and determining if any biological interventions (psychotropic medication, chemical dependency program, etc.) might be effective in the child's overall Treatment Plan.

The following biological factors can play a role in the development of aggressive and violent behavior in youth.

❯ **Genetics** – The contention is that the presence of certain genes might cause some youngsters to be predisposed to aggression and violence. Rapid advances are being made in research that studies the connection between genetics and behavior. However, Blonigen and Krueger (2006) state that at the present time, while "…it is apparent that genes play a significant role in the etiology of aggressive traits and behaviors across development…," it is misleading "…to characterize this as an absolute finding or to suggest that genetic factors are impervious to the moderating influence of other variables."

❯ **Neurobiological processes** – These processes are the electrical and chemical activities in specific regions of the brain that influence the development of certain behaviors, including aggressive behaviors. Simply put, some children may behave in an aggressive manner because certain electrical and chemical activities in the brain are not occurring normally or correctly. In these instances, treatment might be improved through the use of pharmacological interventions (psychotropic medications). Research in this area has produced significant results and is ongoing.

Modern brain research shows that the young brain continues to evolve until the mid-twenties. It isn't suddenly that at age seven or ten a child is capable of thinking like an adult. That's why there is continued education and parenting until a child reaches the age of maturity. But, the actual chemistry and structures of the brain involving the connection between the regions that control and regulate emotions and impulses aren't hardwired until late teens at the earliest and often not until the twenties for many people. That means the brain has yet to mature during adolescence. So it is not surprising that the teenage years are a time when lots of aggression, drug and alcohol experimentation, and other risk-taking behaviors occur.

That is also known about the human brain is that it develops in interaction with the environment. This happens due to "brain plasticity," meaning the environment actually changes structural elements and neural pathways within the brain. If the child's environment is pro-violence and antisocial, those structural elements and neural pathways won't be adequately constructed, which can result in a child who can't control impulses very well. That's why some of the techniques discussed in this book are attempts and strategies aimed at changing the environmental inputs aggressive kids' brains are receiving.

> **Alcohol and drug use or abuse** – Much research has been done in the area of how alcohol and drug use affect behavior. Many studies show that there is a strong correlation between long-term, heavy alcohol use and aggressive and violent behavior. Also, the chronic use and abuse of some psychoactive drugs have been linked to aggressive behavior patterns and unusual hostile or violent outbursts.

Summary

The Boys Town Model's theoretical foundation and subsequent treatment philosophy is based on the belief that aggressive and violent behaviors are learned and evolve from the many influences in a youth's environment. Aggression also can develop as a result of faulty cognitive and perceptual processes (thoughts and feelings). In addition, Boys Town recognizes the important role biological factors (genetics, neurobiological processes, and alcohol and drug use or abuse) can play in aggression, and the importance of considering these factors during treatment planning.

In order for you to develop effective Treatment Plans for the children in your care, it is important that you have a basic understanding of the wide range of research and theory regarding the causes of aggression and violence. This understanding enhances your abilities to identify problems and find solutions.

CHAPTER 3

The Boys Town Ecology and Youth Aggression

Boys Town is a village where five hundred and fifty troubled and at-risk boys and girls live and receive care. The Village is located on a square mile piece of land surrounded by the city of Omaha, Nebraska. There are seventy-two homes here that provide families for children ages ten to eighteen. Six to eight boys or girls live in each single-family home with a married couple called Family-Teachers. Many of these children have serious emotional and behavioral problems, including aggression and violence. They have not been able to stay in their own family's home but can function safely in a community setting. Family-Teachers and their assistants provide compassionate, effective treatment while meeting the daily needs of each child. During their stay, children learn social skills, attend school, participate in extracurricular activities, and take part in daily chores and activities as members of their Boys Town family.

Like many of today's communities, Boys Town is diverse: sixty-two percent of the kids are boys and thirty-eight percent are girls, and they come from various religious, cultural, and ethic backgrounds (four percent are American Indian, twelve percent Hispanic or Latino, twenty-eight percent African American, and forty-four percent Caucasian). Also, the kids come from all over the United States and from rural and urban settings.

The typical boy here has been arrested one time, and seventy percent of the girls have been sexually abused. Most kids arrive two years behind academically. More than sixty percent of the kids have psychiatric diagnoses. Teachers have described these kids as "incorrigible" and "unable to learn." America guarantees education to all children, but many of the kids who come here have not been in school for close to or more than one hundred days prior to their arrival. Also, many have gang backgrounds and affiliations, along with juvenile delinquent histories. In other words, these are the kids who are not wanted in their homes, schools, and communities.

Boys Town has been described as the densest square mile of juvenile delinquents in the United States, yet it is also one of the safest communities. Even though kids arrive with troubled and aggressive histories, they are expected and taught how to be a part of a family, school, team, and community without fighting or using aggression.

In this chapter, we will introduce the elements that help make Boys Town a unique community where, even though many of the kids arrive with major aggression problems, there is very little to no aggressive and violent behavior on a daily basis. The hope is that you can incorporate some of these elements and ideas into your organization, program, school, community, neighborhood, or home to help curb and eliminate aggression problems with kids.

We do not succeed with all aggressive kids. But the fact that we do predominantly have delinquent kids here and we do not have a lot of symbolic aggression, verbal aggression, or physical altercations goes a long way toward making this one of America's safest communities. We are not an institution for delinquents; instead, we strive to create an environment and have expectations that are commonly found in most private school settings.

A Modern-Day Community

Before we discuss the elements, let us dispel the notion that Boys Town is some kind of place out of the 1940s or 1950s. We are a contemporary village where more than forty-one percent are minority children and most are from urban environments. Youth here look like typical, modern-day kids: some have tattoos, some arrive with colored hair or dressed in all black, and others have some of the other concerns that alarm adults and trouble parents all over the country every day. Boys Town is not a throwback to another era; rather, it is a vibrant community and culture filled with modern-day kids who have modern-day problems.

The typical day for boys and girls here starts at 6:30 a.m. They wake up early, shower, make their beds, eat breakfast with five or six other kids in the house, clean their own dishes used at breakfast, and prepare for school. All boys and girls attend school every weekday, even in the summertime, and they typically enjoy school.

Within the first month of arriving here, kids are asked to join a sports team and/or an extracurricular activity. We like to say that "kids swap gang colors for school colors." Girls and boys are expected to participate on sports teams and in clubs like ROTC, cheerleading, chess, or any of the other extracurricular activities or clubs.

Kids here shop, recreate, attend school events and functions, and work in the Omaha community. People in the surrounding neighborhoods and communities often describe our kids as having better social skills and being more polite, well-mannered, and outgoing than the typical grade school or high school youth attending local schools.

The point here is that we are not isolated from the surrounding community. Instead, kids and families are out and about interacting with and involved in the surrounding community each and everyday.

Key Elements of the Boys Town Ecology that Work Effectively with Aggressive Youth

Boys Town has an ecology that is nonviolent, nonaggressive, and prosocial. The elements discussed in this chapter make up the Boys Town ecology that works so well with aggressive kids. Ecologies that influence youth can come in many forms. For example, let's look at the ecology of a football team. On the field, players are taught to be as aggressive as they can be within the rules. Generally, the team with the players who behave most violently within the rules is the team that wins the football game. But, there is an ecology that governs the football environment that involves well-prescribed rules and penalties that keep players safe.

Another darker example of an ecology is a gang. Here, members are required to dress tough, look tough, act tough, talk tough, and carry tough things. The gang creates an environment, through its symbols and behaviors, that is all about one thing – violence. It is not possible to be part of a gang without buying into the ecology of violence.

What Boys Town works hard to do with the elements discussed in this chapter is to create an opposite kind of ecology for aggressive kids – one where all of the symbols, operations, and cultural inputs are nonviolent and nonaggressive.

Behavioral Infection

Gerald Patterson and Tom Dishion developed a peer contagion theory (Dishion & Dodge, 2005; Huefner, Handwerk, Ringle, & Field, 2009). The theory states that when you put aggressive and delinquent kids together, it foments more aggression and delinquency. The classic examples used by contagion theorists take place in therapy waiting rooms where delinquent kids can gather and talk to each other. As these kids meet and speak to each other week after week before their group or individual therapy sessions, they brag about their conquests, fights, drug deals, and other delinquent acts. And, there are instances when these kids meet after therapy during the week and do delinquent things together, resulting in some kids becoming even more deviant. Some of the research that has been cited that supports contagion theory is good research: In unstructured settings, like therapy waiting rooms, delinquents do create more delinquency.

The Patterson and Dishion theory deals only with the negative side of "contagion," where delinquents make nondelinquents delinquent. At Boys Town, we prefer to use the term "behavioral infection." Behavioral infection can be either negative or positive, and we work very hard here to make sure that it is positive. Just as a microorganism can make an individual sick, there are also good microorganisms in a person's stomach and intestines that keep him or her healthy. Behavioral infection can do the same thing – it can be a plus or minus.

At Boys Town, we strive to make the behavioral infection one that is prosocial and nonaggressive. That does not mean kids here are taught to be passive. Simply ask an opposing player after a Boys Town football game. On the football field, players are taught to work hard and knock their opponents on their rear ends, then help the opponent up after the play is over. Also, when an opposing player is injured at a football game, our players have been directly taught by their coaches to respectfully walk away, take a knee, and show concern for the hurt player. This behavior has infected the Boys Town community and fans who come to the games as they grow quiet and do not say a word during the injury timeout. This kind of nonaggressive response and behavior is in direct opposition to the celebrating and hooting and hollering that happens at some high school football games after hard hits and during injuries.

It is possible to teach aggressive and troubled kids respect for an injured player. Now, this response has become an expectation at football games here. How did this come about among a group of aggressive teenagers? How are they so respectful of a kid's injury and their opponents when they have had to "turn in their gang colors for school colors?" How did this transformation take place? We call it behavioral infection and the ecology of Boys Town.

Elements of the Boys Town Ecology

So, what are the elements of the environment here that allow it to work so effectively with aggressive youth? Some of the elements might be considered old-fashioned ideas, but they are the very ones that too many parents, schools, neighborhoods, and communities are struggling with right now. The struggle involves how to take different cultures, ethnicities, religions, and values and create a positive and nurturing society, community, neighborhood, school system, and family.

The way we attempt to do that here is by developing and instituting a common set of values and expectations for kids and adults to follow. One of the greatest common values and expectations is that aggression does not work here and it is not allowed. Kids and adults strive to treat one another well and respect an individual's rights and freedoms. And, we work hard to **teach** everyone exactly how that happens in the Boys Town community.

One of the first things boys and girls do when they come here is "swear in." This is a public ceremony where newly arrived kids pledge to be good citizens of the Village of Boys Town, to study hard, to pray well, to play fair, and to be good brothers and sisters to others in the Village all their days as citizens. This is the kids' commitment to honoring others' humanity. From that day forward, all the adults in this community take responsibility for all children, keeping in mind the common set of values and expectations they will teach to kids.

Unlike what you find in too many communities, neighborhoods, schools, and homes, Family-Teachers (the child's "parents" at Boys Town) are not fighting with the schools and teachers about their child or arguing with a neighbor because he or she found their child misbehaving. In our country's culture at large, too many people want coaches, teachers, and neighbors to want what an individual family wants. In the culture here, we work very hard to establish a community-wide set of expectations. Family-Teachers are responsible for a child's behaviors twenty-four hours a day and have the ultimate authority about removing a child from an activity or a team. Coaches have the authority to make all decisions about sports team issues, like who plays, how much, what position kids play, and any other team issue that might come up. And the teachers decide all classroom issues, like who gets suspended for misbehavior. The Family-Teachers support the decisions of coaches and teachers because they know they have the child's best interests in mind.

Some ideas that people might think are old and cannot work in today's culture with today's kids are the very ideas and reasons why Boys

Town works so well with aggressive youth. As we have said, Boys Town is a modern community dealing with modern-day kid issues and problems. We care for kids with high rates of alcohol and drug use, delinquency, sexual behavior, and all the other problems every community in America faces today and struggles to find solutions to. Yet we put all these problems and kids together – and they get better and succeed.

Your program, community, school, and home can work toward this too by incorporating the elements and ideas discussed in this chapter. Boys Town has had the advantage of having its ecology evolve over ninety-four years of existence. Yes, Boys Town is a small town. Admittedly, the larger and more complex communities are the harder it can be get these elements incorporated community wide; however, these ideas are not hard to incorporate in your home, neighborhood, school, or program.

Boys Town happens to be an incorporated village with its own schools, churches, police, and fire and rescue units. It has made the difficult choices that allow it to come together as a community in the best interests of children. But there are many smaller communities embedded in larger communities all over America where adults have not made the choice to come together. In these communities, the social institutions (churches, schools, teams, police, fire and rescue, etc.) have not made the choice to agree on a common set of values and expectations that define the kind of good life they want their children to have.

We work diligently to define exactly what goodness is for kids, and we constantly strive to teach, coach, and mentor adults on how to come together with a common set of values and expectations. That way, with several months of training and advising, adults who work here can understand exactly what it means to be a guardian of children's welfare.

We have devised a "playbook" that guides adults in parenting children; in interacting with teachers, schools, and neighbors; and with clarifying the roles of coaches, school leaders, ROTC groups, and other adults. We call this playbook our Model of care and we will talk about it later. Many communities have not come close to this kind of preparation and understanding about their children and others in the community. Unfortunately, this means that parents are too often pitted against teachers and schools, and parents and coaches and churches and neighbors are too often at odds with each other. Any one of these community resources might be the very safety net or enclave a child needs to succeed. At Boys Town, the **total** environment is an enclave for kids because all the systems and elements are striving to work together.

Now, let us take a look at each of the elements of Boys Town's ecology.

Family

We believe that the best paradigm for raising a child is in a family; there is no other paradigm as effective as a family. At Boys Town, that paradigm is a traditional family that consists of a married man and woman, called Family-Teachers, who live and work with six to eight kids, twenty-four hours a day, seven days a week. Family-Teachers act "in loco parentis." And, they have the incredible task of working with children who have long histories of failure and attempting to prepare them for a more successful future. Family-Teachers not only work with each child in the home but they also work with parents, teachers, social agencies, and churches involved with their kids. Family-Teachers and the family are the keys to quality and effective care.

There is technical training that Family-Teachers receive in terms of behavior change and assessment of individual children's needs. And Family-Teachers do get professional advice for particular children's needs, as do parents outside of Boys Town whose children are seeing a psychologist or psychiatrist. Here, we do not have a psychologist or psychiatrist for all kids' treatment, only for those with very special needs. We view the family as the change agent responsible for healing. This is certainly something that can be copied outside of Boys Town, and we have demonstrated that by how we run our various programs around the country.

Family-Teachers provide a family where youth can get their physical, emotional, and spiritual needs met in a loving and proactive manner – without resorting to aggression, violence, drugs or alcohol, or in other inappropriate and unhealthy ways. Family-Teachers provide a family setting with stability and security that alone can communicate effectively to troubled and aggressive kids that they are safe and loved – every day.

Family-Teachers work within the context of a family to teach each child what he or she needs to know to be a happy, confident, and caring person. It is within this family that each child learns skills, builds relationships, and is empowered to grow toward spiritual, emotional, and social maturity.

Family-Teachers and their kids have a "playbook" of family expectations that are very well laid out, including:

> A healthy schedule for children.

> Clearly defined parental roles.

> Clearly defined children's roles.

> Prescribed times for the family to play and worship together.

> Prescribed times for prayer as part of the family's daily activities.

> Times for meals together. Our families eat together virtually every night. The typical adult and child will share a meal together five nights a week. The entire family typically has a minimum of ten shared meals together each week.

> Household responsibilities. Upkeep of the house and responsibilities for all of the family's belongings are shared tasks between children and adults. For example, every child has a household task that he or she is assigned to do every day and the child also has weekly chores.

> Fun. Our families make it a priority for family members to have fun together. This is as important an element as any of the other activities in a family's day.

> Expectations. There are strong expectations set for kids regarding issues like appropriate bedtimes, when to get up in the morning, what clothes are appropriate to wear to school, proper manners, reporting whereabouts, and others.

> Role models. All our families have an adult male and female role model. And our role models are taught a set of "adult social skills" so that they model how to appropriately express affection, anger, positive emotion, and/or frustration.

> Religious diversity. There is respect for religious diversity. As Father Flanagan said, "Every boy must learn to pray. How he prays is up to him." The family honors individual religious traditions but builds in family religious traditions to help with family bonding (e.g., prayer before meals).

How do Family-Teachers establish expectations regarding bedtime, prayer, chores, and other daily activities to a group of juvenile delinquents? We strive to develop an ethic among our families that they are teachers of good behavior to children. And, while Family-Teachers have some special technology regarding how to teach effectively, being a teacher has always been the rule of good parenting. Teaching a child anything (how to ride a bike, study, express feelings, etc.) requires teaching him or her skills. And that is what we work hard to do best: We teach kids social skills in our families. For example, we teach cleanliness and prayer skills – everything and anything is an opportunity to teach children skills. And we get rapid and successful changes in children because we do rapid teaching. As children learn and are encouraged for learning, we see less frustration, negative emotion, and aggression.

While our families do have specific technology and techniques to use, **teaching within a family setting** is the main change element at Boys Town – and it can certainly be so in your family as well.

Community

Because Family-Teachers are from different cultures, communities (rural and urban, large and small, etc.), religions, ethnicities, and age groups, we have a lot of diversity among families, just like many other communities and neighborhoods. However, one element unique to Boys Town that bonds the community together is that every family views itself as responsible for its children **and** for the safety and well-being of everybody else's children. This key element is prevalent in the Boys Town community but not prevalent enough in many of today's communities and neighborhoods.

Boys Town families cannot be isolated families and do the job they are asked to do. Our families attend community activities with others, worship with others, and are accountable for the behavior and well-being of every child with whom they come into contact. That means if people see a child doing something dangerous or misbehaving, they are to intervene right away and report what happened to the child's Family-Teachers. This type of community support and communication is a key element in helping kids with aggression problems get better. The more neighbors, teachers, and police all know and support one another, the stronger the community is and the better behaved children are.

Kids here have many eyes and ears on them. These eyes and ears are not here just to catch the problems; they are also there to teach and encourage. Every adult in the community is a teacher. Whether the person is a coach, schoolteacher, police officer, or other adult, he or she is a teacher first before a discipliner or "security guard." We do not need security guards because there are benevolent eyes and ears on every child all the time.

In our families and community, kids are specifically taught how to behave well, befriend an adult, respond to an adult who corrects them, and how to be pleasant around adults. All this teaching makes it easier for adults to "catch kids being good" and encourage good behavior among children. Unlike some environments where eyes and ears are on kids mainly as security guards waiting to catch misbehavior, the eyes and ears here are there as much (and more) to "catch kids being good" as they are there to correct problem behavior. Also, kids know that these eyes and ears are everywhere, that they are going to receive similar instructions from everyone in the community, and that there are similar expectations everywhere in the community. We have a general guideline called the "four-to-one ratio." This means all adults should have at least four positive interactions to one negative interaction with each other and every child they come in contact with.

This key element of community comes through in many ways at Boys Town. For example, something that happens dozens of times every day here is that a family will get a phone call from a person in the community who might say something like, "I ran into your new boy, Julio, today. Boy, he was really polite to me and he seems really enthused about living in your home. And, he was very thankful to me when I gave him directions on how to find the Clinic." We call this a positive report, and it happens all the time between community members.

On the darker side, if Julio "flips off" another kid, an adult is expected to intervene and teach Julio that this is not the right way to handle things. Then, that adult would report the incident and the interaction with Julio to his Family-Teachers. Also, the adult might say to the Family-Teachers, "When I corrected Julio, he immediately apologized and was cordial in accepting the correction. He seems like a nice kid with whom you can work." These two examples show how Boys Town works hard to operationalize community connectedness and how families and kids are not isolated from each other, other families, and others in the community.

Our community connectedness is stimulated by a concern for the well-being and development of children. Father Val J. Peter, a former Boys Town Executive Director, and Father Steven Boes, current Boys Town National Executive Director, regularly say that Boys Town is the only village in the world where every person in the community is there for one purpose: the well-being of each and every child. This is a goal that is challenging to reach here and in any community, but all communities, neighborhoods, schools, and homes should aspire to reach that goal.

School

On the outside, Boys Town's schools look like other U.S. schools – attractive buildings in the middle of the community. And, there are additional ways our schools are similar to other schools, including:

> Kids have a full-day school schedule from 8 a.m. to 3 p.m.

> There is a fully accredited high school and grade/middle school here with fully accredited teachers, along with some special education certified teachers.

> The campus is open. Kids walk to and from their homes to school and extracurricular activities.

> ❯ During lunchtime and class changes, there are hundreds of kids congregating in the hallways and dozens of adults standing outside their classrooms all interacting together.

> ❯ Kids have a full-range academic curriculum, from typing class to trigonometry.

> ❯ There are many student activities available to kids before and after school – sports teams, school activities, clubs, etc.

> ❯ There are regular and special education classes. Some classes have as many as twenty-five kids for regular education classes and ten to twelve kids for special education classes, depending on the individual needs of the kids.

> ❯ Typically, the number of students in each classroom tends to be a bit smaller (fifteen to twenty-three kids), but it is not the size of the classroom that helps these kids learn and succeed.

All this helps to illustrate that schools here look like any other modern-day school, both on the inside and outside. A closer inspection, however, shows that schools here are unique in many ways that allow them to succeed with troubled and aggressive students who previously have not had success in school.

Aggression, fights, and other hostile behaviors do occur at schools here but they are rare, happening only several times per year. The schools are orderly and rival more high-end private schools on the dimensions of low aggression and focus on learning. Yet, schools here are filled with children who have failed in mainstream public education, ninety-eight percent of whom have not had a private school tutelage prior to coming here. This orderliness is seen in the student's behavior toward one another and toward adults. Kids are rarely late for class, and no one misses or skips class, not because adults are following kids around but because everyone is expected to be in class. This is the norm. And, if any adult sees a kid not in school, the adult stops and intervenes in some way to help the child get to school.

Another way that schools here are unique is that students are eager to greet their teachers and other adults who come into the school. When visitors come for a tour, students are enthusiastic and proud to show off the school and its orderliness. Many kids describe Boys Town's schools as the first school where they felt safe. One female student, for example, who came from a large urban city, set an appointment with a key Boys Town leader to talk about the boys at school. She told the person that Boys Town was the first school where no boy tried to grab, grope, or fondle her.

Another characteristic that makes our schools unique and work so well is the common set of expectations between Family-Teachers and schoolteachers. When students do not meet any of the common expectations, Family-Teachers **expect** to hear from the teachers. This results in excellent communication and mutual support between Family-Teachers and teachers. One vehicle for this is a "school note," but phone calls and emails are even more important communication devices. Also, when a teacher reports a problem or success to Family-Teachers, he or she **expects** that they will acknowledge the problem or success when the child gets home. Communication between schools and homes is active and results in teaching activity by schoolteachers and Family-Teachers. Very simply, Boys Town parents and teachers are engaged with one another – and all parents and schools can accomplish this with the effort of community leaders.

The curriculum here is standard. There are special reading programs for kids with special needs, but all schools have those. Our students on arriving, however, are typically two years behind academically and have not had success in school. For example, twelve-year-old Bobby, who was new here, said he hated school. While at home, he previously missed six months of public school – principally for fighting and other aggressive behavior with adults and students. Even though Bobby had his share of adjustment issues early on in the middle school, he told the principal after the first week that this was the best school he had ever attended (and he had attended more then a few). When the principal asked why, Bobby said, "Because nobody 'jacks' with you." Of course, he was telling us that there was no bullying and that other kids were not dragging him down. This is an example of how kids who have been school failures and disruptive school attendees quickly recognize that schools here have a different kind of environment where they are safe and able to learn.

We believe boys and girls are genetically programmed or "hard-wired" to like to be in groups and to learn. Kids having a desire to learn and grow are a big part of what has kept the human race progressing forward since the beginning. This happens best when kids are put in an environment where learning can occur. The real magic of the Boys Town ecology is education and creating an environment where learning can take place. If a community does not provide a place where learning and group bonding to positive norms can occur, kids will join antisocial groups as dropouts or even gang members.

Kids who come to Boys Town quickly bond to the school and people in it. They recognize they are safe and that their desire to learn can be fulfilled. Typically, after one or two months, children say that this is the first school in which they have succeeded, regardless of whether or not they have a learning disability, behavior disorder, or lots of family disruptions that resulted in poor attendance and learning.

At Boys Town, kids with learning disabilities, behavior disorders, and psychiatric problems are all in the same school at the same time, and they all grow and learn every day. Our schools do not segregate kids off into separate classrooms for specific issues. Instead, everyone is in class together – and they thrive. Much of this is due to the common set of expectations and excellent communication between schools and families.

Finally, Boys Town schools are unique in that they have something called the school model. This is the "playbook" for how teachers should organize their school day. Also, teachers receive special training in how to deal with negative behavior and emotions and how to promote and teach prosocial behaviors. This training is important and responsible for a big part of the success, but alone is not sufficient. It is the combination of training, the common set of expectations, and good communication that allows boys and girls to succeed in Boys Town's schools. Finally, it helps having our entire school system on the same page as to what behaviors to correct and how to correct them, and what behaviors to teach and how to teach them.

Religion

When boys and girls arrive here, they indicate their religious preference or practice – e.g., Methodist, Baptist, Jewish, Catholic, Islamic, or other. Kids are required to indicate their religious affiliation and to participate in a religious practice while here. It is not an option to be uninvolved. We want kids to experience their own religious traditions and practices as much as possible, so kids typically begin with their familial tradition.

Upon admission, our kids tend be less spiritual (that is, active members of formal religious communities) than the typical American child. Before coming here, they tend to be on the fringes of many societal institutions and affiliations (less involved in school, more involved in drugs, etc.), including religion. Our girls and boys are expected to join and actively practice a religion in a formal fashion, which is defined as daily prayer, weekly worship, and participation in family traditions and the rituals of their religion.

Kids here are not segregated by religion any more than they are by age or ethnicity. So, for example, it is common to find a Christian observance like Easter discussed and prepared for by all eight kids in a home, including the Jewish, Islamic, and Methodist youth. Also, all eight kids would participate in the major traditions of other religions like Jewish Hanukah or scripture readings.

All kids receive religious instruction at school, and the study of their religion's texts and scriptures is encouraged (e.g., there is a Bible study group that meets regularly that kids can attend). Also, we employ a secular curriculum called "CHARACTER COUNTS!®" (developed by Michael Joesphson) that fits very closely with the social skill and spiritual training and curriculum that occurs here. With CHARACTER COUNTS! kids learn about and practice the six elements of character – trustworthiness, respect, responsibility, fairness, caring, and citizenship – they should use in school and at home. As children learn these elements and observe their use by others, it is remarkable how infrequently they fall back into aggression or "jacking" with one another as the boy in the earlier example explained.

Character formation is one of the primary goals of any religious development activity. Worship in and of itself is valuable for communication and for the community that develops the religious ritual. For children, worship and religious instruction is in place for and helps with character development. We strongly believe that good character, along with positive behaviors and habits, will not generalize without the internalization of the values that religious practice teaches.

Today, there is lots of discussion about spirituality and religion, and there is a difference between the two. Spirituality can be "a walk in the woods" or Transcendental Meditation; however, neither of these practices necessarily would expose people to a community of common values and beliefs. The idea behind getting kids formally involved in religion is that it nurtures the spirit and the person as a whole, because in most religious communities they share activities, worship, and, during important times, even food and drink (church dinners, religious celebrations, etc.). While we promote spiritual development and religious practices, we believe that religious practice supersedes spirituality. It is the routine behavior of praying together, attending services together, and reading scripture together that builds prosocial habits and community identity.

Finally, every boy and girl here has a community service project that he or she works toward. This is a positive movement that exists in many schools. The project is an expectation that kids study and talk about at school in religion class and that is also fostered and monitored at home. This is certainly something that families and schools can come together on in any community.

Relationship with Community Supports

Boys Town's community supports include the police, fire and rescue, public works and services, and recreation leaders. All who work here go through a common training that helps them to set their expectations for how children should behave and under what circumstance to intervene with them. Also, the training sets expectations regarding communication between the community support groups and kids and families. All this helps create excellent communication between all adults in the community. Also, the child experiences a commonality of expectations and interactions throughout the entire community, which makes it very unique and healthy for kids.

So, for example, at Boys Town it would not be unusual to see a group of kids standing around a police officer, all of whom are talking, laughing, and enjoying each other. Or on a Friday night, on-duty and off-duty police, fire and rescue, and public works people attend football games where they interact with kids and help cheer on the team. Community celebrations here are shared beyond the individual family to the community at large.

What one would not typically see here is a group of kids taunting a police officer or throwing things at a police car, and one would rarely see a youth misbehaving around a police officer. If an officer ever has a problem with a child, one would likely see other adults come to assist the officer in any way possible.

As stated earlier, Boys Town is the only village in the country where every adult in the community has the responsibility to ensure that every child is safe and well cared for. A general rule of thumb here is that adults are right and they trust one another to be right because they share the mutual responsibility of caring for and teaching kids the right way. Adults trust the competence and judgment of other adults in the Village. That can only happen when common values and expectations are shared, and it takes day-to-day training and feedback to make it work here.

An example will serve to clarify this. We have a math teacher who is known to be a stickler for neat and accurate work. He will not grade a math handout that is wrinkled or torn. Some other teachers are not so strict. Our Family-Teachers do not spend a lot of time listening to kids complain about how much more strict this particular teacher is than the other teachers. Instead, the Family-Teachers teach the child how to meet the math teacher's expectations with the reason that some day he or she will have a boss who also has high and challenging expectations so the child needs to learn how to meet them.

This is very difficult to emulate today in the culture at large. But, you do not have to hearken back too many years to when parents did not come out of the stands after a game to angrily criticize a coach for not playing their child more, or when parents did not march up to school to criticize the teacher because their child got a poor grade on a test they thought was unfair. Not too many years ago, parents disciplined the child for getting the bad grade because he or she did not study enough, and they sided with the coach by telling the child to work harder in practice. We continue to do this today at Boys Town, and it continues to work well for helping kids learn and grow in healthy ways. Parents and teachers can come together to better work in the best interest of kids.

The entire environment here is one where the activity level for healthy behavior is so high that there is not much time for aggressive behavior. Also, there are role models for healthy behavior in the community and circumstances that promote it. There are not dissident communications between law enforcement, fire and rescue, families, kids, and schools that prompt attitudes of fear, anger, disgust, or disdain. That does not mean there are no disagreements. But even the adults are taught how to disagree appropriately, and they are expected to follow these guidelines. What results are exceptional communications between these groups that result in mutual respect and support.

Sports and Teams

Boys Town values athletics because they teach values and character. We have a program, *Competing with Character*SM (CWCSM), that is used by all sports teams, coaches, players, and fans. The main goal of CWC is for student-athletes, parents, coaches, and fans to learn and use a variety of skills that promote sportsmanship and positive behavior. To build a successful team, every individual has a role to play. CWC outlines specific skill sets for kids, parents, and coaches. These skills benefit children now and for the future, whether that is in athletics, academics, or work. (We adapted the principles of Michael Josephson's CHARACTER COUNTS! when we developed *Competing with Character*.)

CWC skills encourage kids to learn how to listen to their coaches, get along with teammates, win with class, and lose with dignity. Coaches learn to plan practices that are organized and productive, communicate with parents, and understand the big picture – that is, sports are to teach life skills, not merely how to win. Parents learn to voice concerns appropriately, support the coaches, and model appropriate behavior. Together, these promote good sportsmanship and character development. (To obtain a copy of our *Competing with Character* book and for more information about the CWC program, supporting materials, and services go to www.parenting.org/competing-with-character.)

As mentioned earlier, given that we work with a subset of very aggressive kids and groups of kids who were members of gangs or gang "wannabes," we have an important phrase we use with those youth: "swap gang colors for school colors." This is why we want kids to join teams – be it football, basketball, track, wrestling, softball, baseball, volleyball, or others. The whole issue of involvement in student and school activities is vital to the success of these kids.

Some might call athletics an outlet for aggressive behavior, and it is and has been for centuries for young people. Sports are a contributing factor to the lack of aggressive behavior at Boys Town. A bigger factor, however, is the sense of belonging and joining kids get, along with not being an outsider to the culture at large. Teams and games are celebrated by the entire community here, adults and kids. The school band, dance team, ROTC, and cheerleaders all have a role. All this helps create an atmosphere of connectedness that promotes a nonviolent community.

Boys Town teams and players, like other teams and players, compete and play hard, have a desire to contribute, and have various degrees of athletic ability. Some players are extremely gifted athletically, while others are average to below average. Where our kids are unique is that they typically have not participated in organized athletics before their arrival. Even so, our teams still win many of their games. Much of this is due to the focus of athletics being on competing with character and being a "part of" a team – and not on winning.

Our athletic programs and sports teams are important because they help instill a sense of community and pride in troubled boys and girls, most of whom have never before experienced these things. On an individual level, participation in sports is therapeutic; it is another way to help youngsters heal. On a community level, it promotes pride and common identity. Our coaches, players, and fans understand the real value of athletics and work hard to keep it all in the proper perspective. Sports should be only a part of the fabric that makes up a young person's life, not the whole foundation.

Athletic competitions can be one of the discriminators or assessments of a community's or system's health because you see all elements of a community involved – children on the court or field, kids in the stands, and adults on the sidelines and in the stands. We believe how our children and adults behave at athletic events are important moderators of aggression and hostility at games, after games, and in the community at large. That is why you rarely see our kids taunting, arguing with, or getting into fights with referees, other players, or opposing fans. If something like that did happen, the youth would be removed from the game or stands and the teaching process would begin. There just are not the trappings of aggression that tend to take place at many sporting events. For example, in basketball, it is commonplace today to see students and fans screaming at an opposing player to miss a free throw. Boys Town youth and fans are taught and expected to be silent when an opposing player is shooting a free throw; there is no taunting or yelling to distract the player. Also, before a football game, our team lines up at midfield, faces the opposing team, and claps as a way of acknowledging and showing respect for the other team. This type of sportsmanship shows kids how to compete with character and behave in healthy and appropriate ways during good times and bad times.

Expectations

Because some kids have mental health diagnoses, delinquent and aggressive histories, and learning problems, there is a tendency in the culture at large to make allowances for their behavior and misbehavior. From the very first day kids come to Boys Town, they are all expected to behave "normally." What adults work hard to do is to define for kids what "normal" is – and exactly what it looks and sounds like.

The kids here are expected not to be aggressive and instead are taught prosocial skills, like how to greet people in a friendly way, accept criticism, appropriately express their feelings, and many other nonaggressive skills. The expectations for the proper use of social skills are very high priorities.

We expect all our kids, even those who are challenged with learning problems, psychological or psychiatric troubles, and social deprivation issues to behave within a common set of norms. They are all expected to have an overt positiveness for their behavior by using social skills like greeting adults, maintaining composure when being criticized, providing an apology for inconveniencing someone, and others.

Even though we have some of the most aggressive kids in the country, there is an expectation that violence and aggression do not happen here. In fact, the expectation is exactly the opposite – that kids will behave nonviolently by being respectful of adults, authority figures, and peers. And, kids are expected to learn how to build positive relationships and friendships with these people.

Expectations are not in place just for our children; they are there for the adults too, including Family-Teachers, schoolteachers, coaches, police, and other community supports involved with the children. Adults do their best to not role model aggression or hostility. All this helps create Boys Town's interlinked ecology.

We work hard to create a positive micro-social environment and reduce or eliminate behaviors that create negative behaviors like hostile language that leads to aggression or disparaging comments that lead to bullying. It is the micro-social interactions that either trigger violence, passivity, or kindness (Dishion & Patterson, 2006). It is the small interactions that ultimately produce either prosocial or antisocial behaviors. For example, hostile eye contact, an aggressive posture, or a T-shirt with an aggressive slogan or a pejorative phrase aimed at a peer, starts a chain of events that triggers blowups or aggression.

As previously stated, we work hard to capitalize on the concept of behavioral infection. This means that aggression begets aggression and kindness begets kindness. Behavioral infection dictates that one behavior can cause another similar behavior almost in sequence immediately thereafter. Every interaction causes a reaction. By striving to influence the micro-social environment with all these inputs and by being knowledgeable of the concept of behavioral infection, we create healthy and positive micro-social interactions with kids and adults.

The expectations at Boys Town are that we are to be "hyper-nice" and "hyper-respectful." This infects other kids and the whole culture with a tendency to use good social skills and to not be aggressive. When an aggressive or violent child comes into the Boys Town environment, yelling, cursing, and other aggressive behavior from the child is not met with "like" behavior. Instead, the child's behavior is met with a calm voice tone and teaching on how to appropriately express frustration or anger. Whenever aggressive or violent behavior occurs, it is immediately countered by non-aggressive behavior and the child is taught alternative skills to better get his or her needs and wants met.

The failure of some approaches to aggression is that too much focus is put on the individual child and not enough on the ecology. Also, some approaches maintain "institutional tolerances," meaning they have the belief or expectation that kids cannot help but be aggressive because they are emotionally disturbed or have an anger disorder. We have a "noninstitutional tolerance," meaning we believe kids can control their emotions and not be aggressive regardless of background or ability. Our experience has been that by setting noninstitutional tolerances, aggressive and violent kids should not be treated like they have an anger disorder. Even though a child might have a conduct disorder diagnosis or oppositional defiant disorder diagnosis, we expect the child to behave appropriately. In a sense, we ignore the diagnosis and deal with the behaviors. We work hard to teach these kids that it is inappropriate to be aggressive, to curse, to scream at others, to break things. Then, we teach appropriate behaviors, and kids are expected to use them. We give them lots of chances to use these new skills. If they use them, they can expect positive consequences. If they do not, they can expect negative consequences and more skill teaching.

We have expectations for appropriate behavior but we also aim to teach, teach, teach. These changes do not happen right away but they do happen, and they do happen for most children. We are always teaching to build in more competencies with a child so he or she does not have to use over-learned aggressive behavior to get needs met. Instead, we teach the child five or six new ways to get needs met in appropriate, socially acceptable ways that he or she did not known about upon arrival.

The ecology here is most powerful because some of the strongest expectations are placed on children by the other children in the environment – the very kids who once behaved violently. When a new boy or girl comes in using aggressive behaviors (cursing, shouting, etc.), other kids quickly pull the new child aside and say something like this: "I was just like that when I first came here, too. But I learned that kind of stuff does not work here. It is not the way Boys Town is; you do not need to do that stuff to protect yourself. You do not have to watch your back; you now have friends who will watch your back. Here, everyone is going to treat you with respect, and you are expected to treat everyone with respect, too." At Boys Town, some of the most powerful expectations and teaching come from the child's peers.

Social Skills Teaching

There are 182 skills in Boys Town's social skills curriculum, and we work hard to help every child attain competency with as many of these skills as possible. (For detailed information about these skills and the social skills curriculum, see the book, *Teaching Social Skills to Youth, A Step-by-Step Guide to 182 Basic to Complex Skills Plus Helpful Teaching Techniques, Second Edition*, at www.boystownpress.org.) These skills do not encompass the full range of human behaviors by any means, but they do come close to the full range of behaviors children need to succeed with family members, peers, and authority figures at home, in school, sports, and work without ever having to engage in aggressive behaviors. However, it is not just about trying to depress aggressive behavior that is in our expectancy; instead, our expectancy is the social competency that a child gains by learning all these skills.

Let's look at an example of social skill teaching that involves guests who come to dinner at Boys Town homes. Before the guest arrives, Family-Teachers teach the kids how to ask questions about the guest's life and what kinds of questions are appropriate to ask – e.g., what the person does for a living, questions about the guest's family, and other questions that aren't too personal. This teaches kids basic listening and questioning skills that make up the more complex social skill of carrying on a conversation. This kind of complex social skill (and many others) can easily be taught by any adult in any setting (home, school, sports, club, work). This kind of social skill teaching happens every day at Boys Town and guests leave amazed at how Boys Town Family-Teachers can get teenagers to talk with and show interest in adults.

There are twenty-four hours in a day and you can fill those hours tolerating a lot of aggression or teaching a lot of new adaptive skills. Either approach you emphasize is going to depress the time you have to do the other just based upon the sand in the hourglass. The social skill focus at Boys Town is more about competency and learning prosocial behavior than it is just about attempting to reduce aggression. If all we did was attempt to reduce aggression, we would likely fail. There is so much expectancy and reinforcement for learning and using the social skills curriculum that these behaviors replace a lot of aggressive behaviors. Behavioral analysts call this "differential reinforcement of other behaviors" or DRO. A focus on learning new, incompatible behaviors can help reduce unwanted behavior such as aggression.

Social skills are the building blocks of human behavior because they are ways to conceptualize complex human interactions into things that can easily be understood, taught, and learned. In addition, with chains of skills, you get very sophisticated interactions. For example, the skill of being kind involves a combination of listening skills, using a pleasant voice tone, saying certain words in a gentle way, not saying certain words that are aggressive or insensitive, learning how to ask questions instead of make statements, gentle touching, and a tender look. Kindness is a very complex human behavior; some might even call it an emotion. But, we understand that kindness is not communicated to another human being without the skills of look, touch, words, posture, etc. And the building blocks of that concept or emotion of kindness are what we call social skills.

The presence of aggression also is a complex interrelationship of social skills. For example, when two people from different political viewpoints are having a political discussion, there is an inherent conflict and tension in their discussion. They are going to disagree on certain issues. That interaction will remain civil to the extent that both parties have a wide array of social skills to keep the discussion in the civil realm. The interaction will become loud or heated to the extent that one individual in the interaction does not have a wide range of "civilized" ways to express disagreement during conflict.

The secret to Boys Town's social skill curriculum is that we use the concept of behavioral infection to our advantage. As mentioned previously, it is a fact of human behavior that aggression begets aggression, anger begets anger, and loud voice tone begets loud voice tone. But also, calmness begets calmness, praise gets a positive reaction, and gentleness calms nervousness. We attempt to break the cyclic nature of that natural process by teaching our adults to carefully control their own behavior. This begins to infect the micro-social interaction that will continue to escalate the tendency of children to become louder and more aggressive. It now infects them with calmness. That is one aspect of our social skill teaching here that is so important.

We teach and use different sets of social skills that allow aggressive kids to learn new, alternative ways to behave, including sets of social skills related to respect for adults and peers, kindness to others, politeness and manners, problem solving, and others. Aggression comes about due to a dearth of skills that cause kids to express disrespect for adults and animosity towards others. At Boys Town, we strive to identify the over-expression of negative skills and remediate that over-expression by building in tendencies for kids and adults to behave in opposite fashions. (Also see Chapter 3 for further discussion of social skills.)

Values

"He ain't heavy, Father. He's my brother."

These words were uttered long ago to Father Flanagan after an older boy had just carried a younger boy, who had braces on his legs from a disease that weakened them, up three fights of stairs on his back. Reportedly, Father Flanagan had said, "He is getting big. Isn't he heavy?" Today, this boy's words, and the meaning and values behind them, remain alive and well at Boys Town.

When kids first come here, they are told this story as part of their formal introduction to Boys Town and its rich history and culture. This is done to teach kids about the value of "concern for others." Treatment cannot really begin until they buy into something outside themselves. And that something involves caring for others. Change does not happen until youth are willing to give up control and show concern and appreciation for others.

Ultimately, aggression is an act where one is so unconcerned about others that he or she does not care about hurting them, whether that is emotionally, mentally, spiritually, or physically. That is why aggressive kids at Boys Town are taught and use the value of "other-centeredness."

As children begin to learn to be other-centered, it changes them and their thoughts about themselves and others. The contagion theory states that when you put aggressive and delinquent kids together, it foments more aggression and delinquency. The contagion theory works for us and not against us here, because staff work to help kids buy into the value of the "other-centeredness" that is behind the words "He ain't heavy, Father. He's my brother."

When kids come to Boys Town with a propensity for hatred, aggression, lack of understanding, and prejudices, they get caught up in the positive contagion of others here who say that those ways are not the Boys Town ways. This kind of positive contagion is an important element that

58

all good, healthy neighborhoods, schools, spiritual communities, and families impart to its members.

When a community has one or more of its institutions – from neighborhood to church to school to family – out of sync regarding prosocial values promotion, it is harder to create that positive contagion. We have that positive contagion here in all aspects of our ecology. Unfortunately, too many American ecologies or communities have breakdowns within their major institutions which makes aggression and violence extremely difficult to overcome. However, these institutions must be engaged because they are the building blocks for teaching values and prosocial behavior.

It is important to shore up the families and institutions in communities that are struggling. Boys Town strives to help others do this through programs like Common Sense Parenting®, In-Home Family Services℠, and the Boys Town Education Model℠. The types of interventions and services these programs offer can help families and schools all over the country learn how to reduce aggression in their children, families, and schools. In the process, we teach families how to recognize those other social supports outside their family (churches, Scout groups, mentoring programs, other schools and neighborhoods, etc.) that can help them build a better, healthier ecology for their children and other family members. And we help teachers and school administrators build a culture that promotes a positive learning environment.

The value of other-centeredness we teach to kids also comes from traditional Judeo-Christian sources. For example, there is a lot contained in the Ten Commandments that promotes nonaggression ("Honor your father and your mother." "You shall not kill." "Neither shall you steal."). In addition, the Bible asks men and women to love God and to love their neighbor as themselves. These are the basic foundations for being other-centered. Any of the values-promoting systems that we have here – religion, the Ten Commandments, and even our behavior therapy – are trying to get kids to become other-centered.

Community service is another value in the Boys Town community. The psychological literature says that empathy training and development is one of the therapies psychotherapists use to promote less aggression. The literature also states that the psychopathic personality and antisocial personality do not have empathy for human pain and suffering. If they did, they would not lie, cheat, steal, and/or harm others. Community service is currently popular in many U.S. schools as a way to promote and teach kids empathy and how to get outside of themselves. Community service has been a major part of Boys Town and its schools and homes for many, many years.

We also promote values through the programs discussed earlier like CHARACTER COUNTS! and Competing with Character, which are used at home, at school, and in sports. In addition, we promote and teach these values through family discussions at home and classroom discussions at school, and in the discussion of sermons following religious services. As you can see, we spend time focusing on values, and it makes a huge difference. Families can do this. Schools can do this. And churches can do this if parents attend services with their children. We believe some of the answers to reducing aggression lie in the making of positive values promotion an inherent part of major community institutions.

Values (other-centeredness, empathy, community service) are emphasized and taught at every level. This creates the positive contagion where all community systems are coming together to say that values are important. This can happen in any community, and parents can find such supports from leaders, mentors, ministers, and schools if parents seek it out. Even if parents cannot tap into such supports, they can still make values teaching happen in their own family.

Media, Appearance, and Language

When kids surround themselves with the trappings of aggression, they are more likely to be aggressive and violent. This is certainly the case with the models and symbols of aggression represented in the media, personal appearance, and the use of language. Media includes the aggressive and violent content on the Internet, in movies, on TV, in video games, and in music. Youth dress, hairstyle, body adornment, and tattoos also can create an aura of aggression and violence. It is as if the youth is saying, "Look at me; I am angry and you do not like it." What kids say and how they go about communicating with others also is very important.

We limit aggressive and violent communication in these three areas and work hard to replace them with positive, prosocial communication modes. For example, our kids are encouraged to view websites, watch movies and TV shows, and listen to contemporary music that have positive themes and messages. Also, our kids are encouraged not to set themselves apart from others in the community by how they dress and in the language they use.

Boys Town kids enjoy using computers, watching movies and TV, and playing video games like most kids. But, our kids are not allowed to view or watch content that is very aggressive or violent. Also, some music genres heavily represent aggression and violence, especially hip-hop and rap, which are the modern music genres to which many of our kids prefer to listen. We do not eliminate all rap, just specific songs and sometimes certain rappers. Our kids are not allowed to listen to those artists whose music is filled with themes of aggression, violence, and degradation toward others. The very fact that adults teach youth what is violent and degrading is an important communication about values and behaviors.

Some kids can be very countercultural in how they look, which postures them as "flipping off" society. That is why we limit certain dress that postures someone for aggression and violence. For example, we would not allow a youth to wear a T-shirt that reads, "I'm a badass." It is the same thing as helping kids avoid the drug culture by not allowing them to wear T-shirts displaying marijuana leaves or alcohol products. Instead, kids are encouraged to dress well in the mainstream fashion, and not to champion hairstyles, body adornments, and tattoos that promote or glorify aggression and violence. For example, if a boy arrives with a gang tattoo, he is required to cover it up. That way, he cannot use it as a way to try and intimidate other kids. Ultimately, we know we are making progress with very aggressive youth when they ask to have their gang tattoo (or other tattoo representing aggression or violence) removed so they do not have to cover it up anymore.

Also, there is a concept in the literature known as "stimulus-change." The most common example of this is when people dress up for church or religious services. No matter who they are or what walk of life they come from, they know church is a place to be respectful, and appropriate dress is part of that. When people wear nice clothes, they actually behave better. We use the concept of stimulus-change with our kids in regard to clothing to help promote better behavior, whether they are in church, school, or out in public.

Words are very crucial. Obviously, curse words are precursors to arguing and even more aggressive behavior. Slang words like "pimp," "slut," "bitch," or "boy" are out of line in peer-to-peer or adult-to-youth interactions. It is not just what is said, but how words are said that must be taught to children. Voice tone, eye contact, and gestures all create an atmosphere of friendship and approachability or intimidation and aggression.

Ultimately, the goal for our kids is for them to be part of mainstream culture. We ask them to be successful at school and to be ready to do well in the workplace once they leave. In order to achieve and maintain these kinds of successes, kids have to be willing and learn how to give up some of their aggressive symbols related to media, appearance, and language.

Functional Communities

Functional communities have common rallying points. These common rallying points are what make communities strong. For example,

LIMERICK COUNTY LIBRARY

when the American colonies went to war with Great Britain, it was over democracy and the desire for self-rule. When the founding fathers got together to write the Declaration of Independence, they were rallying around this concept of democracy and self-rule. This was the building block that made the thirteen colonies come together to form one country. These kinds of rallying points are essential for forming healthy communities.

We have wonderful examples of subcultures with common rallying points in our country – e.g., a group of Jewish families in a Jewish congregation, a group of Islamic families in an Islamic congregation, or a group of Catholic families in a Catholic congregation. They are rallying around spiritual beliefs and certain tenants on how to live life. And, organizations like Big Brothers/Big Sisters and Habitat for Humanity are secular examples of subcultures rallying around common values and principles.

As society has become more diverse, these common goals and rallying points are somewhat harder to bring to community-wide scale. Even a moderate-sized community like Omaha is divided into smaller communities, neighborhoods, and groups that have widely divergent beliefs and behaviors.

Father Flanagan's famous saying, "There is no such thing as a bad boy," was our initial rallying point at Boys Town and it remains the essence of who we are today. Early on, this became operationalized into "Flanagan's model of care," which was comprised of these four elements:

> Values/spiritual development

> Focus on education

> Focus on employability/functional skills

> Self-determination

Flanagan's model worked brilliantly until the late 1960s and early 1970s when there was a cultural revolution involving family fractionalization, spiritual confusion, and drugs. Flanagan's elements were still potent but another element needed to be added – treatment – for the model to remain effective. Thus, the new Boys Town Model incorporates all five of these elements – the initial four elements and treatment. These elements work together and are empirically related to better social skills, less aggression, and long-term outcomes like lower recidivism and higher graduation rates. That is why our Treatment Family Home^{SM} Model is on two evidence-based practice lists.

The current rallying point that makes us strong is our research-based Boys Town Model, which is still rooted in "There is no such thing as a bad boy." The current Model combines the elements of Flanagan's thoughts with the best available science about youth development and behavior.

Today, we have been able to replicate various elements of the Boys Town Model in twelve communities around the country. This demonstrates that it is not only the Village of Boys Town that can thrive around this rallying point, other communities can, too. We plan to bring these elements to wider and wider circles in each of the twelve communities in which we serve children and families.

"There is no such thing as a bad boy" is as relevant today as it was when Father Flanagan founded Boys Town in 1917. It still inspires and rallies 2,500 employees across the country in our organization every year. It can be a rallying point not only for employees at Boys Town sites but also for advocates, educators, other organizations, and institutions in those communities. It is harder to create common rallying points in diverse communities but we have no choice but to try.

Having a model of care is always better than not having one because you can train, evaluate, and research it. But more than that, it gives you a "game plan" to use every day. It tells you how, what, and when to teach. A good game plan is extremely important for success in any endeavor, especially in helping kids who have problems with aggression and violence.

The Boys Town Model is our common game plan here. It gives staff something to hold onto and an approach to use every day in just about any situation with any child. The only way to effectively work with and help aggressive and troubled children is for adults to be unrelenting in their teaching and in their approach – and in their message that aggression and violence are not allowed, that kids will solve problems peacefully, and that they will use the skills they are taught in their minute-to-minute, day-to-day interactions with others. Our Model of care has become a rallying point because adults see it work so well, and it gives them confidence to successfully deal with difficult kid issues like aggression and violence.

All communities would be much better off if they had some common ways of at least approaching major community issues, like how to educate kids, how kids should behave and dress at school, how kids and teachers should relate to each other, how parents and teachers should relate to each other, and others. This could be a model of care and game plan for how to best approach and reduce aggression and violence in your home, neighborhood, school, and community.

In succeeding chapters, you will learn more about specific techniques and operating principles that flow out of our Model of care.

CHAPTER 4

How Boys Town Reduces Aggression

When Father Edward J. Flanagan founded Boys Town in 1917, he started a revolution in the way America cares for her troubled children. His ideas about surrounding kids with love and teaching them how to be productive citizens were far ahead of their time, and set new standards for child care.

Over the years, Boys Town has helped tens of thousands of children change their lives for the better. And as the problems kids and families face have become more complex and difficult, Boys Town has changed to meet those new challenges. The ability to develop treatment approaches that are innovative and effective, yet still have as their foundation the old-fashioned love and respect championed by Father Flanagan, has always been one of Boys Town's strengths. From that strength and the desire to remain on the cutting edge of child-care technology came the Boys Town Model.

Today, Boys Town has developed its Integrated Continuum of Care℠ (see Figure 1) as part of an ongoing effort to expand the life-changing care we provide to children and families across the United States. The Continuum is unique to Boys Town and enables us to deliver the right treatment at the right time to troubled children and families who are edging toward crisis.

Across the Continuum's service levels and in all programs, treatment is consistently effective because it's based on the research-proven Boys Town Model. As children and families make progress (or fail to make progress) at one level, they can move to other levels that better fit their needs,

Figure 1

Integrated Continuum of Child and Family Services

UNIFYING ELEMENTS FOR ALL LEVELS OF CARE

Safety, Permanency and Well-Being
Family Engagement
Religion and Faith
Behavioral and Medical Research

without starting over in their treatment and all within the same treatment model.

Services toward the top of the Continuum provide more intensive care and interventions to children with serious emotional or behavioral problems. Children receive these services outside of their homes, but the family stays involved so reunification with the family, whenever possible, is always the ultimate goal. Services toward the base of the Continuum provide treatment for and in the family, preventing children from being removed from their homes, and assisting parents through providing training, counseling, and other resources.

To support and further connect the Continuum, certain fundamental ideals, standards, and principles cut across all service levels and programs. We call these our "Unifying Elements," and they enable us to put the needs of children and families first in providing consistent, effective care and treatment. These Unifying Elements are:

Safety, Permanency, and Well-Being

> Children and families must be safe and feel safe in any treatment setting.

> Treatment goals include helping children and families get better so they can live in a safe, stable, and permanent home setting.

> Helping children and families make positive changes can ensure their present and future well-being.

Family Engagement

> In any program, families are active, essential members of their children's treatment team, partnering with Boys Town to plan and develop strategies that best meet the children's needs.

Religion and Faith

> Religion and faith give children and families a foundation of strength for overcoming difficult treatment issues and problems.

Behavioral and Medical Research

> Research develops new programs, measures the effectiveness of Boys Town's care and treatment, determines what's working and what's not, and identifies when changes are needed.

At the heart of every one of these services and programs on the Continuum is the Boys Town Model. The result of extensive research and decades of experience working with children, the Model has evolved and been improved to meet the unique problems that today's kids and caregivers face. It is a proven, successful model of care that is effective in diverse settings and situations with a variety of youth populations. Replicated at Boys Town sites across the country and in many child-care programs and school systems, the Model provides a practical approach to helping troubled kids learn new prosocial ways to solve problems and get their needs met.

The Boys Town Model comprises these main qualities: teaching social skills, building relationships, developing spiritual growth and moral values, and empowering kids through teaching self-control. These components make the Model especially effective when working with aggressive children and adolescents. Social skill instruction gives kids new, positive behaviors that can replace aggressive behaviors. As youth become proficient in using new skills, they are better able to meet their needs in new ways and control their feelings and behaviors. This sense of empowerment helps kids understand and feel confident that they can make good decisions on their own. Spiritual growth and moral development are essential ingredients in teaching kids about change and hope, and about choosing to do the right thing. Finally, relationship-building is crucial because it helps kids perceive the adults around them more positively. Kids are more receptive to teaching if they believe that someone genuinely cares about them. They also learn that getting along with other people is a more positive experience than using force or intimidation, and that respecting the rights of others is the only way to earn real respect.

In this chapter, we will discuss the components of the Boys Town Model and how they are effective in Boys Town's approach to treating aggression. In addition, we will present a summary of Boys Town's research and data that shows that exposure to and treatment provided through the Boys Town Model results in reduced aggression in kids. In following chapters, we will explain the Teaching Interactions – Corrective Teaching, Teaching Self-Control, Effective Praise, and Proactive Teaching – that are used in Boys Town's Common Sense Parenting® Program and are part of the Boys Town Model's treatment approach.

Overview of Social Skill Instruction

The philosophy of the Boys Town Model regarding social skill instruction is that youth who display aggressive or violent behaviors (and other antisocial behaviors) do so because they have not learned, or have learned not to use more positive, appropriate ways to deal with situations that instigate feelings of anger, frustration, and disappointment. They habitually react to situations that arouse unpleasant feelings by lashing out in hostile and, at times, violent ways. In order to help these kids overcome their aggression problem, the Model focuses on teaching and strengthening alternative prosocial skills or behaviors. Aggressive kids are taught new skills – or ways to behave – that allow them to get what they want or need and solve problems in peaceful, productive, and socially acceptable ways.

In the Boys Town Model, social, academic, and vocational skills, as well as spiritual values, are taught in a variety of ways – proactively teaching at neutral times, rewarding positive behavior as it occurs, helping kids practice and rehearse new skills, correcting inappropriate behavior in a positive fashion, and helping youth learn to use alternative appropriate behaviors when they face crisis situations. (We will talk more about each of these methods later in the book.)

According to Combs and Slaby (1977), a social skill can be defined as "the ability to interact with others in a given social context in specific ways that are socially acceptable or valued and, at the same time, personally beneficial, mutually beneficial, or beneficial primarily to others." Thus, social skills are sets of behaviors that can be modified to fit the demands of the social context and particular situation. In addition, using these skills benefits the person who uses them as well as others.

During the entire treatment planning process, it is extremely important for caregivers to view each child individually. This is especially true when determining what social skills are the most appropriate and therapeutic for each youth. For example, even though two kids may have aggression as their primary treatment issue, each youth may need to learn a different set of skills in order to best meet his or her treatment goals.

Boys Town has identified and developed 182 skills as part of its Social Skill Curriculum. These skills help caregivers address a wide variety of youth issues at all levels, from minor school- or home-related problems to more serious problems like aggression, delinquency, depression, and suicide. These four types of skills – basic, intermediate, advanced, and complex – give kids alternative positive behaviors to use instead of the negative behaviors that get them in trouble.

Typically, when youngsters are first introduced to social skill instruction they need to learn the most basic skills *(Following Instructions, Accepting Consequences, Accepting "No" Answers)*. This lays a foundation for learning more complex skills *(Expressing Feelings Appropriately, Being Assertive, Using Spontaneous Problem-Solving)*. Many times, caregivers will need to gradually shape a youth's behavior in order to teach more difficult skills. Caregivers can begin this process by first patiently teaching the basic social skills. Once a child demonstrates proficiency using a certain skill or set of skills, you can introduce and begin teaching the next appropriate, more complex skill. Shaping can sometimes be a slow, arduous process for caregivers and youth, but it is necessary if a youth is to overcome his or her problems.

For some kids, appropriately and consistently using social skills is difficult because it involves an immensely complex chain of rapidly occurring interpersonal events. For example, some aggressive youth have such serious and habitual behavior problems that they meet DSM-IV diagnostic criteria (Conduct Disorder or Oppositional Defiant Disorder). For some kids, these troublesome behaviors occur with such frequency that they interfere with learning prosocial skills and even academic skills. These youth have a difficult time organizing and blending their behaviors into smooth-flowing interactions with others, particularly when they are in conflictual interactions. Since each youth has his or her own unique learning style, you must be able and willing to adjust your teaching techniques, vocabulary, and interpersonal behaviors to best meet each youngster's needs.

Other factors like the age and developmental level of the youngster, severity and intensity of the youth's behaviors, and the length of time a youth has been exposed to social skill instruction play an important role in a caregiver's decisions on which social skills to teach as part of treatment. Often, the success or failure of a youth's Treatment Plan hinges on these decisions. Once caregivers identify and prioritize the appropriate skills for treatment, they can use the various Teaching Interactions (Proactive Teaching, Effective Praise, Corrective Teaching, and Teaching Self-Control) to reinforce and teach youth new prosocial ways of responding to others, and to situations that have caused them problems in the past.

Boys Town's book, *Teaching Social Skills to Youth with Mental Health Disorders: Incorporating Social Skills into Treatment Planning for 109 Disorders* contains a series of charts that list social skills to teach to children and adolescents who require treatment for specific mental health diagnoses. The curriculum in *Teaching Social Skills to Youth* can also be easily integrated into a variety of settings (natural home environment, classroom, foster care program, group home residential program, psychiatric treatment program, and others) for troubled kids with a variety of problems.

The Teaching Interactions that form the cornerstone of treatment planning and active intervention at Boys Town will be presented later in this book. Also, Chapter 12, "Social Skills for Aggressive Youth," in this book contains skills from the Boys Town Social Skill Curriculum that are specific, appropriate, and therapeutic for treating kids who tend to use reactive or proactive aggression.

Flexibility in Teaching

No two children are the same. Each youngster views the world differently and has his or her own unique strengths, weaknesses, and learning history. Therefore, it's important to individualize your teaching to tailor each child's needs.

Think of building a home. In every blueprint there are certain basic architectural guidelines that must be followed so that the house won't collapse in a storm or other natural events. However, you can change or modify various elements of the blueprint to fit your needs (larger kitchen, extra bedroom, two-car garage, and so on) without changing the strength of the structure. The structure of the Boys Town teaching methods works the same way; it provides caregivers with a solid blueprint or framework for teaching to aggressive youngsters, but leaves plenty of room for modification. These modifications may be necessary due to a number of factors which mainly determine the frequency of teaching. For teaching to be as effective as possible, caregivers must look at the following factors and apply them to how they teach to each youth.

A youngster's age is the first factor to consider. Younger children respond better to teaching that is brief and specific. So, it's important to use language and examples in your teaching that are familiar and easy for the child to understand. The attention span of younger children is short, so don't belabor your teaching – get to the point as quickly as possible. In addition, you don't want to bombard younger children with lots of teaching. The younger a child is, the fewer times you will teach. As the child grows and matures, he or she will be better equipped to understand and handle more skills, and teaching can be done more frequently. Generally speaking, this also holds true for youngsters who have learning disabilities or mental or physical health problems.

As children get older and develop a solid foundation of skills, this pattern usually changes. They are more familiar with the behavior that is expected of them and the positive and negative consequences involved. So, the number of Teaching Interactions can decrease and they can be shorter.

The number of skills a child needs to learn is the second factor that will affect how and when teaching will occur. Children who have large skill deficits will require more teaching in order to help them learn new skills as quickly as possible. On the other hand, kids who have mastered a large number of skills will require fewer Teaching Interactions. This also applies to a child's developmental level. Youth who are more mature may require less teaching, while youngsters who are less mature may need more teaching.

For youth-care programs, there are two main factors that determine the amount of teaching that occurs – the length of time a youngster has been in the program and the ratio of staff to children. If a youth is new to a program, he or she will likely require more teaching. This is true because most kids who have been in a program for a short time have not yet learned, don't know how, or are not accustomed to using the basic skills that are necessary building blocks for learning more complex skills. Conversely, a child who has been in a program for a longer period of time has been taught certain skills numerous times, and knows what behaviors are expected.

When there is a lower caregiver-to-child ratio, caregivers will have more opportunities to teach. A caregiver who is responsible for four youngsters will have more time for teaching than a caregiver who is caring for twenty youth.

Finally, the relationships you develop with aggressive youngsters will have a great impact on the direction your teaching will take. At the beginning of a relationship and/or in a weak relationship, teaching will be more structured and take more time. But as your relationship with the youth grows stronger, less teaching should be required and your teaching will become more natural and brief.

Building Relationships

Attempting to help troubled youth change is difficult unless there is a strong relationship between a caregiver and a youth. Unfortunately, the importance of developing a relationship with children who have aggression problems is often undervalued, overlooked, and ignored by some adults. Instead, they try to control aggressive children by demanding obedience and compliance, especially when these kids are upset or in crisis. This mentality only leads to disaster for both the caregiver and the child; a tug-of-war approach is what aggressive kids are used to and, more often than not, they will prevail. In reality, no one wins with this mindset. As a matter of fact, everyone loses. Caregivers and kids end up frustrated and angry with each other, and this ultimately has a devastating effect on the youngster's treatment.

When caregivers focus on building genuine, warm relationships with aggressive kids, they create a bond of trust, and kids begin to feel connected and worthwhile. They are much more likely to want to learn from and try to imitate a person who is warm, fun to be with, and dependable. In addition, caregivers can uncover and develop some of the redeeming and likable qualities that aggressive kids have in their personalities. Instead of continually wrestling to control youth, caregivers can begin to enjoy working with and being around the youth. As the relationship becomes stronger and matures, caregivers and youth start to have more good times together than bad. This can be a turning point for aggressive youngsters because they finally have the understanding and support they need to make the changes in their lives.

When adults are perceived as caring and concerned, it helps all youth, including aggressive youth, learn new ways of thinking, feeling, and behaving. Teaching gives kids the skills they need to become responsible and independent people. But relationships make your teaching sincere and effective. By sending the message to children that you care about them, you give them a sense of belonging and self-worth. For many aggressive kids this may be the first time this has happened! Over time, these positive feelings become reciprocal; in other words, kids also start to care about and like you. When this happens, they are more receptive to your teaching and more willing to change for the better.

Building relationships comes naturally for some people; others may have to work at honing the skills and qualities necessary for creating a solid bond with troubled youngsters. But anyone who works with aggressive youth must make these skills and qualities part of their interaction style and make using them a priority as they work with kids.

Here are some important skills and qualities that can help you create and establish happy and healthy relationships with kids in your care:

> **Smiling** – This quality demonstrates warmth and pleasantness across many different situations. It's also free! Smiling makes people feel good inside. It comforts others when they are sad, lonely, or depressed. A simple smile can be an invitation to friendship, and a signal that a person is approachable and welcomes your presence.

> **Having fun** – Many caregivers hesitate to have fun with the kids in their care for many reasons. Some caregivers are worried about losing authority and control, while others fear that showing a "human" side makes them vulnerable. Some caregivers rationalize that they are too busy dealing with other problems, while others simply don't know how to have fun. But having fun with kids is a great way to create an environment of warmth and acceptance while teaching kids valuable lessons about sharing, respecting others, taking responsibility, following rules, accepting defeat, or being gracious in winning. There are many ways children can enjoy your company and your teaching without you losing any respect or authority (trivia quiz, a board or word game, playing card games, playing catch or shooting baskets, and many others).

> **Humor** – Laughter is great medicine. Seeing or perceiving the amusing and funny events that happen every day and sharing a laugh with kids is extremely healthy both for the youth and for caregivers. Humor and laughter give kids a break from their daily struggle to overcome their aggression problems and from the other stresses in their lives. For caregivers, working with and caring for aggressive children is a tough job. Learning to find humor in what happens, especially during stressful times or crisis situations, can help insulate caregivers from the negative thoughts and feelings that can threaten to overwhelm them.

> **Learn to laugh at yourself** – All of us have shortcomings and we all make mistakes. Laughing at yourself means admitting that you have weaknesses just like everyone else. When caregivers are able to admit their mistakes and laugh at themselves, it sends the message to the kids that it's okay

to make mistakes. But it is also important that caregivers model for kids how to learn from and correct mistakes and shortcomings.

> **Joking and teasing (appropriately)** – Telling funny stories, joking with kids, and teasing in an appropriate way provides relief from the daily tensions of life and usually allows caregivers and youth to better enjoy each other's company. However, joking – and potentially teasing – can be a delicate area and you must know what can and can't be said in certain situations with certain kids. It is risky to joke or tease a child in a sarcastic or condescending manner if a relationship is not yet established. Caregivers should take their time in this area and test the water. Some kids will understand the purpose and intent of your joking and teasing better than others and enjoy it; others, however, may interpret joking and teasing as a "put down" or a "slam." Generally, it is wise for caregivers to wait until they have developed a sound relationship with a child before they begin joking and teasing.

> **Empathy** – Empathy means trying to understand another person's situation and feelings. When aggressive kids are in a treatment program, it is a very emotional and trying time in their lives. These kids are going through many tumultuous changes, and they often don't know how to handle the conflicting and confusing feelings and emotions that these changes bring. Empathy from caregivers can assist kids through these rough times, and help them learn new ways to behave. Caregivers must accept the responsibility of providing a helping hand and an attentive ear to these kids. In order for troubled children to get better, they need to have a caring adult around who is willing to listen and acknowledge their feelings.

> **Praise** – Our society isn't very good in this area. Simply watch the nightly news or look at the front page of the newspaper; negativity and disaster abound. Only acts of unbelievable heroism or kindness are acknowledged, while almost all other good deeds go unnoticed. Adults, particularly those working in treatment programs, have been conditioned to notice the negative things kids do; that means they often ignore positive things kids do. Recognizing and praising kids' positive behavior might seem awkward at first because you aren't used to it, but praising kids is one of the most

important tools in helping them get better. Caregivers must learn to focus on, recognize, and acknowledge kids when they do something right, no matter how small or insignificant it might seem. Kids thrive on your kind words and will likely repeat what they did in order to experience the good feelings that spring from your praise.

> **Listening** – Many troubled youngsters come from environments where parents or guardians live by the axiom, "Children should be seen and not heard." This may be one reason why some kids use aggression. In other words, many children and adolescents have learned to behave and act out aggressively to get the attention they crave. In their young minds, negative attention from adults is better than no attention at all. Kids need to have someone listen to what they have to say, especially when they are trying to change. Many youth with behavior disorders haven't learned appropriate ways to communicate or express feelings, so it's crucial for you to calmly listen and carefully understand what a child's behavior means. Is it attention seeking? Is it coercion? Is it just a generalized means of expressing emotion or excitement? By listening to children, you can better understand the child and his or her individuality, while demonstrating care, interest, and warmth.

> **Thoughtfulness** – This involves doing or saying nice things for someone else. Thoughtfulness is one of the biggest factors in developing relationships. It is extremely powerful and takes very little time or effort. Small things – a note or card, a phone call, a compliment, a smile or word of sympathy, remembering a birthday or special occasion – can mean a great deal to kids. These little acts of kindness add up over time. When troubled children see that you are sincere in your desire to help them get better, they begin to make you a welcome part of their lives.

> **Give and take** – Healthy relationships are not one-sided; there is an equal give and take. However, when you first begin working with and caring for aggressive youngsters, it will seem like you are doing all the giving and the youth is doing all the taking. Be patient! Not surprisingly, many troubled kids think only of themselves. For some time, they will be guarded and skeptical of your motives and intentions. But as the bond between you and youth grows, they will learn to reciprocate your warmth and concern. Teach them

to express thanks, praise others, and apologize after they have made a mistake. In order to overcome their aggression problem, kids have to learn to give their time, their compassion, and themselves. This is the beginning of learning empathy.

Spiritual Growth and Moral Development

From its beginning, Boys Town has cared deeply about children's spiritual growth and moral development. Father Flanagan said, "Successful teaching calls for more than a knowledge of textbooks; it calls for an understanding of life, for an appreciation of human values." Father Flanagan's words are as true today as they were when he first wrote them. Boys Town believes spiritual growth and moral development are essential for healing, health, and happiness. We encourage you to create positive environments where kids can grow strong in mind, body, and spirit.

Because spirituality is such an important part of life, with tremendous potential for healing and hope, we don't want caregivers to avoid it. Instead, we encourage you to embrace the positive role that spiritual growth and moral development can play in effectively and successfully helping troubled girls and boys overcome their problems. With this firmly in mind, let's look at the benefits of spiritual growth and moral development for children.

Father Flanagan said, "The fact is that nothing earthly can fill the void in the human heart." What he knew from personal experience, training, and instinct, we now know from research: Spirituality can help children, teens, and adults manage life's troubles. More than five hundred studies conducted between 1980 and 2000 found positive links between spirituality and good mental health, positive well-being, and lowered rates of substance abuse. Also, involvement in a faith community provides social supports and facilitates acceptance, nurturing, and others' approval (Aten & Leach, 2009). All children need these things.

In its 2003 publication, *Hardwired to Connect: The New Scientific Case for Authoritative Communities*, the Commission on Children At Risk states:

> "Personal devotion among adolescents is associated with reduced risk-taking behavior. It is also associated with more effectively resolving feelings of loneliness, greater regard for the self and other, and a stronger sense that life has meaning and purpose." (p. 31)

Religious beliefs and practices also provide a host of benefits. Dr. Harold Koenig, co-director of the Center for Spirituality, Theology, and Health at Duke University Medical Center, reported in a 2004 article that religious beliefs and practices are associated with:

> Lower suicide rates

> Less anxiety

> Less substance abuse

> Less depression and faster recovery from depression

> Greater well-being, hope, and optimism

> More purpose and meaning in life

> Higher social support

As important as spiritual and religious beliefs are for children and families, especially those in turmoil, it must be emphasized here that Boys Town does not advocate that caregivers should proselytize or promote their individual religious faith to children. This means never forcing personal religious convictions or faith practices on girls and boys or trying to convert them.

It is important to promote and support the faith life of youth who are currently active in it. Also, it is important to discover if kids already have a spiritual/religious belief or practice, learn more about that particular belief, and then assist them in building on that source of strength to reach their goals. If kids don't demonstrate any spiritual or religious outlook, caregivers can suggest that kids make faith a part of their life, and provide them with the knowledge and tools to do so. If you approach kids with openness, respect, and care, you can assess and address spirituality and moral development in a way that builds your relationship with them and leads to better outcomes.

Encouraging Good Character and Morals

It's also important for caregivers to teach good character, regardless of the kids' spiritual orientations. Values like caring for others, respect for others, and good citizenship promote nonviolent attitudes and behaviors. The CHARACTER COUNTS Coalition's six pillars of character are an excellent framework for teaching and reinforcing moral behavior. The six pillars are: trustworthiness, respect, responsibility, fairness, caring, and citizenship.

Good character makes children more successful at home, at school, and in the community. Caregivers can teach skills to reinforce these character traits. For example, you can say, "When you learn to follow instructions, you are showing respect for yourself and your teachers. That helps things run more smoothly here, at school, and at home, too" or "When you report your whereabouts, you show you're trustworthy. That helps bring you closer together with your parents and teachers and helps you communicate with them better." (In the Boys Town Press book, *Teaching Social Skills to Youth,* Appendix B lists social skills by character pillar. You can use this resource to help you learn how to reinforce good character as you teach and work with kids.)

Emphasizing positive character traits, attitudes, and behaviors brings the discussion of aggression into the holistic intrapersonal and interpersonal realm. Aggression is not merely an individual activity by one person. It also is a moral issue. For instance, the Commandment that says to "honor your father and mother" applies to respecting authority. The Commandment that says "you shall not kill" instructs that we should not harm others. And the Commandments that speak to treating "your neighbor" well enjoins us to care about others' feelings and well-being.

Aggressive behavior is an issue of character. Even minor aggressive acts are a loss of control and a violation of the implied social contract between individuals.

Serious aggression is, of course, a crime. It is a transgression against the desired order of a social community. Caregivers should use elements of religion, character, community, values, and personal integrity when talking to children about aggressive behavior and teaching them how to meet their needs in prosocial ways.

At Boys Town, we have learned that if we approach aggression as an individual psychological tendency, we have better success in teaching children that kindness, concern for others, and nonaggressive problem solving are individual obligations for all persons in a culture.

Spirituality and moral development are powerful avenues for assistance and strength in a person's life. As a caregiver, your comfort with and openness to these areas can encourage troubled kids to tap into these important sources of hope. Your own faith can help you face the day-to-day challenges as you work with aggressive and violent youth. Be assured you are making a difference. As Father Flanagan said, "The work will continue, you see, because it is God's work, not mine."

Empowerment and Generalization

By teaching kids skills that help them to control their behavior, you are empowering youngsters to take control of their lives. When kids learn to use a skill in different situations on their own, they have "generalized" the skill. This means that a child who has learned to use a skill in one situation knows how to use the skill in different situations without adult intervention. This also means that a social skill does not have to be retaught in every new setting or situation in order for a child to know how to use it. In the Boys Town Model, the belief is that if children have mastered social skills, they can use them anywhere so long as they find an environment that values good social skills, like schools, jobs, families, churches, etc.

Generalization can be promoted by having the youth thoroughly review and practice targeted skills under conditions that are as similar as possible to the real-life situations they may face. This way, they gain experience in dealing with real-life problems, issues, and events without having to worry about making mistakes or failing. This helps set them up for success in situations where they normally have problems.

With aggressive kids, the ultimate goal of the Boys Town approach is to help them overcome their problems by teaching new, appropriate ways for them to express and control their emotions and behaviors. As kids experience success with these new skills, they become confident in their ability to make the right choices. This improves their chances for success in society. Teaching social skills, building relationships, developing spiritual growth and moral values, and empowering kids through teaching them self-control provides caregivers with a powerful approach to successfully managing and treating aggression in children and adolescents. It also gives youth who might have developed antisocial, bullying behaviors and attitudes a new identity as a person responsible for not only their own well-being but that of others.

A Proven, Effective Treatment Strategy

Caring for and helping aggressive children and adolescents can be a difficult, discouraging, and, potentially, an unsafe task for caregivers. In some situations, these kids can be dangerous; in fact, many aggressive youth are capable of severely and permanently damaging their surroundings, or hurting others or themselves. Aggression is a problem that demands a model of care that has been proven to be effective and reliable. The Boys Town Model is such a model, combining modern, technology-based services along with genuine compassion and care to competently and successfully treat the needs of aggressive kids.

How do we know that one of the Model's hallmarks – social skill instruction – is a therapeutic, effective treatment strategy? For starters, the Boys Town Model grew out of behavioral research conducted at the University of Kansas by Montrose Wolf, one of the pioneers in the applied behavior analysis movement (Baer, Wolf, & Risley, 1968). In the late 1960s and early 1970s, Wolf and his colleagues began their research to design a new treatment model for troubled youth as an effective alternative to the standard programs of the time. The new model came to be known as the

Teaching-Family Model, and it was adopted by Boys Town in 1975 (Risley, 2005). The Teaching-Family Model has been tested time and time again, across numerous settings and behavior problems, with positive results (Fixsen, Blasé, Timbers, & Wolf, 2001).

The Teaching-Family Model combines multiple components including a token-economy motivation system, detailed specification and monitoring of the desired behaviors, and skill teaching of desired behaviors. Originally, all this took place within a family home setting where the primary "teachers" or "house parents" were a married couple (Wolf, Kirigin, Fixen, Blasé, & Braukmann, 1995). The Boys Town Model, which is used in all Boys Town programs, utilizes the components previously listed, with a specific focus on teaching social skills and moral values. Today, the Model is used in a wide range of settings, such as residential homes, school classrooms, outpatient clinics, foster homes, as well as other family and community settings (see page 66 for more on the Boys Town Integrated Continuum of Care).

Over the years, Boys Town has conducted research and evaluation studies in all these program areas and settings. For instance, when youth are treated at Boys Town in our Treatment Family Homes, we know they "get better." In several studies, standardized outcome instruments (CBCL, DISC, etc.) were administered to youth. Improvements on these instruments occurred as youth learned and successfully used the social skills that were taught as part of their treatment. For example, an examination of the admission and departure Child Behavior Checklist (CBCL) scores for youth who left the Boys Town Treatment Family Homes program between 2001 and 2004 revealed that eighty percent of the girls and sixty-three percent of the boys were admitted with a CBCL total score in the clinically significant range. Remarkably, these scores had dropped to twenty-five percent for girls and twenty-four percent for boys by the time these youth departed the program (see Figure 2).

Further, youth admitted during this same time frame arrived with a variety of mental health issues that improved significantly during treatment. For example, seventy-two percent of girls and fifty-four percent of boys were admitted with a DSM-IV-TR diagnosis (this is the clinical term for a mental health disorder diagnosis). Twelve months later, only thirty percent of girls and twenty-four percent of boys continued to meet criteria for a formal DSM-IV-TR diagnosis (see Figure 3) (Boys Town National Research Institute for Child and Family Studies, 2006a).

Keep in mind that all these findings are not limited to Boys Town's residential homes. We find similar results in family settings, such as the families who have gone through our Common Sense Parenting program (Griffin, in press; Thompson, Ruma, Brewster, Besetsney, & Burke, 1997;

Figure 2

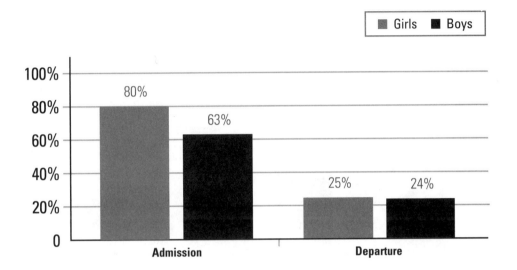

Percentage of Youth with
CBCL Scores in Clinical Range

Ruma, Burke, & Thompson, 1996; Thompson, Ruma, Schuchmann, & Burke, 1996).

Longitudinal outcome research suggests that the effects of treatment at Boys Town continue after youth depart from the program. One such study, an extensive sixteen-year follow-up completed in 2003, involved 211 former Boys Town youth and forty-one "comparison" youth who were accepted for admission to Boys Town but never came. Participants, then ages twenty-seven to thirty-seven, completed a 151-item survey measuring several life domains. Results produced two major findings: 1) As adults, those participants who received treatment at Boys Town were more likely to be functioning as productive, law-abiding citizens than those who did not, and 2) the longer these former Boys Town youth were in the treatment program, the more positive the long-term outcomes. For example, when looking at criminality, the youth who received eighteen months or more of treatment at Boys Town had lower rates of incarceration, recent arrests, criminal activity, and Intimate Partner Violence (IPV) than those youth who received six months of treatment or less (see Figure 4) (Huefner, Ringle, Chmelka, & Ingram, 2007; Ringle, Chmelka, Ingram, & Huefner, 2006).

Figure 3

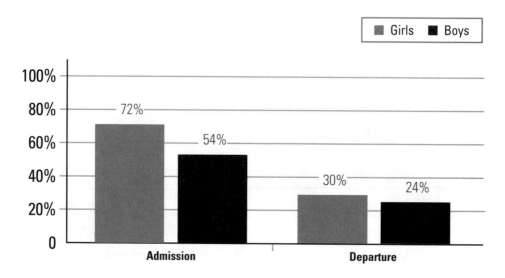

DISC: Any DSM-IV-TR Diagnosis at Admission and Twelve Months

In 2006, the Boys Town National Research Institute completed a five-year follow-up study of Boys Town youth who departed in the year 2000. Approximately two hundred former Boys Town youth (with an average age of twenty-one) responded to an eighty-five-item survey that measured social functioning and quality of life across a variety of domains. These youth entered care with a variety of risk factors, including school problems, being out-of-parental control, aggression, depression, substance use, and interpersonal problems. Five years after leaving treatment, the former Boys Town youth were functioning similar to their peers in the general population in areas like education, employment, and overall positive mental health (see Figure 5). These outcomes provide strong evidence of the efficacy of the Boys Town Model in teaching lasting social skills to youth who are struggling within everyday society (Thompson, Ringle, & Kingsley, 2007).

Finally, childhood aggression can be a primary reason for referral to Boys Town. The Boys Town Intensive Residential Treatment Center[SM] (IRTC) admits youth with high indices of aggression against peers, others, and self. Over the years, we have learned that many attempts to treat such youth involve psychotropic medication. About seventy-five percent of youth admitted to the IRTC are on such medications. It is clear that, in spite of the high medication rates, aggression remains a major problem for these

Figure 4

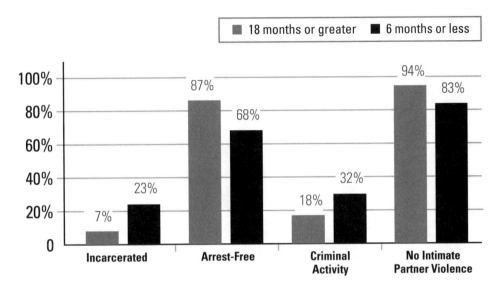

Sixteen-Year Follow-Up: Criminality

youth. At the same time that IRTC staff are teaching youth correct behavioral responses, social skills, and anger control strategies, Boys Town care workers strive to reduce unnecessary and potentially health-aversive medications. In a study of more than 230 youth admitted to the Boys Town IRTC between 2005 and 2007, the intervention provided was successful in reducing both the levels of aggressive behavior (by 63.7 percent) and the medication rates (see Figure 6). The significant reduction in aggressive behavior was key in preparing most youth to "step-down" to less-restrictive levels of care (Huefner, Spellman, & Thompson, 2009).

We believe all the research presented here, as well as numerous other positive findings (e.g., Handwerk et al., 2008; Larzelere, Daly, Davis, Chmelka, & Handwerk, 2004; Thompson et al., 1996), verify that the elements of the Boys Town Model[SM], with its emphasis on social skill training and values development, is an effective treatment option for girls and boys who have aggression problems. Just as other strategies (psychotropic medication; individual, family, or group therapy; and behavioral interventions) are prescribed as part of a youth's Treatment Plan, so too are the specific social skills that youth need to learn. Once youth have mastered these skills, they are better able to appropriately and effectively interact with their environment and those in it.

Figure 5

Five-Year Follow-Up: Positive Outcomes

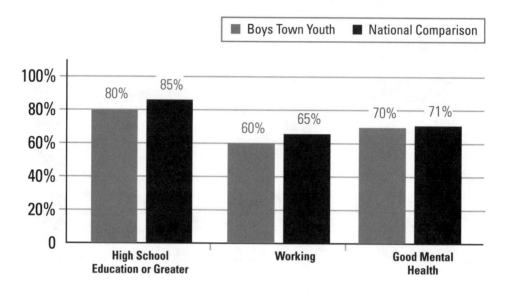

Summary

The core of the Boys Town Model involves teaching social skills, building relationships, developing spiritual growth and moral values, and empowering kids through self-control. The Model incorporates a social skill and social value instruction approach – teaching youth positive alternative skills and attitudes to replace negative behaviors and values. The Model also recognizes the importance of and need for other types of treatment strategies, like medications and therapy, in successfully treating aggression in youth, but the Model emphasizes the social aspects of aggression and antisocial behaviors over the psychotropic or biological elements. Boys Town's research has shown that social skill and social value instruction is a valuable and effective treatment option in a wide variety of treatment settings for helping troubled youth learn that success as a child and as an adult is best achieved in prosocial ways.

Boys Town's teaching methods have a structure that serves as a blueprint for caregivers when they teach to troubled and aggressive kids. But there also is flexibility built into this structure. The goal is to provide effective and therapeutic treatment for each and every child, and this is impossible to do with a rigid, blanket approach to teaching and treatment. In addition to these factors, building relationships with aggressive youth is

Figure 6

Intensive Residential Treatment Center Results

On Medication

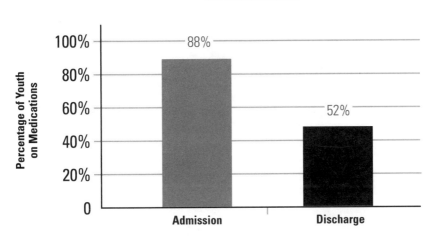

Number of Medications

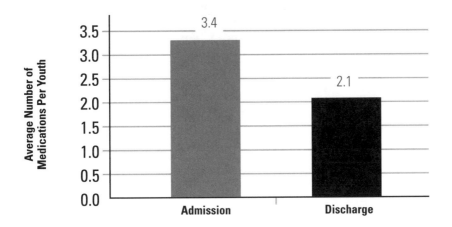

Figure 6 (continued)

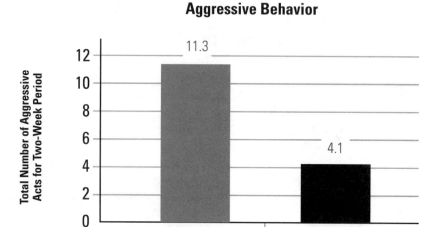

imperative for teaching to be most effective. Spiritual growth and moral development can give kids the strength and hope they need to make difficult changes in their lives. Finally, the Model empowers kids through teaching them self-control. This allows them to gain control over their emotions and behaviors so that they have a better chance of being successful in society.

CHAPTER 5

Correcting Aggressive and Problem Behavior

Kids constantly need teaching. Adults have many opportunities throughout each day to teach a youth something new, praise appropriate behavior, respond to a youth's failure to do what he or she should do, or correct a youngster's misbehavior. Teaching can involve anything from simple tasks like how to tie a shoe or set the dinner table to more difficult and complex issues like how to better control anger or solve a problem.

Kids are faced with new situations and dilemmas every day and they do their best to handle them. They deal with some problems better than others, but generally they need help and guidance from caregivers. Unfortunately, aggressive and violent kids tend to deal with their problems – both familiar and unfamiliar ones – in ways that produce negative and harmful consequences for themselves and those around them. Just as unfortunate, aggressive kids gravitate to other aggressive and violent children, media, music, and settings that reinforce their antisocial behaviors and attitudes. These are the times and situations when you can step in and really make a difference in a youngster's life.

At Boys Town, Corrective Teaching is a process that caregivers use in response to a child's failure to do something he or she should do or to correct a youth's misbehavior. Obviously, this includes aggressive behavior. Through Corrective Teaching, caregivers teach alternative appropriate skills to replace the negative, aggressive behaviors that dominate a child's responses to the situations and people around him or her. Corrective Teaching also allows caregivers to share their experiences, knowledge, and abilities to help aggressive kids learn and grow socially and emotionally.

Corrective Teaching is not limited to the child alone. A child's behavior does not occur in isolation to the environment around him or her. It occurs in context to people (peers and adults) the child interacts with and the places (school, neighborhood, community, etc.) he or she inhabits. For example, knocking someone to the ground in a fight after school with peers cheering is antisocial aggression. Knocking someone to the ground in a football game with peers cheering is a good tackle. Caregivers must teach youth these kinds of differences and access each youth's individual capabilities to know how best to redirect his or her energies, abilities, and needs.

Such teaching is not just focused on aggressive behavior. It also must focus on a wide range of social behaviors. A bully who meets his needs for approval and status by punching a peer on the playground at school needs to learn how to meet these needs in prosocial ways in the classroom, gym, school play, and chess club. A wide range of prosocial behaviors are crucial to reducing a well-learned habit of aggressive acting out.

In the pages that follow, we will describe a process for initiating how to help a child reduce aggressive behaviors. Keep in mind, this is just the beginning. We must first reduce aggression but if we don't follow up aggression reduction with teaching new ways to meet needs, we will not help youth become successful citizens.

Corrective Teaching Steps

1. **Stop/Describe the problem behavior.**
2. **Give a negative consequence (loss of privilege or added chore).**
3. **Describe the positive behavior.**
4. **Practice.**

This proven teaching method consists of four steps and is characterized by three central concepts – description, relationship, and consequence. Description includes specifically describing behavior in words or actions and practice. The relationship concept involves using warmth and pleasantness, and showing genuine concern for the youth. It also involves helping the child to feel good about himself or herself. Consequences include feedback and losing a privilege or adding a chore for using an inappropriate behavior. For your teaching to be effective, there must be a balance among these three concepts.

The four steps that make up Corrective Teaching provide the structure for this teaching method. However, as discussed in the previous chapter, many variables can affect how you use the steps, how many you use, and the order you will use them. Having structure ensures that the critical components are presented and helps make teaching consistent and effective. But if your teaching is to meet each youth's needs and fit the circumstances of the situation, you should be prepared to modify the teaching process. In this way, simple skills and complex skills can be taught to any child using the same basic method.

Let's take a closer look at the four steps and an explanation of each one:

STEP 1 – *Stop/Describe the problem behavior.*

Stopping the problem behavior as soon as it starts is easier than waiting until the behavior goes on for a long time or escalates. Waiting to correct it also might give kids the false impression that the misbehavior is okay or not that important to you. Start by calmly getting the child's attention, describing the problem behavior, and giving him or her a clear instruction such as, "Mark, stop yelling at and pushing Jose. Please come over here and sit down in this chair." Eliminate as many distractions as possible and get at the child's eye level. This will help the child to concentrate on you and your teaching.

Once the problem behavior has stopped, specifically describe it. Here you tell the child what he or she did wrong or failed to do. The description should be simple and brief so that the child can understand it. For example, a caregiver might say, "Sharise, please come over here so I can talk with you. *(Sharise walks over to the caregiver.)* Before you went to watch television, I asked you to pick up your clothes and put away the clean dishes. Your clothes are still on the floor and the dishes aren't put away. But what concerns me even more is that you said, 'Bull----!,' in a loud voice."

For some kids, especially younger children and youth at lower developmental levels, a demonstration of their inappropriate behavior may be necessary. A word of caution: Don't dwell on the description of the misbehavior. Caregivers can come across as "nagging" when they spend too much time rehashing inappropriate behavior, and this can trigger a loss of self-control from youngsters.

STEP 2 – *Give a negative consequence (loss of privilege or added chore).*

This step involves taking away something a youngster likes or giving something he or she doesn't like. For example, a caregiver might tell a youth that she can't use the phone the rest of the evening because she swore at and pushed another youngster. Or a caregiver might have a child do an extra chore for not following an instruction and cursing. (Boys Town uses Motivation Systems in which youth earn negative points for inappropriate behavior and positive points for appropriate behavior. Positive points can be exchanged for privileges. There also are other Motivation Systems, like sticker charts, that can be developed and used to meet the needs of each child and your type of setting.) When giving consequences, it is important that children understand that their behavior earned the consequence and that they are responsible for that behavior. After the consequence is delivered, tell the child that he or she will have a chance to earn back part of the consequence (no more than half) for practicing an alternative appropriate skill with you. At Boys Town, this is called a "positive correction statement," and it gives kids hope that all is not lost.

STEP 3 – *Describe the positive behavior.*

In this step, you give a simple and brief explanation of the skill or behavior the youngster should use in place of the inappropriate behavior. Again, it is important to make sure your words or demonstration match the child's age and developmental level. Let's go back to the example with Sharise who cursed and didn't follow the caregiver's instructions to do a couple of tasks. For this step, the caregiver might say, "Sharise, any time I ask you to do something, I want you to say 'Okay' and get started on it right away. Other comments are not needed."

STEP 4 – *Practice.*

Here, the child is given an opportunity to use the new skill or behavior in a pretend situation. This gives the child a chance to be successful and gain confidence before he or she has to use the skill or behavior in a real-life situation. Each time you have kids practice doing things right, you are increasing their chances for success and decreasing the likelihood that you will see the problem behavior in the future. By practicing, you give kids one more opportunity to learn something new. Practice helps them remember just what they can do to avoid problems and get things right. For example, the caregiver might say, "Sharise, show me how you're going to follow instructions and get your chores done next time." And Sharise might slowly answer, "All right," and walk off to get started on her chores. A little later, the caregiver can tell Sharise, "Thanks for getting started right away. You followed my instruction without any extra comments. Now, you'll finish your chores sooner and be able to get back to what you want to do."

The longer a caregiver works with a youngster, the more natural teaching should become. Over time, a skillful caregiver will be able to determine exactly how to approach each Corrective Teaching opportunity and decide which steps are necessary for the child. By using the steps, a caregiver maintains structure in his or her teaching while continuing to interject personal qualities that strengthen the relationship. The result is a positive change in a youth's thoughts, feelings, and behaviors, and an overall change for the better.

Using the three concepts as guideposts and the four steps as the "path" teaching should follow, let's look at two examples of how Corrective Teaching would look and sound with two different aggressive youth.

EXAMPLE 1 – Bobby is a ten-year-old boy who is new to a caregiver's teaching. During free time, Bobby begins to argue with eight-year-old Tyrone about whose turn it is to choose a TV program. Bobby shouts and swears at Tyrone, and eventually pushes him down and changes the TV to the channel he wants to watch. Tyrone begins to cry and goes to tell the caregiver what happened. The caregiver calls Bobby upstairs, and they sit down at the kitchen table.

Caregiver:	"Bobby, thanks for coming upstairs right away. Let's talk about what just happened downstairs. Swearing and pushing someone down in order to get something you want is wrong. You're bigger than Tyrone and could have hurt him." *(Stop/Describe the problem behavior)*
Bobby:	"But Tyrone was hogging the TV. It was my turn, and my favorite show was on."
Caregiver:	"I understand that you really wanted to watch your program. But for swearing at Tyrone and pushing him down you've lost TV for one hour. *(Consequence)* Remember, you'll have a chance to earn some of that time back after we practice. *(Positive correction statement)* Okay?"
Bobby:	*(nods his head in acknowledgment)*
Caregiver:	"Super job of accepting your consequence, Bobby! Now, let's talk about how to compromise with others. Next time you have a disagreement with someone, the best way to han-

dle it is to remain calm. Then talk to the other person about what you would like to do and what he would like to do, and suggest something that both of you can agree on. If you aren't able to agree, stay calm, and go find an adult to help. *(Describe positive behavior)* That way, you're more likely to get what you want, and no one ends up getting hurt. Do you understand all that?"

Bobby: "Yeah."

Caregiver: "Now let's practice how to compromise with others. Pretend that you're at home in the backyard and you want to use the swing that your sister is on. Do you remember the steps to compromising with others?"

Bobby: "Yes."

Caregiver: "Great. Let's practice what you are going to do and say. I'll pretend to be your sister and you are going to compromise with me about using the swing."

Bobby: *(looking at the caregiver)* "Jane, you've been on the swing for a long time. How about if we switch off and one person can swing for a while and the other person can play on the slide." *(Practice)*

Caregiver: "That was fantastic! You stayed calm and came up with an excellent option. Remember, if both of you aren't able to agree on a solution, continue to stay calm and go find your mom to help out. Since you did such a great job of practicing this new skill, you have earned back twenty minutes of TV time. Bobby, you did a super job of remaining calm this whole time and working hard with me on learning this new skill. I'm really proud of you!"

Now let's look at a similar scenario where a youngster has been exposed to a caregiver's Corrective Teaching for several months.

EXAMPLE 2 – A caregiver asks Beth, a fourteen-year-old girl, to apologize to Michelle for teasing her about her weight problem.

Caregiver:	"Beth, we need to talk for a minute. Michelle just told me you have been calling her names, like 'fatso' and 'blimp,' and teasing her about her weight." *(Stop/Describe problem behavior)*
Beth:	"But she's been such a pain. I'm sick and tired of listening to her talk about her weight all the time."
Caregiver:	"I know it's hard to get along with everyone all the time, but saying positive things to others is something you've been working on. *(Describe the positive behavior)* Remember, when you make positive comments about others you make them feel good about themselves, and Michelle needs that right now. We've gone over this before so you know that. For making negative comments to Michelle, you've earned an extra chore tonight – dusting and sweeping the basement. *(Consequence)* Now I'd like you to go apologize to Michelle. Remember what to do?"
Beth:	"Yes. I'll look at her, use a sincere voice, and tell her I'm sorry for calling her names and teasing her. *(Practice)*"
Caregiver:	"Good. I appreciate you going over those steps. Michelle is in her room. She's still upset, so I'll go with you to see how things turn out."

In the first example, the caregiver used every teaching step in order. This provided structure and ensured that the essential elements were included for a child who is just learning a new way to correct inappropriate behaviors. In the second situation, where the youth was familiar with the caregiver's teaching, the caregiver was able to teach to the child in a brief, more natural style. In both cases, the caregivers dealt with the inappropriate behaviors with effective teaching and taught a skill. This illustrates the flexibility of Corrective Teaching, and how it can be modified as a child makes progress and becomes familiar with your expectations.

Summary

Kids will "mess up" and misbehave; in a sense, that's part of their job as youngsters. Caregivers must address these situations when they occur and view them as opportunities to help kids learn and grow. Corrective Teaching is one way to do this. It is a proven method for helping aggressive youth replace inappropriate behaviors with appropriate behaviors. The four steps provide structure to the teaching process while enabling caregivers to develop and strengthen relationships with kids. What steps you use and how you use them is dependent on the child and his or her situation.

An important concept about Corrective Teaching is to use it often and consistently – particularly with aggressive behaviors like name calling, cursing, shouting, or slamming down objects like books or toys. Adults who consistently address such behaviors and teach children alternative, prosocial skills help them learn to get their needs met in less aggressive ways.

CHAPTER 6

Teaching Youth to Control Emotions and Behavior

As you work with and care for aggressive youngsters, it is inevitable that they will sometimes become upset, angry, or frustrated. Even though you may be making progress in teaching new behaviors, many youth will fall back on their old aggressive behaviors in stressful situations. This amounts to a loss of self-control, which can make teaching difficult or impossible. But kids can learn to control their emotions and behaviors and, in turn, reduce their dependence on aggression. To teach the strategies kids need in order to achieve this goal, Boys Town uses a teaching technique called Teaching Self-Control.

One of the more frustrating aspects of working with aggressive youth is dealing with them when they become very angry or defiant or simply refuse to do what you ask. The child may yell, strike out, swear, throw objects, threaten you, or simply shut down and refuse to respond to you at all. The child's behavior can make you feel powerless, emotionally drained, or just plain furious.

If you have ever felt like this, you're not alone. All caregivers experience situations like this all the time. One thing is certain however: Kids must learn that negative, aggressive behavior is not acceptable. It is harmful to them and others. The sooner children learn to control their actions, the more they will benefit.

Teaching Self-Control helps caregivers calmly deal with kids in a better way when they are upset and refuse to cooperate. It also enables caregivers to teach youngsters better ways to behave when they are upset or refuse to respond to correction. Ultimately, Teaching Self-Control allows everyone time to calm down so teaching can start again.

There are two key parts to Teaching Self-Control: getting the youth calmed down and follow-up teaching. We'll talk about each part in detail later. First, let's take a brief look at what often happens when a youngster yells at a caregiver or refuses to do what is asked.

In these situations, a youth is certainly not interested in, and in some cases, not capable of discussing the situation rationally. A great deal of talking by a caregiver does little to improve the situation. Often, the more the caregiver talks, the louder the child yells. The more the child yells, the louder the caregiver talks – until he or she is yelling, too. This unpleasant exchange of words and actions continues to intensify until someone decides that the argument is too painful and drops out. (See the Conflict Cycle discussed in Chapter 2.) It can be the caregiver who becomes frustrated and angry. If caregivers fall prey to their own emotions, they risk repeating the Conflict Cycle that helped create the problem. Or, it can be the child who stomps out of the room and slams the door shut. In either case, the problem has gotten worse, not better. If you've had to deal with a child who will not cooperate, you know how helpless it feels at these emotionally intense times.

Teaching Self-Control gives caregivers a way to stop the yelling or arguing before things get worse. It also provides you with a structured method for helping kids identify how they are behaving and for teaching them how to deal with these situations in ways that are helpful, not hurtful.

When to Use Teaching Self-Control

Teaching Self-Control should be used when children refuse to cooperate with you, either passively or aggressively. Teaching Self-Control is appropriate in these two types of situations:

1. **When a child misbehaves and will not respond to Corrective Teaching; instead, the child continues to misbehave or the misbehavior gets worse.**

2. **When a child "blows up" – has a sudden and intense emotional outburst – and refuses to do anything that the caregiver asks.**

An example of aggressive out-of-control behavior would be if a caregiver asked a youth to get started on his or her homework and the youth responded by swearing and shouting at the caregiver to get out of the room and then turning the music on full blast. Out-of-control aggressive behavior can be passive as well. In the same situation, the youth might just simply ignore repeated requests to get started on homework.

Think about times when kids got upset when you corrected their behavior or asked them to do something. What triggered their negative, aggressive behavior? What exactly did they do? How did you respond? Looking back at past blow-ups can help you plan for and practice how you will deal with them in the future. Ways to prevent blow-ups include using Proactive Teaching (see Chapter 8) to help children learn more appropriate ways to respond when they feel angry or upset. However, once your child does have an emotional outburst, it's time to use the steps of Teaching Self-Control.

The Steps of Teaching Self-Control

Teaching Self-Control has two goals and two parts. The goals of Teaching Self-Control are:

> To help youth calm down during emotionally intense situations.

> To teach youth to control their behavior when they get upset.

The first part of Teaching Self-Control – Calming Down – is geared toward reducing the intensity of your interaction so that both of you can work on resolving the situation. The second part – Follow-up Teaching – gives you an opportunity to teach kids some acceptable options for behaving when they are upset. Like Corrective Teaching, Teaching Self-Control emphasizes giving clear descriptions of the youth's behaviors, using consequences, teaching youth the correct behavior, and practicing it. Teaching Self-Control gives both you and the youth a chance to calm down when tempers have flared. When everyone has some time to calm down before teaching continues, kids are more likely to learn how to share their feelings in appropriate and constructive ways. Here are the steps of Teaching Self-Control and an example of how it is used:

Part One: Calming Down

1. **Describe the problem behavior.**

2. **Offer options to calm down.**

3. **Allow time to calm down.**

Part Two: Follow-Up Teaching

4. **Describe the positive behavior.**

5. **Practice.**

6. **Give a negative consequence.**

A caregiver tells fourteen-year-old Greg that he can't use the computer for the next two weeks as a consequence for visiting an inappropriate website. Greg laughs and says, "I'll just get on it when you're not around! Or I'll get on a computer somewhere else! You can't stop me!" He walks away from the caregiver and kicks over a stool in the kitchen.

PART ONE: *Calming Down*

STEP 1 – *Describe the problem behavior.*

Caregiver: "Greg, please leave the stools alone and stay in the kitchen."

Greg: *(Glares at the caregiver)* "F... you and your rules!" *(He pushes some mail off the kitchen table and slams his fist on the table.)*

STEP 2 – *Offer options to calm down.*

Caregiver: "Greg, please follow my instructions and show me you're willing to cooperate by going to your room to calm down. *(Greg starts to leave the kitchen but picks up the phone and begins dialing.)* It's up to you to make a better decision about not using the phone. I suggest you take a few deep breaths and think about what you're doing." *(Greg stops, hangs up the phone, and angrily slams it down on the counter.)*

Greg: "This is so f...... lame. Just leave me the hell alone!"

STEP 3 – *Allow time to calm down.*

Caregiver: "I can see that you're still upset. Please go to your room to calm down and I'll be there in a few minutes to talk."

(When the youth is following instructions and willing to talk about the problem, move from the Calming Down phase to Follow-Up Teaching.)

NOTE: It is very important that the caregiver remain calm, talk in a conversational tone of voice, and not allow the youth's aggressive behaviors to stimulate counter aggressive behavior. This is the best way to get the youth calmed down. We will talk more about what caregivers can do to remain calm while dealing with an emotional youth in succeeding chapters.

PART TWO: *Follow-Up Teaching*

STEP 4 – *Describe the positive behavior.*

Caregiver: "Greg, here is what you can do the next time you get upset. Take a few deep breaths and calmly ask me if you can go to your room to think. That also means not using the phone or playing your music."

STEP 5 – *Practice.*

Caregiver: "Let's give this a try. In a little while you are going to earn a consequence for losing control and not following instructions to stop yelling and cursing. Show me how you are going to handle yourself if you start getting angry."

Greg: *(Takes a deep breath).* "Can I go to my room until I feel calm?"

Caregiver: "That was exactly what you should do."

STEP 6 – *Give a negative consequence.*

Caregiver: "As I said, you did earn a negative consequence for refusing to cooperate, cursing, pushing over the stool, and throwing the mail on the floor. You won't be allowed to use the phone for the next twenty-four hours, and you need to pick up the stool and mail."

It's never easy to remain calm when kids are being defiant, disrespectful, and aggressive. What's important is to first focus on helping the youth calm down and regain self-control before you address the original problem behavior. (In the example, the caregiver first handles Greg's loss of control before going back to the issue of his improper use of the computer.) Each of the steps of Teaching Self-Control is a way for you to tell if the youth is ready to cooperate and eventually get back to the initial problem that caused the blow-up in the first place. Not only do these steps act as markers of a youth's ability to remain calm, they give caregivers a proven method to avoid being drawn into power struggles, escalating arguments, or an unsafe situation.

Now, let's look at the steps to the first part of Teaching Self-Control, Calming Down, in more detail.

STEP 1 – *Describe the problem behavior.*

In a calm, level voice tone, briefly tell the youth exactly what he or she is doing wrong. The youth probably will not be interested in listening to what you have to say at this time, so saying a lot won't help. Remember that you will have time to describe the problem in detail once the youth settles down. For now, be clear and specific with what you do say. Don't speak too rapidly or say too much. For example, "Lucia, you're yelling, cursing, and pacing around the room" gives the youth a clear message about what she is doing.

Avoid saying judgmental things like "Quit acting stupid" or "You have a lousy attitude." These are critical, judgmental statements that only serve to fuel the emotional ire in a child. Instead, simply describe what the youth is doing wrong without becoming angry, sarcastic, or accusatory.

Using empathy also helps when a youth is upset or angry. It shows that you understand the child's feelings. For example, you might say, "I can see you are angry right now. And your voice tells me that you're unhappy with what happened." This starts the teaching sequence positively and shows the youth that you really do care about his or her feelings. Plus, using empathy often helps the child to see that you're focused on calming the situation down and not on placing blame or getting the upper hand.

STEP 2 – *Offer options to calm down.*

The purpose of this step is to tell the youth exactly what he or she needs to do to begin calming down. Give simple instructions like "Please stop walking around the room; just stand still" or "Go sit on the couch and cool down." Or, make calming statements to prompt the child: "Take a few deep breaths and try to settle down." Just as when you described the problem behavior, keep your words to a minimum. Don't give too many instructions or repeat them constantly; the child could perceive this as lecturing, badgering, or creating an opportunity to argue. Giving simple, clear options for calming down keeps the focus on having the child regain self-control.

It is very important that you practice these first two steps – describe the problem behavior and offer options to calm down. Practicing how to be brief, specific, calm, empathetic, and clear during intense situations is time worth investing. Besides giving girls and boys an opportunity to regain self-control, clear messages and specific options on how to calm down help you avoid getting sidetracked into useless arguments or power struggles.

STEP 3 – *Allow time to calm down.*

Giving youngsters time to calm down might be a new concept to some caregivers. But if you remain calm and allow kids time to cool down, they are more likely to get themselves together faster. Also, this step helps you to stay focused on getting the situation under control. Simply saying, "Let's take a little time to calm down. We will talk more in a few minutes," can be surprisingly effective. Sometimes giving you and the youth a little "space" helps you both "save face" and calm down.

As you take time to calm down, you can think of what you are going to teach next. This also allows the youth to make a decision – to continue misbehaving or to calm down. Come back to the child as often as necessary. Ask questions like, "Are you ready to talk about what happened?" or "Are you calmed down enough to talk to me?"

Move to the next phase, Follow-up Teaching, when the youth is able to answer you in a reasonably calm voice and is willing to cooperate. You're not going to have the happiest child at this point, but it's important that he or she can pay attention and talk without losing self-control again.

If the youth tries to use this "cool down time" as an opportunity to blare music, sleep, talk on the phone, or go from room to room disrupting others, then you should remind the youngster that this behavior will only make things worse for him or her later. For example, if a youth gets upset when you tell her to turn off the TV and then refuses to stop watching, part of her consequence will be losing TV time. Don't make angry threats; simply inform the child that continued misbehavior will earn larger or more negative consequences. Do not be specific at this time; it will only prompt more arguing. This is a good time to prompt the youth to make better decisions and to give a brief reason that's meaningful to him or her.

It's important to take your time here. You are in control. The child's behavior has not paid off and you are sending the strong message that he or she needs to start making better choices. Give descriptions and instructions as needed to test the child's readiness to move on to Follow-Up Teaching. Most importantly, remain calm and in control of what you say and do. Do not end Step 3 until the child is calm. Step 4 should not begin until you reach this point.

STEP 4 – *Describe the positive behavior.*

Describe what the youth can do differently next time to remain calm. Explain other, more positive ways to express frustration or anger. Children

101

have to learn that if they blow up in aggressive ways when something doesn't go their way, it leads to more negative consequences and less time doing the things they like. This is an opportunity to explain the prompts you gave in the "offer options to cool down" step and to encourage the child to remember how to calm down.

You can use the "Instead of..." phrase to describe positive behavior. It goes like this:

> ➤ "Instead of yelling and kicking the door, the next time you get upset, please tell me you're mad and ask if you can go to your room to calm down."

> ➤ "Instead of swearing, why don't you ask if you can sit on the couch until you are ready to talk about it."

The purpose of this phase is to teach kids positive behavior they can use the next time they get upset. Part of this teaching can include helping them recognize when they are beginning to get upset and teaching them to say something like, "I'm getting mad. Can I have some time to calm down?"

Once children calm down, they can talk about the circumstances that triggered their anger and talk with you about a solution. If kids can learn to talk about how they feel in these situations, they can successfully solve the problem rather than attack others.

STEP 5 – *Practice.*

Now that the youngster knows what to do, it's important that he or she knows how to do it. Ask the child to take several deep breaths with you, count to ten, or repeat a request for time to calm down such as "I'm really upset right now. May I go to my room for a few minutes?" After the practice is over, let the youth know what was done correctly and what needs improvement. Be as positive as you can be, especially if the child is making an honest effort to do what you ask. Practice allows you to see if the youngster is in control of his or her emotions and willing to cooperate with your instructions as well as to accept responsibility for the behavior.

STEP 6 – *Give a negative consequence.*

This is a crucial step to Teaching Self-Control. Some caregivers might forget to give a negative consequence for the out-of-control behavior because they are so pleased to have the aggressive behavior stop. Others might forgo a negative consequence because they don't want to upset the child any further. Sometimes, after a blow up is over, adults might want to ease up or the youth's remorse convinces them to forgo the consequence. These feelings are understandable, but they don't contribute to changing a child's behavior. Consequences do help change behavior, but only if you consistently use them.

With Teaching Self-Control, you should always give an appropriate negative consequence and follow through with it. Kids must learn they cannot blow up or lash out when things don't go their way. At school, these behaviors can result in detentions, suspensions, expulsions, or other disciplinary actions. At work, they could cost them their job. And most likely, kids won't keep friends for very long if they can't control their tempers. As caregivers, it's important to teach boys and girls how to respond in less emotional and less harmful ways even when they get upset. Consequences increase the effectiveness of your teaching, and the whole process of Teaching Self-Control helps kids learn better ways of behaving.

Let's go back to the example of the boy who walked away, cursed, and knocked over a stool after being told he lost computer privileges for two weeks. As a negative consequence for the misbehavior, you might extend the loss of computer privileges for two or three more days.

Example of Teaching Self-Control

Let's take a look at another example of Teaching Self-Control. Here's the situation: A caregiver tells ten-year-old Marques that he can't play video games because he didn't come straight home after school as instructed. Marques yells, "That's so f...... stupid! I hate you! You never let me do anything!" Then, he stomps into the living room screaming and swearing.

PART ONE: *Calming Down*

STEP 1 – *Describe the problem behavior.*

> Use empathy and understanding.

> Clearly and calmly describe the misbehaviors.

Caregiver: "I understand you are upset about not being able to play video games, but you are yelling and swearing."

STEP 2 – *Offer options to calm down.*

> Describe what you want him to do.

> Give options for calming down.

Caregiver: "Please stop yelling and either go to your room or stay out here and sit on the couch. Whatever you decide, take a couple of deep breaths to help calm yourself down."

STEP 3 – *Allow time to calm down.*

> Give each of you a chance to calm down. Minimize further instruction unless damage or injury will occur without intervention.

(Take a few minutes to catch your breath. Monitor child's safety without close engagement and ask him if he is willing to talk.)

> Check for cooperative behavior.

Caregiver: "Marques, how are you feeling now? Are you ready to calmly talk to me?" or "I can see that you're still upset. We will talk in a few minutes."

(When Marques is following the caregiver's instructions and is willing to talk about the problem, the caregiver moves from the Calming Down phase to Follow-Up Teaching.)

PART TWO: *Follow-Up Teaching*

After the youth is calm, it is important that caregivers engage in Follow-Up Teaching. This is a crucial part of any strategy to stop and prevent aggression for two reasons: 1) It minimizes the risk that the youth's aggressive behavior paid off; 2) It maximizes the probability that the youth can use better, more appropriate skills next time.

STEP 4 – *Describe the positive behavior.*

> Think of a better way the youth can react when he gets upset. Describe what he can do differently.

Caregiver: "Here's what you can do the next time you get upset, Marques. What I'd like you to do is take a deep breath, let me know that you are getting upset and ask me if you can go to your room – or sit in a private place – and calm down."

STEP 5 – *Practice.*

> Practice increases the chance that the child will learn what to do next time.

> Let him know how he practiced.

Caregiver: "Okay, let's practice this. I'm going to tell you that you can't play video games. What should you do?"

Marques:	(*Takes a deep breath.*) "I feel really mad right now. Can I go to my room until I feel calm?"
Caregiver:	"That was great! You asked me in a nice tone of voice."

STEP 6 – *Give a negative consequence.*

> Help prevent the problem from occurring again.

Caregiver:	"Remember, there are negative consequences for yelling and swearing. You did that just a few minutes ago. Tonight, you'll have to do the dinner dishes, even though it's not your night to clean up, and you won't get a snack."

In real-life situations, a youth probably won't cooperate this quickly. He or she may go from arguing and swearing to being calm, and then suddenly start arguing again. Some kids have a lot of stamina when they're upset so it's best to realize it could take a while to resolve the problem. You may also have other distractions to deal with in these situations: Other kids might need something, the phone rings, and so on. Interactions with boys and girls do not occur in a void; other things are always taking place that affect your behavior. In those instances where other children are present, instruct them to go to another room so the upset youth doesn't "feed" off of them, and adapt the teaching steps and your teaching style to the situation. Stick to simple descriptions and instructions, continue to use empathy, and stay calm. Also, when kids misuse privileges when they're upset (blaring music or watching TV), they should lose access to those privileges (no radio, iPod, or TV for the rest of the day) as part of the consequence.

Make Good Teaching Better

While there are several steps to effective teaching like allowing time to calm down, describing negative and positive behaviors, practice, etc., there are some important stylistic elements that adults should attend to and use that can help make their teaching better.

Stay on task

Don't lose sight of what you're trying to teach. Implement all of the steps of Teaching Self-Control; concentrating on the youth's behavior is much easier when you have a framework to follow. Teaching Self-Control gives you that framework. It helps you stay calm and avoid arguments that take you away from what you want to teach.

Kids may try to argue with what you say or call you names. They may say you don't like them or tell you how unfair you are. They may say things to make you feel guilty or angry. Expect these statements but don't respond to them. If you get caught up in all of these side issues, you lose sight of your original purpose – to calm the child and to teach him or her self-control. At Boys Town, we ask our staff to avoid getting caught up in the kids' content. If you get caught in content, you can lose sight of the original problem and how you need to deal with it. If you find yourself responding to what the youth is saying, remember to use a key phrase: "We'll talk about that when you calm down." Staying on task ensures that you won't start arguing or lose your temper.

Be aware of your physical actions

These times can be emotionally explosive. Don't use threatening words or gestures that might encourage physical retaliation or an aggressive response from kids. Attend to your posture, voice tone, and facial expressions. It might help to calm the situation if you are sitting down rather than standing up. When adults stand up – particularly males – children see them as more threatening. Any action the child views as aggressive will only make matters worse and increase the likelihood that he or she will respond aggressively.

Pointing your index finger, putting your hands on your hips, scowling, glaring, and leaning over the youth are all examples of physical actions that tend to increase tension in these volatile situations. Try your best to avoid these gestures. Keep your hands in your pockets or fold your arms across your chest – just find something to do with your hands and arms other than waving them at kids.

Plan consequences in advance

Think of a variety of appropriate negative consequences beforehand, especially if losing self-control is a problem for a youngster. Making decisions when you are upset can lead to giving consequences that might not be appropriate or that you can't follow through on.

Find time when the child is not upset to explain the future consequence for arguing and being aggressive with you. You might say, for example, "Maria, when I tell you 'No,' sometimes you argue with me. Then you get real mad and start yelling and cursing. From now on, if you do this, you will lose your computer privileges for two nights." Then explain to Maria why she needs to accept decisions and why she shouldn't argue, scream, or swear. Knowing what the consequence will be may help the youngsters to think before losing self-control in the future.

Follow up

As the child calms down and you complete the teaching sequence, other side issues can arise. Some situations may call for an understanding approach. Kids may cry after an intense situation. They just don't know how to handle what they're feeling inside. Then you can say, "Let's sit down and talk about why you've been feeling so angry. Maybe I can help. At least, I can listen."

Some youth want to make up with you after an emotionally intense situation. They probably have avoided or gotten out of consequences by "making up" in the past. In these situations use a firm, emphatic ending to Teaching Self-Control and keep your follow-up brief. Accept an apology but indicate that the child's behavior is unacceptable and that your interaction is finished: "I am glad you are sorry. Thanks. We've practiced what to do. Now, go and pick up the chairs you knocked over."

Earlier, we emphasized that you shouldn't get sidetracked with complaints and accusations that kids may bring up when they are angry. But that's only during the Teaching Self-Control process. Afterwards, when everyone has calmed down and the youth has accepted his or her consequences, you should discuss with the youth those statements that upset or concerned you and/or the youngster. This is your opportunity to find out the reasons behind the outburst.

Kids may make more negative comments during these emotionally intense situations especially when you first start using Teaching Self-Control because these words may have distracted others (parents, teachers) before. Kids may think they can avoid getting a consequence or doing what was asked if they just keep the pressure on you. In other situations, kids may make these comments because they sincerely don't know how to express their feelings in healthy ways. Sometimes, children make negative comments simply because they are mad. Other times, kids really do have concerns, or they feel frustrated. Some children won't have a clue why they said what they did, but discussing it and allowing them to share their feelings helps the healing begin.

When you have finished Teaching Self-Control and both you and the youth are calm, you may want to discuss some of these comments. Tell the child you're concerned about what he or she said. Talk about trust. Ask the child to share feelings and opinions with you. Regardless of why the comments were made, take time to hear what the youngster has to say. Whenever possible, implement the suggestions the child makes. By doing so, you will be opening the door to more constructive conversations with the youth. You will also be reducing the likelihood that the child will express negative feelings in destructive, aggressive ways. But remember, cursing, calling names, yelling, or throwing objects is never acceptable, and you should always give that message to the child.

Finally, as part of following up, you should sit down with the child at a neutral time (when he or she is not upset) and develop a plan that helps the youth stay calm when he or she becomes upset. Help the youth identify what upsets him or her and select a method of calming down (deep breathing, counting to ten, journaling, drawing, taking time alone to cool down, etc.). Having a plan of their own helps children recognize when they are beginning to feel upset and familiarizes them with ways to stay calm. Then, when you must use Teaching Self-Control, the youth may need only a prompt from you to realize that it's time to get negative emotions under control.

Summary

Teaching aggressive kids various individual, effective, and prosocial ways to maintain self-control is one of the more important treatment objectives of the Boys Town Model. These children and adolescents experience many unpleasant feelings (sadness, anger, jealousy, and so on) due to traumatic events in their lives. These overwhelming feelings often are expressed in aggressive, violent, and self-destructive behaviors when a crisis occurs. Yet, our experience and research firmly suggest that even the most traumatized youth can learn new, socially acceptable ways of behaving and expressing emotion.

There are two phases to Teaching Self-Control and each phase has its own steps. However, it's important to remember that each child's needs and situation is unique, so be flexible during a crisis and use what works. Teaching Self-Control is what helps troubled kids deal with unpleasant feelings, anticipate crisis events, and calm themselves instead of exploding with combative, antagonistic, and damaging behaviors. In this way, youth learn different methods to successfully manage crisis situations and get their needs met in a more socially appropriate manner.

CHAPTER 7

Using Praise to Encourage Positive Behavior

Kids make mistakes – that's to be expected. It comes with the territory of being a young person. But for every mistake or misdeed, there are many, many things that a youngster says or does that are positive and should be praised and reinforced. With some children, caregivers have to look much longer and harder to find these positive qualities, skills, and behaviors. When working with and caring for aggressive and violent youngsters, this is often one of the most challenging tasks for caregivers.

In today's society, adults have a tendency to expect kids to behave appropriately and make the right choices. But when kids do, many rarely receive praise and encouragement. And without praise and encouragement, many children see no reason to continue to do good things; their positive skills and behaviors are not reinforced and likely won't occur again. In the Boys Town Model, "catching kids being good" and reinforcing them with praise when they do something right, correctly using a skill, and engaging in a prosocial behavior – no matter how small or insignificant it might seem – is a critical component to helping aggressive kids get better.

It isn't always easy for kids to "do the right thing." Many factors – friends, television, Internet, music, and others – can influence or encourage youth to take a dangerous or destructive path. That is why you must be able to recognize and praise positive behavior and accomplishments when they occur. At Boys Town, Effective Praise is a teaching component that caregivers use to identify and reinforce positive qualities, skills, behaviors, and accomplishments so that kids will repeat them and, ultimately, make them a permanent part of their lives.

As a matter of fact, praising kids' prosocial behaviors is so important to effective teaching that Boys Town recommends that caregivers recognize or praise four to ten or more positive behaviors for every one negative behavior that an adult corrects. This means, for example, that caregivers should recognize and praise at least four positive behaviors for every Corrective Teaching interaction they do with kids. This ratio is based on the needs and circumstances of each child. For instance, kids who are younger, new to your teaching, or have severe treatment issues will likely require a higher positive-to-negative ratio than kids who are older, familiar with your teaching, or have less-severe problems.

As you can see, Effective Praise should be your most frequently used Teaching Interaction. That's because people – especially kids – thrive on the attention of other human beings. Kids need words of approval, pats on the back, smiles, and recognition of their accomplishments in order to become happy, healthy individuals.

This chapter will focus on how to use Effective Praise to bring about changes in aggressive youth.

Factors that Make Praise Powerful

Praise can be one of the most powerful teaching methods you use. But it also can be misused and ineffective if you aren't aware of some important principles. Here are five principles that must be incorporated into a caregiver's Effective Praise interaction to make praise powerful, effective, and therapeutic:

> > **Immediate** – Praise works best when it is given immediately after the desired behavior or skill occurs. This means that the connection between the praise and the positive behavior that is being praised is clearer and stronger. This, in turn, makes it more likely that the child will use the behavior again because he or she wants to be praised. For example, a caregiver observes a child ignoring some teasing from other kids. In order to effectively reinforce and strengthen the positive behavior of ignoring the teasing of others, the caregiver praises the youngster immediately. If the caregiver waits until the end of the day or the next day to praise the youth for his positive behavior, the praise either will not be as powerful or won't have the desired effect.

> **Contingent** – Caregivers should provide praise (i.e., positive reinforcement) only when the desired behavior or skill is correctly displayed by the youngster. Keep in mind that a behavior is strengthened when it is immediately followed by praise or some other type of positive reinforcer (pat on the back, tangible reward, etc.). Thus, the behavior must occur before a reinforcer is given. In this way, the praise or reinforcer is directly linked to the youngster's accomplishment.

> **Specific** – Caregivers should be as specific as possible when describing positive behavior or accomplishments to a youngster. This helps the youth understand exactly what he or she said or did, making it easier for the child to duplicate the appropriate behavior again in the future. Using only vague statements like "Nice job" or "That was great" can leave a child confused about what he or she did that was so nice or great. In fact, there is a danger that another, less desirable behavior may be accidentally reinforced when the reason for the praise isn't clear. Specific praise would be something like, "Fantastic! You ignored the teasing by walking away and saying nothing."

> **Credible** – Praise is only effective if it is personal, sincere, and focused on improvement. If a caregiver praises kids all the time without any apparent purpose, the youth will become confused and not believe that a caregiver's praise is sincere. Therefore, praise is no longer effective in bringing about change. For example, a swimming instructor constantly and indiscriminately tells his pupils, "Great job" and "Way to go." When a mother asks her daughter how she is progressing in swim lessons, the girl replies, "I don't know." The mother, confused, says, "But I just heard your instructor tell you that you were doing a great job." "Yeah," the young girl says. "But he tells everyone that, even the kids who can't swim." Praise loses its "clout" when it is used for everything a child does. Be selective and make praise count. Also, make sure your facial expression, voice tone, and mannerisms match your praise. A dour look and a bland, monotone voice are not very reinforcing and won't lend credence to your words.

> **Praise Approximations** – Kids will not always do something exactly right, so it is important to praise and acknowledge effort. For instance, a boy might ignore teasing for a couple minutes and try to walk away before he finally yells and curses back at the teaser. It's important recognize that with

111

specific praise like, "I saw you start to walk away from Kenny. That was a good start."

The Effective Praise Interaction

Effective Praise is crucial to developing healthy relationships with kids, and is very important in developing and strengthening appropriate behavior. This teaching technique allows caregivers to sincerely and enthusiastically recognize the progress each youngster is making. Like Corrective Teaching and Teaching Self-Control, there is a structure to Effective Praise. And the same factors that affect other types of teaching also affect how you use these steps.

Effective Praise Steps

1. **Show approval.**

2. **Describe the positive behavior.**

3. **Give a rationale.**

(Optional) Give a positive consequence.

Let's take a closer look at these steps and their descriptions.

STEP 1 – *Show approval.*

Caregivers should begin each interaction on a positive, upbeat, and enthusiastic note by praising youth for their appropriate behavior. Be sure to identify the skill that is related to the behavior you are praising. Hearing the name of the skill will help many youth, especially younger children and youth at lower developmental levels, gain a clearer understanding of what you are praising and what they should continue to do.

STEP 2 – *Describe the positive behavior.*

Here, caregivers should specifically describe, or demonstrate if necessary, a child's verbal and nonverbal behavior. In other words, tell the child exactly what he or she did right and what he or she should continue to do in the future. Keep in mind that it is important to use words or a demonstration that matches the child's age and developmental level.

STEP 3 – *Give a reason.*

A reason is a rationale given by caregivers that explains to children why it's important to use a skill and helps them "buy into" the behavior. In Effective Praise, caregivers will focus on two types of rationales: how using the skill benefits the youth (personal-benefit rationales) and how using the skill benefits others (other-centered rationales). (Avoid using

112

rationales in which children are told they should use a certain skill only to avoid negative consequences.) Caregivers should shift from using personal-benefit rationales to other-centered rationales as soon as it is appropriate for each youth. Make sure youth understand the rationale you give. If the child doesn't understand the reason, give another one, and don't proceed until you feel that the youth understands.

OPTIONAL – *Give a positive consequence.*

Here, the child earns a positive consequence as a reward for his or her appropriate behavior. This increases the likelihood that the behavior or skill will be used in similar situations. The positive consequence should be something the youth likes or wants; what reinforces one child may not reinforce another child. Positive consequences can range from social reinforcers like verbal praise, pats on the back, and smiles, to tangible reinforcers like extra time on the computer or phone, a soft drink with dinner, or going to a movie. It's important to keep in mind that the positive consequence should be large enough to keep the child interested in continuing to use the desired behavior. For example, a positive consequence of two extra minutes for playing video games may not be large enough to motivate a child to use a behavior again. However, ten or fifteen minutes of extra time might better capture the child's attention.

Over time, the size and type of consequences you use should be faded away so that kids don't rely on external rewards. For instance, during the time it takes for a child to master a given skill, a caregiver should gradually switch from giving tangible types of rewards when the child is just beginning to learn the skill, to social kinds of rewards like pats on the back or verbal praise as the youth gets better at using the skill. Eventually, a simple nonverbal signal like a thumbs-up or a smile will be a sufficient consequence for recognizing the child's mastery of the desired skill or behavior. The goal here is to help youngsters eventually internalize a positive behavior and use it because it's the right thing to do, not because they'll get something they like or want.

Ineffective "levels systems" stay with external reinforcers the whole time a child is in care. Such systems are aptly criticized for this feature. The goal must always be to have a youth become self-motivated. On the other hand, many programs struggle to motivate difficult-to-treat youth because they staunchly refuse to adopt any system of external rewards. The balance is to use just enough external rewards to help a youth develop new behaviors and habits.

Now, let's take a look at two examples of how Effective Praise would work with two different children.

EXAMPLE 1 – Julie is an eleven-year-old girl who is new to the caregiver's teaching. One of her primary treatment goals is reducing incidents of aggressive behavior. In this scenario, the caregiver asked Julie to begin her homework. This time, Julie responded appropriately. In the past, Julie refused to follow this instruction, and the caregiver used Corrective Teaching and even Teaching Self-Control. Here, the caregiver will respond with Effective Praise.

Caregiver:	"Julie, that was great! Just a second ago, you did a fantastic job of following instructions." *(Show approval)*
Julie:	*(smiling)* "Thanks."
Caregiver:	"When I asked you to get your books and begin study hour, you looked at me and said, 'Okay, I'll get on it.' Then, you went upstairs, got your books, and told me you were ready to go. That's a great job of following instructions. *(Description of the positive behavior)* When you follow instructions right away, you're more likely to finish your homework and other tasks quicker. That way you'll have more free time to do some things you like to do, like riding your bike. *(Reason)* Does that make sense?"
Julie:	"Yeah, it does."
Caregiver:	"Since you did such a super job of following instructions, you've earned an extra fifteen minutes outside after study time. That way you'll be able to ride your bike a little longer." *(Positive consequence)*
Julie:	*(smiling)* "All right!"
Caregiver:	"Julie, you've been trying real hard lately. Keep up the good work!"

EXAMPLE 2 – Jerome is a fifteen-year-old boy who has been living with a caregiver for three months. The first couple of weeks, Jerome had problems accepting "No" for an answer. Since then, Jerome has consistently responded appropriately to "No" answers. In this example, Jerome asked to go to a movie and his caregiver told him he couldn't because the movie was not appropriate for his age. Jerome responded appropriately by saying, "Okay."

114

Caregiver:	"Jerome, nice job of accepting 'No' when I said you couldn't go to the movie. *(Show approval)* Caregiver pats Jeff on the back. *(Positive consequence)* Remember that if you can accept 'No' answers without arguing, you have a better chance of getting a 'Yes' answer in the future, if possible. *(Reason)* Now, let's look for a different movie."

Summary

Learning and using a new skill or behavior is difficult for kids and involves many behavioral steps. That is why caregivers must take great care to recognize, validate, and reward even the smallest signs of progress. Praising these accomplishments encourages kids to keep trying, and lets them know that their efforts are worthwhile. In order for aggressive children and adolescents to get better, they need recognition and appreciation. The more ways and times a caregiver can find to praise youngsters for their efforts to learn, the faster they will learn. Effective Praise allows caregivers to sincerely and enthusiastically recognize the progress that each youth is making, while enhancing each youth's confidence and feelings of competence.

CHAPTER 8

Teaching Social Skills to Prevent Problems

When aggressive kids are just starting to learn new social skills to replace problem behaviors, caregivers will spend a great deal of time doing what we call Proactive Teaching. Proactive Teaching is used to teach new skills before a youth will need to use them and to anticipate and head off problems and crises before they happen. When you prepare youth for problems before they occur, kids are set up for success in situations where they previously behaved poorly. As a child starts using these newly learned skills and begins experiencing success, you will be viewed as helpful and concerned, which helps to further develop and enhance positive relationships. Proactive Teaching can be a real key to a youth's success and your sense of accomplishment. At Boys Town, we make some basic assumptions: All behavior is learned, even bad behavior. Also, children behave in certain ways because it has "worked" for them in the past. Our job is to teach new, appropriate behavior that will "work" even better for youth.

Proactive Teaching can be used to teach youth basic and advanced social skills, prepare youth for specific situations or circumstances, and address specific skill deficiencies. This type of teaching can be done individually or with a group of youth, depending on the circumstances.

There are many opportunities for this type of preventive teaching during the course of a day. As youth make progress and begin to use their new skills and behaviors, you can spend less time doing Proactive Teaching and rely more on cues and verbal prompts instead. Eventually, kids will consistently and correctly use these skills as they begin to successfully resolve problems and conflicts on their own. Achieving this goal isn't always easy; in fact it often can be slow, arduous, and frustrating. Caregivers must remain patient and continue to make the most of their opportunities to teach proactively if they are to help aggressive youngsters learn new, nonaggressive ways to respond. Remember, there is bad behavior, but there is no such thing as a bad boy or girl.

It's important to use Proactive Teaching during "neutral times." These are times when the youth is calm and not misbehaving, is not involved in an activity, and the environment is relatively free from distractions. This makes it easier for the youngster to remain attentive and focused during the teaching sessions, and makes the child more receptive to your teaching.

Caregivers should keep these teaching sessions as short as possible, while maintaining high quality. Proactive Teaching opportunities generally occur at times when kids could be doing something they like to do, so if caregivers spend too much time teaching, kids get bored and "antsy." If this happens, teaching actually can become counter-productive and it can sabotage future sessions because the youngster views this time as a nuisance. In addition, it is essential to keep the teaching session upbeat, positive, and interactive. Kids learn better when the teaching atmosphere is fun, and when they are active participants instead of passive observers. So have fun, joke, and be animated and generous with words of encouragement.

Proactive Teaching is a great way for you to teach aggressive youth new, nonaggressive skills that help them get their needs and wants met in more appropriate and socially acceptable ways. So use Proactive Teaching often! And make sure the skills you choose for and teach to a child are good, positive alternative skills to the ones he or she is currently using.

The Proactive Teaching Interaction

Proactive Teaching has three steps; caregivers should use all three in every teaching session. This is necessary because each step has an important function in teaching children new social skills and preparing them for new situations.

Proactive Teaching Steps

1. **Describe the positive behavior.**
2. **Give a reason.**
3. **Practice.**

Let's take a closer look at the steps and their descriptions.

STEP 1 – *Describe the positive behavior.*

Caregivers should tell the youngster what they will be discussing and identify the specific skill area that will be taught. Also, you should give examples of the settings (home, school, sports team, work, etc.) where the skill can be used so that kids understand that the skill is important to their success in many different environments. It's important that caregivers break the skill down into specific, understandable steps. If necessary, you can provide a demonstration to ensure that the youngster knows the skill steps and how to use them.

STEP 2 – *Give a reason.*

As in the other Teaching Interactions, caregivers provide a reason for why it's important to use the new skill or behavior. Keep in mind that reasons should be brief and to the point, not long-winded explanations or lectures. One way to make Proactive Teaching more interactive is to ask the youth why he or she thinks it's important to use the skill. Ask the child if he or she understands the rationale given. This also helps get the youth involved in the teaching session and can be used all throughout the interaction.

STEP 3 – *Practice.*

In this step, caregivers should have the youth practice the skill immediately so he or she can become comfortable with the component behaviors. This also allows caregivers to assess their teaching. A role-play or pretend situation that is appropriate to the age and developmental level of the child can be used to give the youth a realistic opportunity to practice the new skill. When the practice is set up, caregivers should carefully explain what will happen and review the skill components again. To make teaching even more effective, practice sessions should be as fun and reinforcing as possible.

Since the skill is new to the youngster, it is unlikely that he or she will initially get all the steps right. Caregivers should encourage the youngster by praising behaviors that are performed correctly, and nonjudgmentally describe those that need improvement. If the youth is having difficulty with some components, caregivers should make sure that the steps are not too difficult and have been explained clearly, and that the skill is age-appropriate. The youth can practice the skill again, as long as this step doesn't become too lengthy.

Caregivers are strongly encouraged to give positive consequences to kids (when appropriate) for practicing and learning a new skill. Remember that this teaching is usually done when youth could be doing other things they like to do, so a positive consequence helps ensure that kids will want to participate in Proactive Teaching again.

Preventive Prompts

After using Proactive Teaching several times to teach a skill, you may need only to provide a reminder to kids rather than going through all three steps when it comes time for them to use the skill. This reminder is called a "preventive prompt." For example, let's say that you and a youngster have practiced how she should accept "No" for an answer a number of times. Before you enter a store, you could say, "Tara, if I say 'No' about something, remember to stay calm and accept it just like we practiced." The purpose of a preventive prompt is to remind the child what she practiced before, just before the situation occurs again.

Now, let's see what a Proactive Teaching example might sound like.

EXAMPLE – Carla is a thirteen-year-old girl who is receiving help for her aggression problem. Being new, Carla needs help learning some of the basic social skills that can be used to replace her aggressive behaviors. One skill she needs to begin working on is "Accepting Criticism."

Caregiver:	"Carla, let's take a few minutes to talk about a new skill called 'Accepting Criticism.' It's not always easy to do, but it will help you be successful here, and at home and school. It will even help when you're playing volleyball for your school. I know that volleyball is really important to you. Does your coach ever give you feedback and tell you to do things differently?"
Carla:	*(laughing)* "Yeah, she's always telling us to change something or to hustle and stuff like that."
Caregiver:	*(smiling)* "When I played sports, my coaches were like that too! So, when you're given criticism by someone – your mom, or teacher, or volleyball coach – you should look at the person, say 'Okay,' and don't argue. *(Describe the positive behavior)* That way people like your volleyball coach will be more likely to want to help you, and you'll have a better shot at making the

	team and getting playing time. *(Reason)* Make sense?"
Carla:	"Yes."
Caregiver:	"Great! Now let's practice accepting criticism. Let's say I'm your volleyball coach and I'm going to give you feedback on your serve. Remember to look at me and say 'Okay' without arguing. Got it?" *(Practice)*
Carla:	"Sure, I got it."

(Caregiver gives pretend criticism and Carla responds appropriately.)

Caregiver:	"Outstanding, Carla! After I gave you that criticism, you looked at me, said 'All right, coach,' and didn't argue at all. That's the way to accept criticism! Because you did such a nice job here, you've earned an extra snack after dinner. Super job! Now, later today I'm going to come to you and give you some criticism. It may be pretend or real, so be prepared to use the steps we just went over, okay?" *(Prompt)*

Summary

Proactive Teaching is a valuable teaching tool for both caregivers and kids. This teaching technique helps caregivers prepare youth for unfamiliar situations and promotes gradual behavior changes in areas where youth have previously had problems. When youngsters learn how to change their behaviors and handle problems, they feel good about themselves and their confidence in their abilities soars. Proactive Teaching allows caregivers and aggressive kids to work toward goals together, which strengthens relationships. Taking time to set kids up for success through Proactive Teaching is one of the most valuable teaching methods a caregiver has at his or her disposal in helping children and adolescents overcome their aggression problem.

CHAPTER 9

Preparing to Do Treatment Plans

Aggressive youngsters come to you with varied histories and assorted problems, and they require help for different reasons. But the treatment goal for every aggressive child is essentially the same: To reduce and, when possible, eliminate aggressive behavior so the child can become a productive and valued member of his or her family and society. Unfortunately, there is no "magical cure" for every child's aggression problem. Helping aggressive kids is a complex and demanding goal for caregivers because each child is unique and requires individual treatment. That is why being prepared for the treatment planning process is the single most important task for caregivers as they try to help aggressive kids get better.

In the previous chapters, we've laid a foundation to help prepare you for developing effective and therapeutic Treatment Plans for aggressive kids. So far, we've discussed what aggression is and what it is not, how to distinguish between proactive and reactive aggression, and the important role that the Boys Town Model and its specific teaching methods can play in treating aggression. But there's still a little bit more to know before you begin choosing and using strategies for treatment. Specifically, this includes an explanation of some principles of behavior and a look at a unique evaluation approach that helps you determine why a youth uses aggression. This information will allow you to become better at selecting appropriate strategies for each child's Treatment Plan.

Successful treatment planning begins with an in-depth, thorough, and careful evaluation process. Beginning the journey to reduce aggression is pointless unless caregivers know what has happened in a youngster's life and understand why he or she uses aggressive behavior. Neglecting this information is like a doctor trying to treat patients without knowing what is wrong with them. The doctor may get lucky and occasionally prescribe the right remedy, but more often than not he or she will miss the mark and the patient will not get better. In many instances, the patient's condition will worsen because the doctor prescribed the wrong medicine or treatment. An inadequate evaluation frequently leads to a misdiagnosis, which results in ineffective and even harmful treatment.

A good doctor is trained to complete a comprehensive evaluation that requires a thorough examination, tests, and questions about a person's ailment and medical history. The doctor takes time during this assessment process because it is essential for an accurate diagnosis, which ultimately leads to responsible treatment. Skilled caregivers must use the same care and consideration in their evaluation of aggressive youth. Caregivers and others involved in a child's treatment must complete a thorough assessment so they can choose the best strategies. Once caregivers discover the scope and depth of a child's aggression problem, then and only then can they confidently begin constructing an effective and therapeutic Treatment Plan.

This chapter contains a discussion of some principles of behavior that are important for caregivers to be familiar with. In addition, we will present an evaluation process that can help you uncover the reasons kids use aggressive behavior. In Chapters 10 and 11, we will offer some specific ideas and strategies for developing effective, workable Treatment Plans for kids who tend to use proactive or reactive aggression. Those two chapters also will include samples of Treatment Plans that can be used in different programs and treatment settings.

Principles of Behavior and Assessing Aggression

Caregivers can't simply provide custodial care or just be passive observers or "baby-sitters" for troubled youth and expect results. In the Boys Town Model, caregivers are active participants, teaching social skills and developing close and caring relationships with kids. Those closest to the kids are the ones most likely to be effective agents of change so long as their energies and activities are on target. Teaching a wide range of social skills is an important treatment strategy and a big part of a Treatment Plan because it enables caregivers to be direct agents of change and to guide and adjust a youth's treatment.

In order to competently assess a youngster's problem and confidently choose and assign appropriate skill sets for a Treatment Plan, caregivers must have a fundamental knowledge of some basic principles of behavior. These principles make up some of the "science" behind the Boys Town Model. The Model applies these basic principles of behavior in answering the question of why youth engage in aggression and why they have few nonaggressive options when faced with conflict or stress.

Behavioral principles are the fundamental laws or assumptions concerning the nature of behavior. They attempt to define and explain the relationships between a behavior and the specific conditions surrounding the behavior. In other words, these principles are statements of the natural causes and effects of behavior.

In order to understand how to assess and identify the "payoff" – or reasons – for aggressive behavior in children and adolescents, it is necessary to become acquainted with the terms and definitions of some principles of behavior. These are discussed in the following sections.

The ABC Pattern

SAM IS A FOURTEEN-YEAR-OLD BOY *who has been in an out-of-home treatment program for about four weeks primarily due to physical aggression toward others. One day after study hour, Sam and the other kids were asked to go to their rooms and put away their school books. As they walked down the hall, one boy dropped his homework folder and all his papers scattered over the hallway floor. Sam and most of the other kids had not gotten along with this younger boy since he arrived four days earlier. Laughing loudly, Sam called the boy a "clumsy a——." The other youngsters in the hallway laughed at Sam's comment, patted him on the back, and said, "Way to go! You finally shut up that little s—." The younger boy began to cry, got up, and ran down the hallway to "go tell on" Sam.*

Behavior does not occur in a vacuum. Events that happen in the environment or are present before and after a behavior can have a major impact on that behavior. For example, in the situation with Sam, seeing the boy drop his homework papers (what happened before) prompted Sam to call the younger boy a name (Sam's behavior). The other kids in the hallway laughed at Sam's negative comment (what happened after). The attention from the other kids was Sam's "payoff" for his aggressive behavior. It is important to understand what happens before and after a behavior so that the behavior itself can be fully understood. This enables caregivers to choose the most effective treatment strategies and, in the case of social skill instruction, the best social skills to target for teaching.

The terms used to identify these events make up the ABC pattern:

A = Antecedents – the events or conditions present before a behavior occurs.

B = Behavior – anything a person says or does that can be observed and measured.

C = Consequences – the events or conditions that occur after a behavior.

Antecedents

The events or conditions that are present before a behavior occurs can range from simple to complex. For example, a telephone ringing is a simple antecedent to the behavior of answering the phone. In this case, a single event (the phone ringing) occurred prior to someone answering the phone. However, other conditions that affect the behavior of answering the phone could be present. A person who is expecting bad news from a bill collector on the phone may feel anxious, begin thinking about what excuse to give, and hesitate before answering. A person in the middle of a heated argument might answer the phone with a harsh voice tone or not answer the phone at all. A person who is high on drugs might hear the phone ring but not answer it because it would interrupt the drug experience.

When analyzing the antecedents of a behavior, it is important to pay particular attention to what you can observe: the who, what, when, and where of the situation. In other words, who was present, what activities were occurring, when did the behavior occur (the time of day or day of week, season of the year, and so on), and the location or physical setting. Other important conditions, which are more difficult to observe, can include a person's history of reinforcement, thoughts, emotional arousal, or other physiological influences such as illness or drugs. These events or conditions may combine in different ways to become antecedents of behavior.

When examining the antecedents of aggressive behavior, caregivers are looking for characteristic patterns that appear to frequently precede aggressive words and actions. For instance, a boy may usually bully younger boys and typically do so when he has an audience of peers. Or, a girl may shout and curse when given criticism from female authority figures. Knowing the characteristic patterns of antecedents to aggression is one important part of diagnosing "why" the child uses aggression.

Behavior

Behavior is anything a person says or does that can be observed and measured. It can be observed directly or indirectly. For example, caregivers can directly observe a youth sweeping the floor, cursing, or apologizing. (Concepts such as intelligence, anger, or depression are not behaviors; they are labels for sets of behaviors that people often group together for ease of reference.)

Indirectly observing behaviors involves observing the results of behavior. If someone swept the floor, you could see a clean floor; if someone hit another person, you could see bruises or scars; if someone injected drugs, you could see marks on a person's skin; or if there is broken glass, you could infer that a child aggressively threw a plate. In addition, physiological "behaviors" that happen "inside" a person can not be directly observed, but some can be measured with special equipment.

In the Boys Town Model, we assume that behavior is not a random event. It occurs lawfully in the context of observable antecedents and consequences. Anger is not typically the result of spontaneously generated internal energy, but rather a reaction to a set of external circumstances.

Consequences

Events or conditions that follow a behavior are known as consequences. Consequences can be pleasant, unpleasant, or neutral. In terms of the teaching methods we've discussed, consequences can involve something that is given or added or something that is taken away. A pleasant event that occurs following a behavior and the removal of an unpleasant event after a behavior are both likely to increase the use of that behavior. Receiving an "A" on a test (pleasant event) as a result of studying hard should motivate a student to study hard in the future. Hitting the "snooze" button to turn off the alarm clock in the morning (removal of an unpleasant event) may result in increased use of the snooze button.

A behavior tends to decrease if an unpleasant event occurs, or if a pleasant event is taken away, following the behavior. For example, calling a friend and getting cussed out (an unpleasant event) may decrease your behavior of calling that friend. Having to pay a fine for speeding (money – something pleasant – is taken away) can result in less speeding.

Knowing the events and conditions that occur following a behavior can help you analyze why the behavior is occurring, determine whether it is likely to increase or decrease (or stay the same), and plan effective treatment strategies.

Understanding Aggressive Behavior:
A Three-Dimensional Approach

Generally, children (and adults) tend to repeat behaviors that in the past have resulted in pleasant events for them or the removal or avoidance of unpleasant events. For example, an aggressive child may tease and belittle others in school because it draws the attention of his classmates (like Sam in the earlier example). Another child may engage in noncompliance, yelling, threatening, cursing, and hitting in order to get out of having to go to school. Many suspension policies assume that children want to be in school. For children who dislike school, such policies might be counter-productive.

Understanding the reasons for human behavior is so challenging because behavior is so complex. It's clear that a wide range of antecedents and consequences can influence behavior. For example, a child may regularly use certain physically aggressive behaviors like hitting and fighting only under certain antecedent conditions, perhaps when peers tease or shun him. Under other antecedent circumstances, the same child may use different aggressive behaviors to get out of doing an unpleasant task. Since

Figure 1

The Three-Dimensional Approach

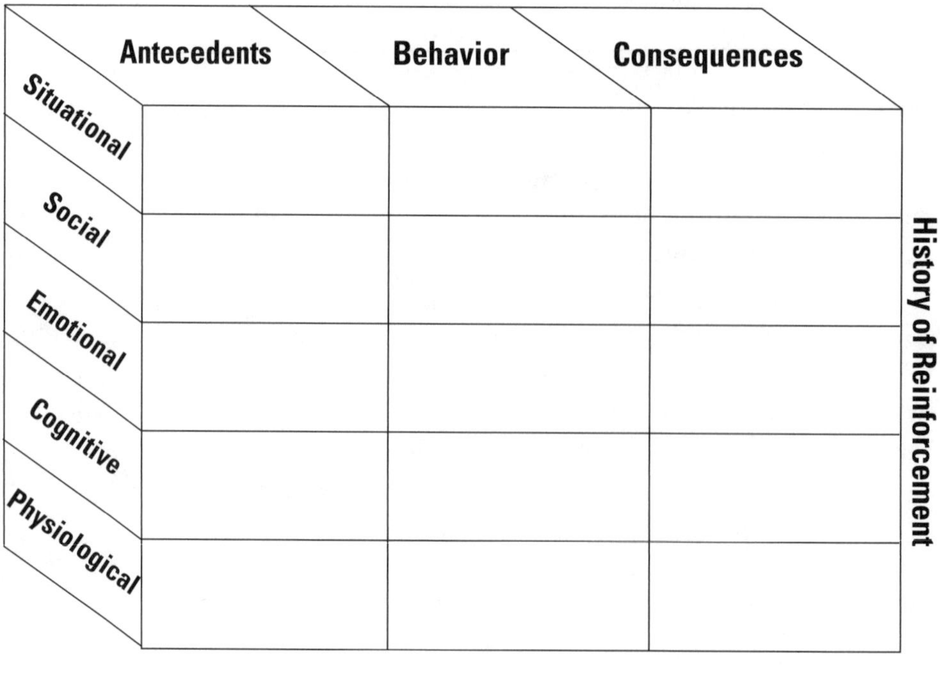

such aggression has helped him avoid tasks in the past, he uses the same aggressive behaviors whenever he's told to do a chore.

In analyzing the difficult behaviors that make up aggression, it may be helpful to use a three-dimensional approach. (See Figure 1.) According to Stumphauzer (1986), this involves breaking antecedents, behaviors, and consequences (dimension one) into specific categories (dimension two), while also recognizing that each category has a complete history of reinforcement (dimension three). We've already discussed the ABC's of behavior that make up dimension one. Here is a description of the categories that make up the second dimension:

> **Situational** – the influence of the situation (other than social influences)

> **Social** – the influence of other people in the environment

> **Emotional** – the influence of emotions or states of arousal

> **Cognitive** – the influence of thoughts

> **Other physiological** – physiological influences other than those that are emotional

It is important to stress that the total of all these events and conditions contribute to making up an antecedent, behavior, or consequence. Categorizing the ABC's of a behavior is an arbitrary process and simply a way to help one understand the reasons for certain behavior.

While this categorization is helpful, it is not complete without the child's history of reinforcement. The reinforcement history represents the third dimension to understanding the function of behavior. Each category included in the second dimension has a complete history of being reinforced, not reinforced, or punished under certain circumstances. This reinforcement history influences whether or not a behavior occurs.

Let's look at how this three-dimensional approach applies to an example of an older boy who engages in physically aggressive behaviors (hitting and fighting) to get a younger child's music player. (See Figure 2, adapted from Stumphauzer, 1986.

As you can see, the various influences on antecedents, behavior, and consequences, coupled with a person's learning history, can result in a complex matrix of behavior. But there is yet another analysis to be completed. That involves looking at the payoff for each category of behavior. In the example of an older youth hitting a younger child to get a music player, here are some possible payoffs or functions:

> **Situational** – The older youth easily obtains the music player he wants and does not get caught. This may increase the likelihood that such behavior will occur in the future.

Figure 2

The Three-Dimensional Approach

	Antecedents	Behavior	Consequences
Situational	Younger, smaller child no adults present	Punched younger child to get music player	Now have a new music player
Social	Peers suggest, support hitting other youth	Peers continue to support	Now have a new music player
Emotional	Aroused due to anger over not having a music player	Heightened arousal and excitement	Excited, relieved, arousal decreasing
Cognitive	"This kid is a wimp. I won't get caught"	"You can do it, no adult is around"	"I did it, this is great, my friends are impressed"
Physiological	Inhibitions reduced by alcohol	Alcohol effects: reduced reaction item, etc.	Continued effects of alcohol

History of Reinforcement

> **Socially** – Lots of reinforcement from peers in the form of praise, approval, and admiration may increase the likelihood that such behavior will occur in the future.

> **Emotionally** – The emotions felt by the older youth (initially anger, followed by a general increased arousal) may be reinforced by the success of obtaining the music player, and increase the likelihood that the same behavior will occur in the future.

> **Cognitively** – Thoughts of being strong, dominating others, being too smart to get caught, and peer approval are being reinforced and will likely lead to a repeat of the behavior in the future under similar circumstances.

> **Other physiological** – Using alcohol or drugs may have reinforced all of the above events, and the positive effects or sensations that come with being drunk or "high" may outweigh the long-term negative physical and emotional effects of drinking or using drugs (hangover, fatigue, depression, etc.).

Given this hypothetical situation, do you think the older youth will continue to use physical aggression in order to get what he wants under similar antecedent conditions in the future? Because the behaviors of hitting and fighting are being reinforced at all these levels in this situation, there's a good chance that this youth will hit and fight again.

You may not yet know the child's learning history but even one observation of such aggressive behavior gives you some hypotheses to follow and questions to ask, including:

> How did he learn to bully to get what he wants?

> Did he have role models who were bullies (dad, mom, brother, etc.)?

> Is he more aggressive when using drugs or alcohol?

> Does his history support aggressive tendencies?

> Which is greater motivation, peer support or gaining a desired object?

You can get at some of the learning history by reading a child's social and psychological history. Another way is by having a trusted adult ask the child. Knowing the child's learning history, helps you decide how to set up new learning situations to gain more prosocial skills and engage in less aggressive skills. For example, if peer approval is a major motivator, you can use it to support new learning.

Summary

When planning treatment for children who engage in any aggressive behavior (noncompliance, yelling, cursing, verbal threats, stealing, harming animals, punching, fighting, and so on), it is extremely helpful to look at antecedents, behavior, and consequences, how these are directly influenced by the various categories, and the history of reinforcement for each category. Using this three-dimensional approach to gain an understanding of the "payoff" of aggressive behavior for children helps caregivers to choose the best treatment strategies.

In addition to this assessment process, there are several other sources of information at caregivers' disposal that can help provide valuable insight into understanding why a child uses aggressive behavior. Some of these include psychological reports, social histories, and other admission reports; parent or guardian interviews and reports; youth interviews; caregiver observations; and others. The point here is that caregivers should gather as much information as possible during the evaluation process so that they are able to determine why a child is using aggression. Once caregivers collect all this information and identify the reasons for a youth's aggressive behavior, they are better prepared to develop therapeutic, effective Treatment Plans.

CHAPTER 10

Treatment Strategies for Reactive Aggression

Planning and providing treatment for aggressive children is an awesome responsibility and a tough job for caregivers. When caregivers are able to evaluate and identify the reasons or motivation for aggressive behavior, they can better determine whether the behavior is proactive or reactive. Once a child's aggression problem is classified, a caregiver can select strategies that are designed to tackle specific inappropriate behaviors and integrate those strategies into a Treatment Plan.

Reactive aggressive kids tend to be bothered and upset by the actions and reactions of others. They are impulsive and respond to what happens around them in an emotionally charged manner. When they become upset, reactive aggressive youth have great difficulty controlling their aggressive behaviors. Typically, they use their aggressive behavior to avoid and/or escape problems that stem from their contact or relationships with others. This aggression regularly harms and, many times, severely damages these relationships. That's why one focus of treatment planning for reactive aggressive youth should be teaching new skills that enable kids to solve their problems in ways that are socially acceptable and not harmful to relationships.

The following sections discuss and explain some treatment strategies that Boys Town has found helpful and effective in treating reactive aggression in children and adolescents. It's important to keep in mind that using only one of these interventions in a Treatment Plan is not likely to bring about the desired changes in a troubled youth's aggressive behavior. Instead, selecting and implementing a combination of strategies helps to make a Treatment Plan therapeutic and successful. The last section of the chapter includes two case studies and sample Treatment Plans from two different treatment settings. These are presented to demonstrate this multidimensional approach to treating aggression.

Social Skill Instruction

As we have stressed throughout this book, social skill instruction should play a major role in the treatment of any aggressive youth. An integral component of the Boys Town Teaching ModelSM, this treatment strategy has been proven to dramatically reduce both proactive and reactive aggression in children. Treatment Plans for kids with these behavior problems are much more likely to succeed when they focus on teaching skills that foster self-control and provide several options for children to meet their needs.

Several factors can enhance the use of social skill instruction when caregivers are helping reactive aggressive youth. Those factors are discussed here.

Accentuate the positive

Many reactive aggressive youth have a history of unhealthy and hurtful relationships with others. Because these kids have directed unpredictable and impulsive acts of aggression toward others, those "victims" have reacted negatively toward the youth or developed a negative perception of them. As a result, many reactive aggressive kids are not well-liked and have experienced much criticism. When these kids come to you for treatment, they may be extremely wary and distrustful of others; many times they don't seem to want help. That is why Effective Praise is such an important Teaching Interaction for caregivers.

You should try to "catch" reactive aggressive kids using positive behaviors as often as possible. Boys Town recommends that you praise kids much more often than you correct them during treatment. Depending on the child's problems and his or her situation, a positive-to-negative ratio of at least four-to-one and up to ten-to-one can be appropriate and therapeutic. (You may recall that this means trying to do up to ten Effective Praise Interactions with a youth to recognize appropriate behavior for every one Corrective Teaching or Teaching Self-Control Interaction.)

Because many aggressive kids have such severe relationship problems, it's vital that caregivers establish a strong, healthy bond with each youth as soon as possible. Building good relationships by having fun, showing interest, staying calm while the child is struggling, and simply showing care and concern is very important. Effective Praise also can help accomplish this goal. Over time, as caregivers point out and reinforce the good things youth do – often some of these may seem small or insignificant – kids begin to feel good about themselves. As they come to realize that the caregivers' praise is genuine, the confidence kids have in themselves and their ability to overcome aggression problems soars. Creating this sense of self-efficacy is an important factor in helping youth learn new ways of behaving.

Catching kids being good through lots of Effective Praise helps build trust with kids; they begin to believe you really want to help them get better. Eventually, the walls these kids have put up around themselves crumble, and they start to work with you instead of against you. When kids allow you to enter their lives, you have a much better chance of helping them overcome problems.

Set kids up for success

Life is full of new people and experiences; not all of them are good or pleasant. A large part of succeeding in life depends on how well a person learns to deal with difficult and unpleasant circumstances. When people have the opportunity to plan and rehearse for these upcoming difficult events, they are much more likely to succeed than if they go in cold and unprepared.

Unfortunately, reactive aggressive kids have learned to respond in harmful and destructive ways when they face new experiences that cause upset and turmoil. Oftentimes, they don't think about the consequences of their aggressive behavior – they just erupt. So an important treatment goal for many reactive aggressive youth is to learn how to "look before they leap." In other words, caregivers should teach kids to stop before they act and to think of the best, most appropriate way to handle a given situation.

Incorporating extra Proactive Teaching sessions into a Treatment Plan is a strategy that can help achieve this goal. Caregivers can set kids up for success by preparing them to properly respond to situations that have caused problems in the past or new situations that will likely lead to an aggressive response. For example, if a child is about to have a meeting with the school principal, helping her practice conversation and staying calm skills that she can use in place of aggressive behaviors will help lead to a successful outcome. A youth who has a history of becoming aggressive when other kids tease him should practice skills for appropriately dealing with teasing before his first day of school. When youngsters are given the opportunity to rehearse prosocial skills and proper responses before difficult situations, they are much more likely to succeed and learn how to react in similar situations.

One way to make Proactive Teaching even more powerful is to use a **preventive prompt**: Just before a difficult event or situation, or when a child is beginning to cycle into an aggressive outburst, a youth is given a prompt or reminder of what he or she practiced in a Proactive Teaching session. For instance, just before a child meets with the principal or walks into the school for a new school year, you give a quick reminder to use the appropriate skills and responses that were practiced earlier. Or, just as a youth is starting to raise his voice or curse in response to being called a name, you can remind him how he practiced lowering his voice and slowing down his speech.

Another type of preventive treatment strategy involves helping kids recognize physiological signs (quick breathing, fast heartbeat, flushed face, racing thoughts, tingling in hands, etc.) that precede aggressive responses. Youth then learn to respond to these signs by using strategies that help them with self-control.

Proactive Teaching, preventive prompts, and recognizing physiological cues that precede aggression are extremely effective with reactive aggressive children and adolescents because each strategy acts as a stop sign, signaling youth to pause and think about how to appropriately handle a difficult situation. As children learn to better recognize and handle difficult situations on their own, caregivers won't have to use prompts and Proactive Teaching as often. When kids experience success where they once experienced only failure, they will view you as concerned and helpful. This helps to further develop and enhance positive relationships. Mastery of skills develops confidence and a sense of empowerment and self-efficacy.

Don't fuel the fire

Reactive aggressive kids are especially likely to react with extreme outbursts in Corrective Teaching and Teaching Self-Control situations. Why? One reason is that youngsters resist consequences that they don't like or think are unfair. While consequences are a necessary component of effective teaching, how caregivers give them often determines how a child will react.

To avert a negative reaction when doing Corrective Teaching with a reactive aggressive youth, it's effective to follow up a consequence with a "positive correction statement." In other words, tell the child that he or she will have an opportunity to earn back some of the consequence for practicing the appropriate alternative skill. Remember, positive correction lets kids know that all is not lost; it helps soften the blow of a negative consequence and helps prevent a negative outburst.

Teaching Self-Control – when a child is beginning to unwind and erupt – can be a real juggling act. A crisis is looming, but caregivers often can skillfully manage its severity and duration by staying calm themselves and giving the child opportunities to use a self-control strategy (more on this in the next section) to help them calm down. Also, avoid giving a barrage of consequences by moving slowly and carefully through each step of Teaching Self-Control. Remember, the goal here is to get the child to stop his or her aggressive behavior and initiate and correctly use a self-control strategy. Quickly delivering consequences and racing through the interaction doesn't give the reactive aggressive child enough time to process what he or she should do. In fact, counter aggression and consequences may trigger or increase aggression. It almost guarantees that the child will revert to old, familiar aggressive behaviors instead of trying to use new, appropriate skills. Moving too quickly also can perpetuate and escalate a crisis.

Self-Control Strategies

Self-control strategies are behavioral and cognitive techniques that empower kids to calm themselves down. Generally, these strategies are used during crisis situations and other times when there is upset and turmoil in a child's life. The goal when teaching youngsters self-control strategies is to enable them to recognize the need for, choose, and correctly use a calming strategy like deep-breathing or positive self-talk (see Figure 1 for other examples of self-control strategies) on their own before they erupt in aggressive and violent ways.

Since it will be difficult for youth who have been so locked into aggressive responses to change their behavior and use new strategies, progress often will be slow. Youth will face many setbacks and sometimes they may feel like they're not getting anywhere. That's why it is important that caregivers use Effective Praise to reinforce a youth's efforts to make even the smallest improvements in behavior. Youth who see that you are behind them, providing support and guidance because you genuinely want them to get better, are more likely to stick with the treatment program, even when times are tough. Getting youth to commit to and believe in the goals they are trying to achieve is a major accomplishment, and Effective Praise can help you get there.

Frequent Proactive Teaching sessions also should be incorporated into a youth's Treatment Plan. These teaching sessions are most effective when they occur during "neutral times," when the child is neither upset

Figure 1

Examples of Self-Control Strategies

Deep-Breathing
- Take a deep breath in through your nose and hold it for about two seconds.
- Let the breath out slowly through your mouth.
- Repeat this process two or three times until you feel yourself calming down.
- When you are calm, tell an adult.

Journaling or Drawing
- Go to a designated place where you won't be disturbed.
- Write down (or draw a picture that shows) how you are feeling and what you are thinking.
- When you are calm, tell an adult.

Take Time to Cool Down
- Go to a designated place where you won't be disturbed or distracted.
- Take an agreed-on amount of time to calm down.
- If you need more time, calmly ask for it.
- When you are calm, tell an adult.

Positive Self-Talk
- Make a positive comment about how you can handle a situation appropriately. Use a phrase like, "I can get myself under control"; "I've done it before, I can do it again"; "If I stop now, things will get better"; or "I can do this."
- Repeat the statement you choose until you are calm.
- When you are calm, tell an adult.

Muscle Relaxation
- Clench and squeeze your fists for five seconds and slowly release them.
- Slowly roll your neck in circles for five seconds.
- Scrunch your shoulders and slowly roll them in circles several times.
- Slowly rotate your ankles.
- Raise your eyebrows as high as you can and slowly lower them.
- Scrunch your face and release.
- When you are calm, tell an adult.

nor displaying negative behavior, and there are few or no distractions in the environment. When using Proactive Teaching, caregivers should set up role-plays that are realistic and as close as possible to the issues and situations that have caused the youth to lose self-control in the past. For example, if a child who is new to your teaching consistently becomes upset and begins to yell, curse, and throw things when she is told she can't do something she wants to do, it is important to review and practice the new skill of *Accepting "No" Answers,* and review and practice how to choose and correctly use a self-control strategy. (This is especially critical when kids are first learning a skill or are having difficulty using a particular skill.) In this type of situation, there may be many instances when Teaching Self-Control and self-control strategies are needed. However, as the child becomes more proficient at accepting "No" answers, Teaching Self-Control and the use of self-control strategies will be required less frequently.

Choosing Individual Self-Control Strategies for a Treatment Plan

It is extremely important to choose the right self-control strategies for kids who are not able to appropriately express or deal with anger, frustration, conflict, and crisis. These strategies should meet a youth's individual needs, and work best for that youth in times of crisis. As you consider the strategies presented in Figure 1, these factors should serve as guidelines for matching techniques with the needs of each child.

> **Age and developmental level** – Some self-control strategies are geared for and are more suited to older youth, while other strategies are more appropriate for younger children. For example, drawing would be a better strategy than writing in a journal for a younger child who has not yet learned to write or a youth who is unable to express himself or herself through writing. In these cases, choosing the wrong strategies can actually worsen a crisis situation because the child becomes frustrated by the inability to perform them. Strategies like drawing, deep-breathing, and taking time to calm down that divert the child's attention away from the crisis situation are most effective with younger or developmentally handicapped children.

> **Severity of behaviors** – Many troubled youth have behavior problems that are quite severe. Problems that jeopardize the safety of the child or others may initially call for self-control strategies that are appropriate for a situation, simple to teach, and easy for the youth to use anywhere. For example, with a boy who has a history of being physically aggressive toward

others, giving him a pen to write in a journal with could create an extremely dangerous situation. Instead, calming techniques like deep-breathing, muscle relaxation, or positive self-talk would work better and be safer.

> **Exposure to teaching** – The length of time you have been working with a youth on self-control issues also will play a role in determining appropriate strategies. A child who has been participating in treatment for some time and has been making progress in using calming techniques may be ready to learn more advanced strategies. With these kids, calming strategies such as writing in a journal, progressive .muscle relaxation, positive self-talk, anger logs, hassle logs, and others may be extremely effective and therapeutic. On the other hand, children who are new to your teaching would concentrate more on basic calming techniques like deep-breathing or muscle relaxation.

As a youth gets better at using self-control strategies, you can begin to teach new ones. For example, a child may progress from going to his bedroom to draw in a notebook when he gets upset at home, to writing in a journal at the kitchen table, to using deep-breathing while physically remaining in any situation where he experiences frustration or anger. This process usually develops and improves slowly over time, so be patient. The longer a child is exposed to your teaching and has opportunities to practice and use a self-control strategy, the better he or she will get at initiating and using the strategy independently.

> **Setting** – Some settings are more suitable for specific self-control strategies than others. For example, a child can use the strategy of drawing in his room at home. However, this may not be an appropriate strategy to use outside the home. That's why it is important for children to learn a number of self-control strategies that can be used in different settings (school, sports, church, work, and so on).

> **Child's response** – This factor involves a child's willingness to learn and use a particular self-control strategy, and its observed effectiveness. It is fruitless to try to teach a strategy that a youth does not want to use. In addition, if you observe that a child is not using a certain calming technique, then it may be necessary to replace it with a different strategy. One of the best ways to prevent this from happening is to have the child help choose which strategies will be taught and

used. This gives the child a sense of ownership and involvement, and makes it more likely that he or she will use these strategies in crisis situations.

Keep in mind that the five self-control strategies listed in Figure 1 are examples of calming techniques that Boys Town has effectively used to help aggressive kids. This is by no means an all-inclusive list of self-control strategies. With some kids, caregivers may have to create and develop effective calming techniques. The point here is that it's very important for caregivers to teach strategies that work best for each youth.

Distorted Thinking

One factor that can cause a child to react aggressively is distorted thinking. This means that the youth is either inaccurately perceiving cues from others or is misreading their intent. In order for children to change their reactive aggressive behaviors, they must learn how to recognize their distortions and how to change their thinking so they can assess situations more accurately and more positively.

Before discussing how to help children in this area, it is important to understand some of the common cognitive distortions that play a role in reactive aggressive behavior. Here is a list of some of these distortions:

> **Filtering** – This occurs when a youth dwells exclusively on a single negative detail of a situation, ignoring all the positive aspects. Consider this example: Jack writes a paper for English class. The teacher returns it with the remarks, "Well written, Jack. Good subject matter and keeps the reader interested. Next time, provide more detail about your subject." When Jack reads this, he ignores the teacher's positive comments and concentrates only on her suggestion to provide more detail next time. Jack takes this criticism to mean that he is lazy, and he gets mad.

> Everyone "filters" information differently. Many people tend to focus on the areas that they consider to be weaknesses. In the example, Jack thinks he is inadequate, so he looks for things that reinforce this belief. Unfortunately, when Jack's thoughts become negative, he becomes angry. If Jack does not change or control these negative thoughts and unpleasant feelings, he will act them out, often in an aggressive manner.

> **Overgeneralization** – This occurs when a person bases his or her conclusion about a situation on only one piece of information or one experience. For example, a boy asks a girl

for a Friday night date and she turns him down. From that experience, he concludes that this girl will never go out with him. He asks another girl and she turns him down. He concludes that no girls will go out with him. The boy uses these incidents to conclude that all girls don't like him, and ignores any other evidence to the contrary. Later on, when the boy's mother asks him what he is going to do on Friday night, he shouts, "It's none of your business!" The mother has no idea that her son thinks she is teasing him about not having a date.

> **Mind-Reading** – In this situation, the youth makes an assumption without having any evidence to support the assumption. An example would be a situation where a teacher asks a child to stay after class for a few minutes. Even though he believes he hasn't done anything wrong, the child immediately thinks, "Man, I'm probably going to get a detention or something." He is irritable and on edge for the last two hours of school. This youth thinks that everyone has the same thoughts and feelings that he has; if he sees the worst in everyone and every situation, he assumes that people feel the same way about him.

> **Personalization** – This occurs when a child thinks that everything that happens is related to him or her, and that the child is responsible for every situation. For example, if a girl's best friend is angry, the girl will assume that she did something to make the friend angry. This child also compares herself with others: "She's prettier than me...,"; I'm not as smart as him...,"; "I'm a better soccer player than her...," and so on. The child sees everything that goes on around her as a measure of her worth. And because she thinks everything is related to her, even the most innocuous event can lead to anger, frustration, disappointment, and an aggressive response. Often, other people don't know how to respond to this aggression because they don't see an incident as being related to the child at all.

> **Control Fallacies** – There are two possible ways children can distort their feelings of being in control: They can see themselves as being totally under others' control, or as being totally responsible for everyone around them. The child who feels that everyone else is in control is more likely to be a reactive aggressive child. This child feels that he doesn't have any control over his life, and that he just responds to

everyone else's decisions. Because the child feels like everything is being done to him, it is easy for him to be angry with and resentful of those around him. He also feels helpless because he does not think he can influence anything that goes on in his life. This leads to poor decision-making because the child does not think any solution he comes up with is going to matter anyway.

> **Fallacy of Fairness** – In this situation, children view everything in terms of "fairness," or how much others care for them. A youngster's thinking follows this kind of logic: "If my teacher liked me, she wouldn't give me a 'D'"; "If my parents loved me, they wouldn't make me baby-sit my sister all the time"; "If my girlfriend really cared for me, she'd go out with me Friday, instead of staying home for her sister's birthday." Since no one can live up to this child's expectations, he begins to resent almost everyone with whom he has a relationship. Over time, these feelings of resentment can lead the child to try to punish others or to constantly test a relationship with inappropriate behavior.

> **Blaming** – When a child distorts her thinking in this way, she blames others for her decisions and responsibilities. An example of this would be a situation where a child "blames" her friend for always wanting to play the same game. The child could insist on playing something different or play with a different friend, but it is easier for her to hold the friend responsible. Another example would be a child who gets upset with his mother for suggesting that he work on his model car. The child does not explain that he is watching an exciting part of a movie; he just assumes she knows this.

> **Heaven's Reward Fallacy** – Children who view things this way always expect to be "paid back" for something they do. For example, a child helps her mother clean the house and wash the car. Later, when Mom tells the girl that she cannot go to a movie that night because it is not appropriate for a thirteen-year-old, the child blows up and says, "It's not fair. I did everything you wanted all day. You owe me something." She feels cheated and robbed, and responds by trying to "punish" her mother for "tricking" her.

It is easy to see how children who are experiencing any one of these cognitive distortions (and many aggressive children are prone to several) would begin to see people in a hostile, angry light. These children misread situations, and since other people cannot know their thoughts, no one is able to help the children process information more clearly and accurately.

Often, people whose intentions are neutral or positive are caught off guard by the aggressive child's behavior. They have difficulty "reading" what the child is thinking, which makes the child's behavior seem totally unreasonable and irrational. Because other people are unprepared for the child's aggressive response, they are more likely to respond inappropriately as well.

It is not necessary to be a therapist to learn about what form of distorted thinking a child might engage in. However, if you are a treatment team member or a parent of a child in therapy, the easiest way to find out is to ask the therapist.

The therapist learns about the child's distorted thinking by listening to the language the child uses when describing why he or she gets angry, who he or she is angry at, and situations that cause anger. The therapist asks questions and listens carefully for patterns of responses. You can do the same thing. For example, you might ask why a boy blew up at his teacher in the classroom. The boy says, "She does not like me and criticizes me a lot. She's just like the other teachers." Such response patterns might signal overgeneralization, so you ask, "Did any other teacher criticize you today?" The child says, "No." Next, you ask, "What did you think about when your teacher criticized you?" The child responds, "I thought she was tearing me down just like all the teachers." This tells you that overgeneralization is one of the child's distortions, and you can begin to help him change how he interprets information in similar situations. We will describe additional ways to learn about distortions and how to help change them next.

Helping a Child Change Distorted Thinking

This section will look at several ways caregivers can help children overcome distorted thinking and get better at picking up and accurately translating such cues from others.

> ❯ **Describe the situation or event.** Each time the child engages in aggressive behavior, have him write a description of the event. With younger children, you may want to have them tell you about the event while you write out the simple details. When the child first begins this treatment strategy, it might be helpful to have an adult present while the child is working. Initially, the child may have a difficult time figuring out how the incident relates to others. Most aggressive children develop a view of the world by internally processing events, rather than looking at external factors and considering

144

the views of others. In other words, they think only of themselves and not of others. Talking with the child can help draw out more details, not just a slanted description of what others did to provoke the child.

> **Identify thoughts.** Go over the situation with the child. Help him identify his thoughts, particularly those that occur just before the aggressive behavior. Help the child to recognize distortions that may have occurred. When a distortion is identified, have him write it down, or write it down for him.

> **Change the distortion.** After the child has identified the distortion and written it down, have him rewrite the phrase or sentence without the distortion. For instance, in our example about the child blowing up when getting criticized by the teacher, you might help the child do the following. First, the child writes, "She doesn't like me and criticizes me a lot. She's just like the other teachers." Next, you would direct the child to write, "Mrs. Green criticized me for not raising my hand. She criticizes other kids for the same thing. Most teachers do not like kids talking out in class." Initially, children will need a great deal of guidance to do this. Over time, however, older children should be able to do it by themselves. Once that happens, it's important to reinforce this behavior with positive consequences.

Helping the child to recognize distorted thinking and teaching him to change it can be a big step toward changing his aggressive tendencies. Showing the child how to look at things from another person's perspective by providing "other-centered" rationales, and periodically asking the child how he thinks others feel in a given situation also may prove worthwhile. The idea is to help the child realize that other people have feelings and that, just as the behaviors of others affect him, his behavior affects others.

> **Thought-stopping.** This is a simple process where the child is asked to picture a stop sign inside his head when he has a thought that could lead to aggressive behavior; he then tells himself to "stop" the thought. If you are working with a younger child, explain that he should just picture the stop sign again if the thought returns. With practice, the child eventually will be able to remove himself from the situation or think about other things. Older children can be told to try to replace the negative thought with an alternative positive

thought. So if a child is thinking, "Nobody likes me," he should try to think, "Well, some people like me; my friend, Jamir, for instance." The goal is to help the child change the thought before it leads to aggressive behavior.

Earlier, we mentioned that a child's distortions can lead to feelings that may result in aggressive behavior. Often, when we act spontaneously, we are reacting to our emotions. Children are no different. Aggressive children often report feeling anxious, alienated from others, angry, fearful, frustrated, hurt, or inadequate before they display aggressive behavior. Certain situations are more likely to cause these feelings than others. These situations include being teased, getting criticized, receiving consequences, being rejected, being told "No," or having a trust betrayed. These situations are difficult for most of us to deal with, so it is not surprising that a child whose distortions already make him see others as hostile would find them even more challenging. Changing distorted thinking itself is not a "cure" but it gets one of the complicating factors out of the way.

Using Time-Out

One treatment strategy that works well with young children or kids at lower developmental levels is Time-Out. Time-Out involves having a child sit in one place for a certain amount of time, away from all the enjoyable things in the child's life. Time-Out works with most young kids because they eventually begin to realize that avoiding aggressive behaviors and using appropriate behaviors helps them to stay out of Time-Out, allowing them to do things they like to do.

When using this intervention, caregivers should follow these basic guidelines.

> Immediately following a problem behavior, describe the behavior to the child and send (or take) him or her to the Time-Out area. Stay calm and describe the behavior only once. Do not reason, explain, lecture, argue, threaten, raise your voice, or use physical punishment (e.g., spanking). In fact, avoid giving the child a lot of attention at this time.

> Choose a convenient place for a Time-Out area. It doesn't have to be the same place each time. A kitchen chair, a couch, a footstool, or a step will work. Make sure the area is safe, well-lit, and away from enjoyable distractions like the TV or toys.

> Before you ever begin using Time-Out, explain to the child what it is, which problem behaviors it will be used for, and

how long it will last. For example, you could say, "When I ask you to put your toys away and you start crying and throwing your toys, you will have to go sit on a chair in the kitchen for three minutes. I'll start the timer on the stove and when it buzzes you can get up." Then practice having the child go to the chair when you ask. Do this when the child is calm and in a good mood.

> As a general rule, a child should spend one minute in Time-Out for every year of his or her age. In other words, if a child is five years old, quiet time should last no longer than five minutes. Kids may think it's fun the first time you practice, but it's quite likely they won't enjoy an actual Time-Out situation. Therefore, it's very important to specifically explain the process beforehand and prepare the child for the real thing.

> During Time-Out, the child is to sit calmly and quietly in the designated area. If the child complains, makes angry statements, cries, or throws a tantrum, it does not count toward "quiet time." On the other hand, fidgeting and talking in a soft voice can count. Don't start the time until the child is quiet; if you start the time and the child starts to cry or begins a tantrum again, wait until he or she is quiet and start the time over again.

> The child must stay seated and quiet during Time-Out. If the child decides not to cooperate and tries to leave, calmly return him or her to the Time-Out area. If this continues (and it often does when you first begin using Time-Out), keep returning the child to the area. If you get tired or other activities take you away from the Time-Out, you can have the child leave the area, but be sure to use a different consequence. The child may lose play time with toys or TV privileges, or friends may have to go home. When the child is calm, practice using Time-Out again so that the child will learn to stay in Time-Out during actual situations.

> Early in the process, the child may cry, say nasty things about you, throw objects, or make a mess. Ignore behaviors that are not dangerous to the child, you, or the surroundings. Kids use these negative behaviors to try to get your attention and stop the Time-Out; remember that Time-Out is a time when the child doesn't get any attention.

> ❯ When the Time-Out is over, ask the child, "Are you ready to get up?" The child must answer in a way that's agreeable to you – a nod or an "Okay" work just fine. Then you can tell the child that time is up and that he or she can leave.

Keep in mind that Time-Out is most effective with younger kids and kids at lower developmental levels. It shouldn't be used with older children or adolescents; for these kids it's usually more effective to deliver a consequence that removes something they like (loss of phone, TV, or computer privileges, etc.) or adds something they don't like (extra chore). Job lists are great to use with adolescents.

Aggression Log

An aggression log is a treatment intervention that can provide youth and caregivers with valuable insight and information about a youth's aggression problem. The log, which is filled out by a youth during a quiet time after an aggressive incident has been resolved, helps track the cause, severity, and frequency of aggressive behaviors. It is one of the ways previously discussed that adults can get insights into what's going on inside a youth's head. It also is a way for youth to reflect on the thoughts and feelings that go with those behaviors. Over time, youth and caregivers can use the log to identify progress and areas where improvement or more teaching is necessary.

Before caregivers decide to use an aggression log in treatment, they should do a lot of Proactive Teaching with the youth. The youth must understand the purpose of the log, how it is to be completed, and how it fits into the Treatment Plan. Caregivers also must make sure that a youth has the necessary writing skills and the ability to reflect on and analyze his or her behaviors. Youth who are not capable of completing a log might become angry or frustrated by the task, and find the treatment to be more punishing than helpful. Keep in mind that aggression logs work best with older children and adolescents, and are probably not a good intervention for younger children or kids at lower developmental levels.

A youth should enter the information about an aggressive incident in private during a quiet time. Caregivers should allow sufficient time after the incident so that the youth is calm and in control of his or her emotions and behaviors. If a youth is not comfortable with the process the first few times a log is used, a caregiver may have to ask the youth questions and record the youth's answers in the appropriate column.

Figure 2

Sample Aggression Log

Date_____ Time_____ Place_____

Who Was Present _____

_____

Trigger (What happened before) _____

_____

_____

_____

Thoughts _____

_____

_____

Feelings_____

_____

_____

BehavŠrs_____

_____

_____

Consequences_____

_____

_____

Figure 2 presents a sample aggression log. The following section explains the different entries the log contains and how the information can be used to help kids get better.

> ❯ The areas labeled "Date" and "Time" help monitor when and how often incidents are occurring. This helps the youth and caregivers measure whether a youth is making progress, staying the same, or getting worse. It also gives a picture of any patterns of behavior that might be developing. For example, a youth might react with more serious aggressive behavior on days when he has to do a certain chore or has a lot of homework. Identifying these types of patterns enables caregivers to make adjustments in a youth's treatment.

> ❯ The "Place" and "Who Was Present" entries identify where the aggressive behavior took place and who was around, respectively. For example, most of a youth's aggressive incidents might occur at school, and be directed at females more often than males. Again, this data can help caregivers detect behavior patterns.

> ❯ The area labeled "Trigger" is where a youth writes what happened just before he or she responded with aggression. This can provide valuable clues about what antecedents may be contributing to a youth's decision to respond with aggression. For example, one day a youth might write, "Some friends were teasing me about my new haircut" in reference to a fight he had with those friends. The next day, the same youth might have another altercation with a different person, and write "Ethan was rubbing it in that he beat me at basketball." These entries would indicate that the youth is having trouble dealing with teasing, and the caregiver could do more teaching in that area.

> ❯ The "Thoughts" and "Feelings" entries are where a youth writes down what he or she was thinking just before the aggressive behavior occurred. These responses let caregivers know whether the youth needs help with correctly identifying feelings or changing distorted thinking.

Identifying feelings is an area where many youth will require help. Generally, aggressive kids know three feelings: mad, glad, and sad. Oftentimes, they will mistakenly say they were mad before an aggressive incident when they actually were feeling lonely, anxious, frustrated, irritated, or something else. In order for kids to learn to appropriately deal with unpleasant feelings, they must be able to correctly recognize and label what they are feeling. This might become a priority in a Treatment Plan.

> The "Behaviors" area is where the youth writes down the aggressive behaviors he or she used during the incident. Examples might include, "I yelled and swore"; "I punched Keisha in the back"; or "I threatened to hurt the caregiver." Information in this column helps caregivers gauge the severity and intensity of a youth's aggressive behavior, and determine whether the child's problems are getting better or worse. For example, if over a five-week period a youth has gone from hitting and kicking during problem situations to yelling and cursing, he or she has made progress. This indicates that the treatment strategies that are in place are working. On the other hand, a deterioration of behavior to more extreme forms of aggression indicates that treatment is falling short and changes are necessary.

> The final area is labeled "Consequences." Here, the youth lists the consequences that resulted from his or her aggressive behavior. Caregivers must teach youth that these consequences include not only those that are obvious and personal, like losing privileges or earning an extra work chore, but also those that are more far-reaching, like damaging a relationship, losing a person's trust, or causing physical injury. This enables young people to understand that their aggressive behavior has a destructive and harmful effect on their lives and the lives of others.

Once the youth has completed the entries on the aggression log, the caregiver and youth should discuss the content. The main teaching should focus on how the youth can better deal with similar problems in the future. Afterwards, the youth also should earn a positive consequence; the type and size of the consequence should be based on how thoroughly the youth completed the log and the youth's participation in the discussion. If the youth sees this as a reinforcing event, he or she will be more willing to participate again.

Aggression logs are excellent evaluation tools for measuring the success of or need for change in Treatment Plans. Equally important is their value as self-assessment and self-monitoring tools for the kids who use them. The aggressive youngster can use this activity to reflect on and analyze the many different factors that lead up to and follow an aggressive incident. This is extremely valuable for reactive aggressive kids, who don't usually take the time to stop and think about how their aggression negatively affects them and others.

Individual and Group Therapy

Psychotherapy is a popular type of therapy that is often used as part of a troubled youth's overall Treatment Plan. Psychotherapy is based on "intrapsychic" views of the nature of deviant behavior in youth. Intrapsychic processes are those that are viewed as being responsible for maladjustment in youth. Therapy is primarily directed at helping a youth develop or increase awareness of certain thoughts, feelings, and experiences; the youth then works through these issues with a therapist. Because reactive aggressive youth tend to have problems in these areas, this treatment strategy can be appropriate and effective. As with other treatment strategies, it is necessary for the youth and the therapist to have a strong relationship. Youth who trust their caregivers usually are more open in their expression of important thoughts, feelings, and experiences, which can contribute to efforts to bring about therapeutic change.

Having said that, it is important to point out that psychotherapeutic techniques tend to be relatively nonspecific, making it difficult to judge treatment effects or to replicate psychotherapeutic procedures. Consequently, the outcome evidence regarding psychotherapy is not strong enough to determine the effectiveness of psychotherapeutic treatment modalities. Although individual psychotherapists may experience clinical success in treatment, there is little evidence that individual or group psychotherapy alone impacts aggressive behavior (Kazdin, 1985). Kazdin's review of the psychotherapeutic literature indicated that relatively few studies focused specifically on the treatment of aggressive youth and adolescents. In general, intrapsychic approaches are laden with untested theory, both in the development of aggression and the key variables necessary to treat it. However, the value of psychotherapy as part of an overall Treatment Plan for reactive aggressive youth should not be underestimated nor discounted.

Pharmacotherapy

Pharmacotherapy involves the use of various drugs (stimulants, antidepressants, antimanics, etc.) to control aggression in children and adolescents. This therapy is based on evidence that suggests that for some youth, there may be a biological basis to their aggressive behavior. Our experience at Boys Town has been that reactive aggressive kids are more likely to have medication as part of their overall Treatment Plan than proactive aggressive kids.

To date, there is no established drug treatment that can be broadly applied to treating aggressive behavior in youth. This is due, in part, to the fact that aggression is correlated with a wide variety of other nonbiological attributes (family history, sex, age, etc.). However, certain classes of drugs such as stimulants and antidepressants have been effective with some aggressive youth.

The use of pharmacotherapy as a treatment strategy for aggression is worth exploring for some specific types of aggressive youth, including those who tend to use reactive aggression. However, pharmacotherapy should be used with other nondrug therapies. In addition, due to the short- and long-term side effects of certain drugs, pharmacotherapy as a treatment for youth should be carried out only under the direct supervision of a professional who has been clinically trained to evaluate, diagnose, prescribe, and monitor psychotropic medications for children and adolescents.

Sample Treatment Plans

Now, let's put all this together. This section contains sample Treatment Plans for two reactive aggressive kids who are being treated in different settings. The first example takes place in a Treatment Foster Care setting, while the second occurs in a psychiatric environment. Each example includes a short summary of the youngster's behavioral history and a completed Treatment Plan.

The information in each summary is the result of a thorough and careful evaluation. The treatment strategies appear in bold face type and targeted skills appear in bold italic type so that you can see how these skills and strategies can be incorporated into a Treatment Plan.

Example 1

Latonya is a ten-year-old girl who has been placed in a treatment foster home. The Treatment Foster Parents have a fifteen-year-old son at home. Latonya has been in and out of various placements since she was three; this is her fifth out-of-home placement. Her history includes placement in two different psychiatric hospitals for a total of four months, placement in a traditional foster home for two years, and a three-month stay at an emergency shelter. Latonya has lived at home in-between these placements. Latonya's primary referral problem is aggression toward others. She also has been sexually abused by her mother's boyfriend and has experienced academic difficulties and depression. The Treatment Foster Parents have observed that Latonya has great difficulty controlling her aggression. They report that Latonya "loses it" without warning when she doesn't like what someone tells her or when she can't have something she wants. When Latonya loses self-control, she slams doors, yells and curses, and occasionally hits others. Latonya also frequently forgets to close the door when she is in the bathroom. Furthermore, she makes sexual jokes, talks about sexually explicit movies her mother has allowed her to see, and stands too close to people when they are talking. Latonya's Treatment Plan follows.

Treatment Plan

Date _____

Youth: Latonya

System: Motivation Chart

Problem at Admission: Aggressive Behavior

Target Behavior: (1) Controlling Emotions: Using Anger Control Strategies

Baseline: Frequency of Problem Behavior: 5 per day (average)

Problem Definition

When Latonya is angry, frustrated, or upset, she tends to suddenly lose self-control. Generally, this happens when she is told something she doesn't want to hear or when she can't have or do something she wants. During this time, she slams doors, throws things, and sometimes hits others. She also swears, refuses to listen to adults, tells them to "shut up," and refuses to follow instructions.

Goal: Frequency of Problem Behavior: 2 per day
(0 per day for physical aggression)

Treatment Strategies

Proactive Teaching

Latonya will practice and review every day before and after school, and every morning and afternoon on weekend, the steps of two self-control strategies that she has helped to choose and develop. The strategies are:

1. **Deep-breathing** (take a deep breath in through the nose and hold it for about two seconds, let the breath out slowly through the mouth, repeat this process two or three times until calmed down, when calm tell an adult).

2. **Ask to listen to music in room** until calm.

When Latonya has mastered these two strategies, she will begin working on others, including:

1. **Self-talk.**

2. **Telling someone she trusts what is bothering her** (using the skill of *Expressing Feelings Appropriately*).

3. **Problem-solving.**

Latonya will be given an opportunity to review or practice the steps to her **self-control strategies** prior to situations where she frequently loses control. Latonya will earn a checkmark on her chart for role-playing her **self-control strategies** twice each day. She also will earn two check marks each day she doesn't lose self-control. At the end of each week, Latonya can exchange these stickers for:

- a candy bar (nine stickers).

- staying up an extra thirty minutes on a nonschool night (twelve stickers).

- thirty minutes of playing video or computer (fourteen stickers).

- a video rental and eating popcorn during the movie (sixteen stickers).

Social Skill Instruction

Latonya will earn stickers for using her **self-control strategies** at home and at school. Latonya will earn a **Time-Out** and/or lose privileges for not using the skill of *Expressing Feelings Appropriately*. When this happens, Latonya can earn back some of her privileges by role-playing the skill of *Expressing Feelings Appropriately*. Latonya will lose from one to five stickers when she loses self-control. **Effective Praise, Corrective Teaching,** and **Teaching Self-Control** will be used.

Family Meeting

There will be a Family Meeting at least twice during the first week Latonya is in the home, and as often as needed each week after that. During these meetings, any problems that any of the children in the home are having with physical aggression will be discussed. (It is important not to "single out" Latonya during these meetings, and not to discuss her private treatment issues in public.)

Relationship Development

The Treatment Foster Parents will use **Effective Praise** to help Latonya recognize when she is using the steps of her **self-control strategies**. The Treatment Foster Parents will look for opportunities to praise Latonya for using the steps of her self-control strategies. Latonya will be given rationales for how these strategies will benefit her at home, at school, and during visits with her family.)

Medication and Individual Therapy

Latonya will continue to see Dr. Smith twice a month for individual therapy and to monitor her medication.

Example 2

Tom is a thirteen-year-old boy who has a learning disability. He has recently been placed in an intensive residential treatment facility, his sixth different placement since he was eight. Tom displays little impulse control and tends to be overly active and "scattered" in situations that involve groups (classrooms, group therapy sessions, unit outings, etc.). Tom is easily distracted and overstimulated, and frequently loses his orientation and focus on tasks. The other kids on the unit dislike Tom, and he has great difficulty in his relationships with adults. For example, Tom is likely to argue when someone corrects his behavior, has a hard time completing tasks, and often engages in activities without asking permission. Tom frequently loses self-control and claims that he is "picked on" and treated unfairly by other kids and caregivers on the unit. When he loses self-control, Tom becomes physically aggressive, damages property, and eventually becomes self-injurious. On two occasions during his last three-month placement in a group home setting, Tom lost self-control and cut his arms and hands with glass from windows he broke. Both situations involved an argument with another youth in which a caregiver initially intervened and gave Tom a consequence for his part in the fight. During these two occasions, Tom alternated between threatening to kill himself and the caregiver. The self-inflicted cuts to his arms were serious enough to require stitches and could have been fatal had there not been immediate intervention. Tom has not destroyed property or hurt himself at school; however, one reason for his placement in a more-restrictive psychiatric setting was because he hit a teacher.

Comprehensive Treatment Plan
Intensive Residential Treatment Center

Date of Admission: January 1

Name: Tom   Date of Initial Treatment Plan: January 10
Medical Record Number: 00-00-00

Priority Treatment List

Priority Yes	No	Problem List
X		History of self-harm statements and attempts.
X		Acts out aggressively (including assault).
X		Difficulty expressing feelings appropriately.
X		Symptoms of depression (withdrawn, tearful, easily distracted, low self-esteem).
X		Poor coping skills.
X		Family relationship issues.
X		Poor anger/impulse control.
X		Difficulty accepting decisions of authority.
X		Behind on school credits.
	X	History of drug and alcohol use – The other placements report that, to the best of their knowledge, Tom has not used drugs or alcohol in the last year.

Each "No" response requires a rationalization to be listed following the problem.

DOB 6/17/20xx
M.R. # 00-00-00

Comprehensive Treatment Plan

Date of Admission: January 1

Medication: Zoloft (50 mg.) in the morning.

Goal : Tom will decrease self-harm statements and self-injurious behaviors while increasing his ability to express feelings appropriately.

> **Objective #1:** Tom will increase his ability to use the skill of ***Expressing Feelings Appropriately*** to a rate of 90% as measured across all areas by February 15.
>
> _____ **Date Achieved**

> **Objective #2:** Tom will increase his ability to use the skill of ***Expressing Feelings Appropriately*** regarding family issues in individual, family, and group therapy to a rate of 90% as measured across all areas by February 15.
>
> _____ **Date Achieved**

> **Objective #3:** Tom will increase his ability to use the skill of ***Making Positive Self-Statements*** to a rate of 90% as measured across all areas by February 15.
>
> _____ **Date Achieved**

> **Objective #4:** Tom will increase his ability to use the skill of ***Participating in Activities*** to a rate of 90% as measured across all areas by February 15.
>
> _____ **Date Achieved**

Persons Responsible: Doug Smith, MD; Dawn Johnson, MSW; Rick Doe, Unit Coordinator

* See the Boys Town manual, *Teaching Social Skills to Youth,* for the steps of the skills listed in the Comprehensive Treatment Plan.

Tom
DOB 6/17/20xx
M.R. # 00-00-00

Goal : Tom will decrease his aggression while increasing his ability to accept decisions of authority.

Objective #1: Tom will increase his ability to use the skill of ***Accepting Decisions of Authority*** to the rate of 90% as measured across all areas by February 15.

_____ **Date Achieved**

Objective #2: Tom will reduce the number of aggressive incidents (i.e., assaults) to zero for thirty days by February 15.

_____ **Date Achieved**

Objective #3: Tom will increase his ability to deal with frustration and anger by using the skill of ***Controlling Emotions*** to a rate of 90% through using the self-control strategies of deep-breathing and visual imagery and an aggression log by February 15.

_____ **Date Achieved**

Persons Responsible: Doug Smith, MD; Dawn Johnson, MSW; Rick Doe, Unit Coordinator

Tom
DOB 6/17/20xx
M.R. # 00-00-00

Goal :   Tom will improve confidence and competence in his academic abilities and study skills.

Objective #1:   Tom will remain on task when directed and demonstrate this by using the skills of ***Accepting Help or Assistance, Asking for Help,*** and ***Participating in Activities*** in the classroom in four out of seven class periods by February 15.

_____ **Date Achieved**

Objective #2:   Tom will use the skill of ***Completing Tasks*** (i.e., school assignments) at 80% accuracy in five out of seven class periods by February 15.

_____ **Date Achieved**

Objective #3:   Tom will use the skill of ***Using Spontaneous Problem-Solving*** with peers and staff when conflicts arise in the classroom in four out of seven class periods by February 15.

_____ **Date Achieved**

Objective #4:   Tom will attempt to be more assertive and resist peer pressure by using the skills of ***Being Assertive*** and ***Resisting Peer Pressure*** in four out of seven class periods by February 15.

_____ **Date Achieved**

Person Responsible: Cathy Wilson, MA

Comprehensive Treatment Plan Review

Treatment Strategies: *Individual, group,* and *family therapy* using cognitive-behavioral strategies, family system strategies, level system, therapeutic milieu, and medications.

Data Collection: Weekly medical chart probes, professional observation, and motivation system card data.

Treatment Team Reviews

Review 1 – Date: February 17

During this review period, Tom has made minimal progress on all objectives. He has engaged in nine incidents of physical aggression and has been physically assaultive toward peers and staff on four occasions. Tom also has made five self-harm statements and engaged in two incidents of self-destructive behavior. Due to these statements and behaviors, Dr. Smith placed Tom on suicide evaluation on three separate occasions. A new objective will be designed so that the occurrences of these statements and behaviors can continue to be monitored and measured. The treatment team will meet within twenty-four hours to discuss and disseminate the new objective.

Review 2 – Date: _____

Review 3 – Date: _____

Review 4 – Date: _____

Discharge Plan

Estimated length of stay: Three to four months.

Criteria For Discharge: No incidents of aggression for thirty days.

Projected Placement: Group living environment.

Transition: 15-30 days.

Psychiatric Consultation: Ongoing for monitoring **medications** and mental health needs.

Therapy: Individual and **group sessions** with unit therapist.

Medical: None.

Other: Parents will attend and complete a Boys Town Common Sense Parenting® course.

Treatment Team Reviews

Review 1 – Date: February 17

Review of Discharge Plan and Reason for Continued Care:

During this review period, Tom has had several behavioral difficulties within the classroom setting; this environment seems to be a great source of frustration. Tom also has had difficulty *controlling his anger* impulses and has made several self-harm statements instead of *expressing his feelings appropriately.* Continued practice, effort, and improvement is needed before Tom will be able to move to a less-restrictive level of care. Tom's parents are enrolled in and will attend a Boys Town Common Sense Parenting® course next month.

Review 2 – Date: _____

Review of Discharge Plan and Reason for Continued Care:

Review 3 – Date: _____

Review of Discharge Plan and Reason for Continued Care:

Summary

Every youth who receives treatment deserves and requires individualized treatment. This can be accomplished through the use of a comprehensive evaluation of a youngster's problem. From that evaluation, a Treatment Plan can be developed that includes interventions designed specifically to treat the youth's aggression problem. Children and adolescents who meet the pattern of reactive aggression have a unique set of issues and problems that require special attention and treatment. Some strategies that have proven effective for these kids include social skill instruction, changing cognitive distortions, aggression logs, individual and group therapy, medications, and others. Remember, however, that the therapeutic power of a Treatment Plan lies not in each strategy alone, but in the sum of the values of all interventions.

CHAPTER 11

Treatment Strategies for Proactive Aggression

The major payoff for proactive aggressive kids is acquiring things. Proactive aggressive youth bully, control, or dominate to get what they want, regardless of whether others are hurt in the process. The proactive aggressive child uses aggression as an instrument; he or she has learned to manipulate others by using verbal or physical attacks. This type of aggression is more thought out and calculating, and less emotional, so the youth may or may not be angry, upset, or experiencing any unpleasant feelings. Thus, one of the major goals during the treatment planning process should be to target skills that teach these kids sensitivity toward others and how to build healthy, lasting relationships.

This chapter will focus on some of the treatment interventions that Boys Town has found effective in helping caregivers achieve treatment goals for proactive aggressive children and adolescents. Also included are sample Treatment Plans for two proactive aggressive youth in two different settings.

Keep in mind that the following strategies in and of themselves are not meant to be "cure-alls" for proactive aggression. When putting together an effective and therapeutic Treatment Plan, caregivers should carefully evaluate and choose a variety of these interventions.

Social Skill Instruction

Social skill instruction is a powerful and effective intervention for treating proactive aggression. But several key issues should be incorporated into your teaching to help enhance its effectiveness and therapeutic value. These issues are discussed here.

Focus on the positive

When working with proactive aggressive youth, it is important to change certain patterns that have developed and contributed to the continuation of negative behavior. One such pattern involves situations where children have received no praise or attention for positive behaviors, and are noticed (and punished) only when they use aggression. After a while, these kids turn exclusively to aggressive behaviors to get attention and other things they want.

Focusing on catching these kids being good, praising, and reinforcing positive behavior through lots of Effective Praise is one important way to break this pattern. Believe it or not, these kids will engage in prosocial skills while in your care. In the beginning, it generally will be something very small and inconspicuous, such as not making a negative comment to or teasing another youth, or picking up another child's dropped fork from the floor during dinner.

Caregivers may have to look long and hard for these kinds of opportunities to praise kids. But it's a place to start! Remember, the goal is to teach these kids skills that will help them become sensitive to others and interact with adults and kids in appropriate, friendly ways. Including a lot of Effective Praise in a Treatment Plan helps proactive aggressive kids see the rewards and benefits that come from using positive behaviors. Over time, with plenty of determination and patience from caregivers, these kids will begin to realize that they can get their needs met in positive ways, and will become less and less dependent on their old aggressive behaviors.

Effective Praise also allows a caregiver to show an aggressive child how to respond to others in a positive fashion. Caregivers model the qualities and skills needed to teach these kids sensitivity toward others and how to build and maintain a positive relationship. For many kids, the real-life demonstration you provide as part of Effective Praise may be the catalyst they need to begin making the necessary changes in their lives.

A final benefit of frequently using Effective Praise (along with other relationship development strategies) in a Treatment Plan is that it strengthens your relationship with the child. Over time, the child begins to like the positive attention, and seeks to please you instead of disappoint you. As kids begin to see that you are truly concerned about them, they start to use more of the positive, prosocial behaviors that you have taught them.

166

Use all the teaching interactions

Proactive aggressive youngsters respond very well to the contingencies and consequences that are built into Corrective Teaching and Teaching Self-Control. Kids who are calculating in their use of aggression are better able to understand that there are negative consequences attached to their aggressive actions. Unfortunately, if you let an aggressive act pass by without responding with Corrective Teaching or Teaching Self-Control, you are likely to see that same aggressive behavior again. Therefore, caregivers need to address and teach to every incident of aggressive behavior when it occurs.

Proactive Teaching also can contribute to the effectiveness of a Treatment Plan. This type of teaching can be extremely effective with proactive aggressive kids and should be used frequently, especially when a child is new to a program. During these teaching sessions, focus on making your expectations clear, and consistently give consequences (both positive and negative) when a child meets or fails to meet those expectations. This not only sets the child up for success, but also shows him or her that you are fair, and strengthens the relationship.

Stay the course

"I'm gonna kick you're a--- if you don't let me have that!"

"Why are you always so unfair to me? I want to call my mom!"

"You son of a b----! I hate your guts!"

"You don't like me! You're just like all the others who treat me like s---!"

Proactive aggressive kids are masters at using verbal statements like these. The outcome here usually is baiting a caregiver into a frivolous argument or a fruitless discussion that will sidetrack the caregiver's teaching and draw attention away from the youth's aggressive behavior. When kids do this, caregivers must not get "sucked in." Remember, this is only a ploy kids use to avoid or escape negative consequences they've earned for inappropriate behavior.

It is tempting to want to respond to "baiting" statements when they happen. But a good rule of thumb is to ignore them or simply acknowledge the child's concerns by saying you would be happy to talk about them later. Above all, stay focused on your teaching. Once a youngster has calmed down, you can follow up on any concerns or problems he or she brings up. During Corrective Teaching and Teaching Self-Control it is important to keep the focus on the child's aggressive behavior.

Many caregivers make the mistake of taking these statements personally. This causes them to react in an emotional manner and, suddenly, caregivers find themselves defending or explaining what they said instead of finishing their teaching. To avoid this situation during Corrective Teaching or Teaching Self-Control, stay calm and keep the responsibility squarely on the child's behavior, not yours. When you follow up with the child later, you usually will find that the youngster either forgot about what he or she said or no longer believes it is important.

Do more than choose the right skills

When choosing social skills for Treatment Plans for proactive aggressive children and adolescents, it is important to always keep the primary treatment goals in mind. These kids need to learn the skills that relate to the concepts of getting along with others and building healthy relationships. This might include teaching skills like Volunteering, Making an Apology, Compromising with Others, Showing Sensitivity to Others, and so on. (See Appendix A, "Social Skills for Aggressive Youth," for more examples of social skills for proactive aggressive kids.)

In addition to assigning appropriate skills as part of a child's overall Treatment Plan, there are many other creative ways to go about teaching these concepts. For example, you can take youth to homeless shelters to help serve meals, to homes for senior citizens or veterans to spend time with residents, or to a women's shelter to read stories to the young children. Kids also can volunteer for community projects like neighborhood clean-ups, painting houses or cleaning yards for the elderly or economically disadvantaged, food drives, and many others.

Proactive aggressive kids must learn to stop focusing on themselves and turn their attention to others. Choosing and using the right social skills is one way to accomplish this. But if you take it one step further by incorporating many types of real-life activities into a Treatment Plan, the child can learn very powerful and influential lessons about what it really means to put others ahead of self. Keep in mind you need to teach the skills as well as provide the activities. If you do not do both, the activities will seem to be unrelated to their treatment and the skills will not generalize to the activities.

Work Chores

Because many proactive aggressive youth understand that there are negative ramifications to their aggression, work chores are effective consequences to incorporate into a Treatment Plan. Work chores require a child to sacrifice time and effort that could be spent playing or doing something enjoyable. And the process of adding work chores is simple. Take, for example, a situation where an older boy has verbally threatened a younger boy in order to get his candy. As you begin to use Corrective Teaching, the older boy begins arguing and making excuses. Once he calms down, you finish the Corrective Teaching interaction and deliver a consequence (loss of privilege related to the behavior) for making threats. Then you can add the work chore of helping to clean the bathroom for arguing with you. Both consequences should be effective at reducing those behavior problems in the future.

In some instances, a chore can relate directly to the problem behavior. For example, if a youngster knocks over a couple of kitchen chairs during a tantrum, a good work chore might be having the youth straighten up the rest of the kitchen after he picks up the chairs.

Here are some examples of how work chores can be used as consequences for aggressive kids.

> A girl breaks another youngster's radio. To make restitution, she must do chores to earn money to buy the other child a new radio.

> A boy steals another child's video game. Later, the boy wants to call his best friend. As a consequence for stealing, you decide that the youth has to do the other child's daily chore as well as his own daily chore before he can make the call.

> A girl is yelling at another youth to get off the phone so she can make a call. Her consequence is folding a load of laundry that the other child was supposed to fold as a regular chore.

> A boy pushes another child to the floor during an argument over whose turn it is to put away the clean dishes. As a consequence for his aggressive behavior, the boy has to put away the dishes for the next three days.

Here is a list of work chores that can be added as consequences, where possible. Add chores in areas that are different from the chores kids do as part of their daily routine.

Folding laundry

Putting laundry away

Making another child's bed

Vacuuming

Raking all or part of the yard

Mowing the grass

Taking out the trash

Collecting the trash from throughout the house

Helping another youth with his or her chores

Dusting furniture

Sweeping the porch

Washing some or all of the windows

Washing the car

Vacuuming the carpet in the car

Washing the car windows

Cleaning the garage

Helping a youth put toys away

Washing, drying, or putting away the dishes

Sweeping the kitchen (dining room) floor

Cleaning the bathroom

Cleaning the kitchen sink

Cleaning the bedroom

Shaking the rugs

It's very helpful to keep a list like this handy so you can pick a chore at a moment's notice when needed.

It's up to caregivers to decide how often a chore should be done, and to define exactly what the child should do. Take into account the age and ability of the child. Also, adjust the consequences to fit the severity of the problem behavior. Remember to use the smallest consequence necessary to change the behavior.

One variation in this area is called a **chore jar**. Here, caregivers write different, extra chores on small pieces of paper and put them in a jar. When a child engages in an aggressive act, the child must select a chore from the jar. This is easier for caregivers because the consequences are made up ahead of time and are readily available. It's important that caregivers tell kids ahead of time about the chore jar and how it will work. Caregivers can use a chore jar for less severe aggressive behaviors like noncompliance, arguing, sarcasm, and so on.

Problem-Solving

The aggressive youth has learned a pattern of behavior that is self-destructive and self-defeating with respect to successful community living. This pattern of behavior is played out daily in every facet of the youth's life (home, school, and work) and results in numerous interpersonal confrontations. Research has shown that aggressive youth usually interpret inter-personal encounters as hostile and are less sensitive to interpersonal con-flict (Kazdin, 1985). Additionally, they generate fewer alternative solutions to interpersonal encounters than other youth and their solutions are almost always aggressive in nature. While caregivers should actively inter-vene when confrontations occur and teach the youth alternative behavior patterns, the ultimate goal is to help youth develop a wide range of effec-tive skills that they can use on their own to avoid confrontations.

Problem-solving is one of those skills. This step-by-step process enables youth to accurately identify a problem, come up with options, review the pros and cons of each option, and finally reach a solution.

The next sections will discuss various aspects and benefits of problem solving and a structured, problem-solving method known as **SODAS**.

Problem-Solving Counseling

Problem-solving counseling involves actively teaching an aggressive youth how to explore his or her feelings and develop more appropriate responses to these feelings. Such counseling can help youth learn to think through an issue before making a decision and can provide caregivers with the opportunity to guide the decision-making process.

Caregivers should not appear shocked by anything an aggressive youth might say. For instance, a child might say, "Josh is a wimp. He shouldn't be afraid when I push him." This indicates the child's lack of compassion. It is very important for you to accept a youth's feelings and let him or her know that it's okay to express these feelings to you. This helps the youth feel comfortable about expressing emotions, fears, and concerns about intimate or embarrassing events. This also helps caregivers to better understand the youth and to assess his or her current behavior in the con-text of those feelings.

In the Boys Town Model, problem-solving counseling goes beyond the traditional exploration of feelings and seeks to help youth work out new, more appropriate ways to express them. The message here for youth is that it's okay to feel a certain way, but it's not okay to behave any way you want. Society holds us accountable for what we do.

Goals of Problem-Solving

A caregiver's goals during problem-solving counseling sessions are to help the aggressive youth arrive at a viable solution to his or her problem and to teach the youth problem-solving skills. Because such counseling sessions also promote and establish trust between the caregiver and the youth, another benefit is the opportunity to build relationships during such sessions through expressions of concern, affection, respect, and interest in the youth's problems. As an aggressive youth confides in you and sees that you respond with respect, concern, and helpfulness, he or she will feel more and more comfortable problem solving with you in the future.

When to Use Problem-Solving

Problem-solving counseling is most appropriate when an aggressive youth needs to develop a plan to deal with a problem. The problem may be one that he or she is currently experiencing or one that is anticipated, and might involve the youth's parents, siblings, teachers, friends, employer, girlfriend, or boyfriend. Such problems can range from how to talk with an employer whom the youth feels is unfair, to how to resist peer pressure, to deciding whether to participate in an activity. Problem-solving also can be used retrospectively to help a youth make a better decision in the future. For example, a caregiver may help an aggressive youth review a problem that resulted in a fight at school and arrive at a more acceptable solution to a similar future situation.

There are some situations when problem-solving counseling is not appropriate. These can include times when a caregiver is attempting to teach an aggressive youth a new skill, or is dealing with inappropriate behaviors such as skill deficiencies, rule violations, or inattentive ongoing negative behavior. Such youth behaviors should be consistently addressed with consequences, Proactive Teaching, and Corrective Teaching. At times, caregivers may be tempted to counsel when a youth is passive and withdrawn or when the child complains about unfairness. In such cases, it is important to stay on task, regain the youth's attention and cooperation, and complete the necessary teaching. Later, when the youth is calm and his or her behavior is appropriate, the caregiver may choose to initiate a problem-solving counseling session. Bad behavior should never be tolerated or receive a "neutral" consequence like counseling.

When serious issues arise, caregivers should seek professional guidance from a therapist. For example, you can help a youth through a divorce or a death in his or her family. But you must recognize that these events can be so traumatic that the youth might need counseling from a therapist who specializes in this area. Another example of a time when professional help is needed is when a youth threatens to commit suicide. Suicide threats should always be taken seriously and a supervisor or therapist should be consulted immediately.

Caregivers also should not attempt counseling when a youth is under the influence of drugs or alcohol. An intoxicated youth is incapable of good decision-making. Counseling may even provoke violent behavior from an aggressive youth. Therefore, there should be no counseling or consequences until the youth is sober.

Caregiver Counseling Behaviors

The following qualities are critical for effective and successful problem-solving counseling with aggressive youth. Mastering these qualities requires practice and reflection, and will enhance your effectiveness in working with aggressive youth.

> **Listening skills** – Caregivers who have good listening skills are better able to encourage the youth to discuss issues and express feelings and thoughts. A caregiver can indicate that he or she cares about and respects what the youth is saying by looking at him or her, not interrupting, frequently nodding, and generally being attentive.

> **Verbal behavior** – Caregivers can keep an aggressive youth focused on the subject and involved by offering verbal encouragement and praise ("It's really good that you're thinking this through."). Asking clarifying questions and requesting more information will encourage the youth to participate even more ("Tell me a little more about what happened after that.").

> **Empathy** – Providing empathy during the discussion lets the youth know that you are trying to understand his or her feelings and point of view ("That must be very upsetting to you" or "It looks like you're really angry about that."). Empathy is very important in establishing rapport with an aggressive youth and encouraging him or her to discuss issues.

> **Physical proximity** – Caregivers should avoid sitting behind a desk or table, or having other physical barriers between them and the youth. This can make caregivers appear to be less open and accessible to the youth. Sitting on a couch with a youth or sitting in a chair directly across from him or her establishes a relaxed and comfortable setting for the youth.

While all these qualities are important to facilitate problem-solving, they also should be used in your day-to-day interactions with each youth. Caregivers need to express care and concern, listen, offer empathy, and be open any time they are working with or talking to a child. Nurturing and caring occurs daily. When you consistently express your concern and act in ways that demonstrate your commitment, aggressive kids are more likely to come to you with problems.

Problem-Solving Process

Caregivers guide the counseling and rational problem-solving process by using the **SODAS** method, a revision of a counseling process developed by Jan Roosa (1973). SODAS is an acronym that stands for the following steps:

S Define the problem **situation.**

O Examine **options** available to deal with the problem.

D Determine the **disadvantages** of each option.

A Determine the **advantages** of each option.

S Decide on the **solution/simulation.**

While using the SODAS method, caregivers should use all the supportive nonverbal and verbal behaviors previously discussed. Each of the SODAS components is explained in more detail on the following pages.

Starting the session

In the first session, caregivers should teach the SODAS acronym to youth, explaining what each letter of the method means. Then use SODAS on one or two simple, pretend issues. For example, you might ask, "How would you solve the problem of finding a lost coat at school?" This is an easy way to introduce SODAS. Then you are ready to use SODAS on real-life issues.

Situation

The problem-solving process begins with the caregiver helping the aggressive youth clearly define the situation or problem. In some cases the youth initially will present vague and emotional descriptions ("I'm sick of school" or "My folks don't care what happens to me."). Caregivers can use general clarifying questions or statements to help the youth more fully describe the issues ("Why don't you explain that some more."). However, it may be necessary to ask direct, specific questions ("Why are you sick of school?" or "Did something happen during your home visit?"). By calmly and skillfully asking these questions, caregivers can keep the youth involved and help the youth articulate a realistic description of the situation.

As questions are asked and the youth responds, the caregiver should provide empathy, concern, and encouragement. Without empathy, concern, and encouragement statements, the questions can become more of an interrogation that could cause the youth to withdraw.

As the youth more clearly defines the situation, the caregiver should summarize what the youth is saying. This summarization is particularly important before any options are discussed. The summarization helps assure that all relevant information has been reviewed and that the caregiver has an accurate picture of the youth's situation. If the summarization is inaccurate or incomplete, the youth has the opportunity to correct any misperceptions. This is especially important at this point since the remainder of the process is built around the defined situation. Without an accurate or clearly defined situation, it will be difficult to generate useful options and a viable solution.

Options

After the situation is clearly defined, the caregiver helps the youth generate options for solving the problem. It is important to have the youth generate these possible solutions since the goal is to have the youth develop the ability to solve problems on his or her own.

To help the youngster generate options, the caregiver should specifically ask the youth how he or she might solve the problem or deal with the situation ("Can you think of a way to handle that?" or "What do you think you can do about this?"). After the youth suggests an option, the caregiver should continue to solicit additional options ("Can you think of any other ideas?").

Initially, a youth may have difficulty generating options. The suggestions he or she offers may not be very helpful or realistic. Whenever a youth does come up with an option, the caregiver should remain nonjudgmental and make a positive comment about the youth's participation in the process ("Well good, you've come up with a second option. You're really trying to think this through."). The caregiver also can offer a neutral comment and a prompt for more options ("Okay, that's one option. Can you think of another one?").

Remaining nonjudgmental can be difficult for caregivers, especially when the youth suggests an option that would only result in greater difficulties ("I'll just have to punch him out."). The caregiver should remember that his or her role at this point is just to get the youth to generate options. In that sense, this phase of the process is a "brainstorming" session. If a caregiver discounts or denies the youth an opportunity to come up with options, it may harm the relationship with the youth and may diminish the likelihood that the youth will come to the caregiver with problems. (During the next phase of examining the advantages and disadvantages, the caregiver can help the youth judge the "wisdom" of the suggested options.)

After the youngster has given all of his or her ideas, a caregiver may give suggestions as well. Options should be phrased as questions ("What do you think about talking to the teacher after class?") so that the child still feels involved in the process. Over time, kids will be better able to generate options and will be more comfortable doing so.

Disadvantages and Advantages

After a number of options have been generated, the caregiver helps the youth think through and discuss the disadvantages and advantages of each one. In a sense, the caregiver is trying to teach the aggressive youth that there is a cause-and-effect relationship between making decisions and what happens to him or her.

As in generating options, it is important that the youth come up with some advantages and disadvantages. Again, the caregiver's role is to skillfully guide the youth by asking general questions ("Can you think of any problems if you do that?" or "Are there any benefits for doing that?"). If the youth has difficulty thinking of the disadvantages and advantages, the caregiver can help by asking more specific questions ("Well, what do you think your teacher will do if you start a fight in his class?" or "Do you think she might be more willing to listen to you if you did that?").

There may be a number of disadvantages and advantages for any given option. Since a goal is to help the youth learn to think, it is important to solicit as many disadvantages and advantages as possible ("Can you think of any other advantages? Any other problems?"). Caregivers should remain nonjudgmental and not argue with the youth about his or her perceptions of the disadvantages and advantages. This can be difficult when the youth is enthusiastic about the advantages of an option that may be unrealistic or problematic ("Yeah, it'd be great to fight it out because then he'd leave me alone and everybody would think I was tough."). Rather than argue about an advantage, the caregiver can simply acknowledge the youth's view ("Okay, so you think that an advantage would be....") and guide the youth's judgment during the discussion of the disadvantages ("What happens if you don't win?"; "Could you get hurt?"; or "What will your boss do if he hears you've fought with another employee?").

If the youth clearly does not see or cannot be directed to verbalize an important advantage or disadvantage, caregivers should offer their viewpoint and allow the youth to react.

The caregiver can finish this step by summarizing each option and its advantages and disadvantages. This summary further helps the youth see the cause-and-effect relationships.

Solution/Simulation

In this step, the youth selects a solution and prepares to successfully implement it by practicing. Typically, as a result of examining disadvantages and advantages, the youth selects a workable option. It may not

176

always be the best option in the caregiver's opinion, but it must belong to the youth. If the youth feels some ownership of the choice, he or she is more likely to be committed to making the option work.

After the youth has selected an option, the caregiver should provide encouragement and reassurance that the youth can successfully implement the solution. Caregivers also can help make the youth comfortable with the solution by answering any questions the youth may have about how to use it.

Another important aspect of improving the youth's chance for success is setting up a role-play or practice session. These role-play sessions should be as realistic as possible. Often, caregivers will know the people the youth will interact with as he or she implements the solutions (parents, friends, employers, teacher). Because they know the individual(s), they can behave like those people. For example, if an employer is fairly abrupt and somewhat stern, a caregiver can best help the youth by portraying the employer in that manner. The caregiver can make the role-play more realistic by giving the youth several different responses; this can help prepare the youth for the unexpected.

Caregivers should express confidence in the youth's ability to implement the solution. However, they should not promise the youngster that the solution will work. As the practice session ends, caregivers should prompt the youth to check back after he or she has tried to implement the solution. If the youth succeeds, caregivers should praise the child for doing so and for going through the problem-solving session. If the solution does not work, caregivers should be supportive and empathetic. Caregivers and aggressive youth can then return to the SODAS format to find another solution.

SODAS is an appropriate and effective intervention for both proactive and reactive aggression. With proactive aggressive kids, this problem-solving approach will most likely be a primary intervention; that is why it is included and discussed in this chapter. The SODAS process teaches proactive aggressive kids to become more empathetic and to begin thinking about how their aggression negatively affects others. In addition, these kids learn how to generate options that are nonaggressive , and how to improve rather than damage relationships. These, if you recall, are the main treatment goals for proactive aggression.

The principal treatment goal for reactive aggressive kids is to learn to stop their explosive reactions before they happen and to control their behaviors by using calming techniques. This will take a lot of time and effort, but once reactive aggressive kids have demonstrated they can do this, caregivers can add the SODAS problem-solving process to their Treatment Plans. Kids can use SODAS to help choose their preferred anger control strategy or how to avoid situations likely to trigger their aggression. The SODAS problem-solving method is a higher level skill for reactive aggressive kids that can and should be taught once the fundamental treatment goals are reached.

Learning to problem-solve is a complex task, but it is critical to an aggressive youth's eventual success. It is important that a youth can earn some type of reward to reinforce his or her cooperation and participation. Further, because aggressive youth have "solved" their problems in inappropriate ways in the past (running away, becoming angry), it is important to praise a youth when he or she indicates a desire to talk about a problem ("I have a problem at work. Can we talk about it?").

Using the entire SODAS process during a private counseling session is important in teaching rational problem-solving skills to aggressive youth. However, there are many other types of informal and formal ways to model and directly teach this problem-solving approach. For example, a caregiver and youth may be riding in a car together and observe a young person speed through an intersection, run a red light, and squeal his car's tires. At that point, the youth may say that she can hardly wait until she can have a car and be "bad." The caregiver could use this opportunity to ask the youth if she sees any problems (disadvantages) with running red lights or speeding. The caregiver also could ask the youth for ideas (options) about how to impress people with a car without engaging in unsafe or illegal activities. Such informal discussions can help aggressive youth learn to think ahead, get their needs met in appropriate ways, and connect their actions with future possible consequences. All these behaviors are keys to thinking and problem-solving.

Formal opportunities to use the SODAS method arise when an aggressive youth needs to develop a plan for the future. For example, planning for a career, employment, or college, or deciding how to develop an area of interest all lend themselves to the SODAS process.

There may be times when you will initiate a counseling session and use the SODAS process to help a youth develop a plan for more personal issues (making friends, personal hygiene, etc.). Take a future-oriented approach to these sessions, and be receptive to the youth's attempts to initiate sessions.

Problem-solving counseling has two important goals – to help aggressive youth arrive at sound solutions to their problems and to teach them how to solve problems in a systematic, rational way. The SODAS process, coupled with important quality components (empathy, listening skills, etc.) can help caregivers accomplish both goals.

Contracts

One effective way to change behavior with proactive aggressive children and adolescents is to use contracts. Basically, contracts are agreements between you and a youth that clearly spell out what the youth will earn from you when he or she behaves in certain ways. With contracts, privileges are contingent on specific behaviors you want to see from your kids. For example, you could tell a youth, "When you finish cleaning your room, you can go out and play." If you were to write down this proposal, you would make a contract. Contracts motivate children to try new strategies. No behavior changes without motivation.

Contracts have three main points: 1) specify the behavior the youth needs to change; 2) specify what positive consequences and privileges can be earned; and 3) specify how long the agreement is in effect. They can be used in a variety of situations, including:

> **When you want to focus on a particular aggressive behavior.** A child may frequently lose self-control, take things he or she wants from others, or yell and curse when asked to do something.

> **When a child has a goal in mind.** A child may want to work toward earning money for a new bike, having a later bedtime, or being allowed to go out with friends.

> **When you have a particular goal you'd like a youth to achieve.** You may want a youth to stop bullying younger children, decrease the number of times he or she loses self-control, decrease the severity of aggressive behaviors, or increase the number of positive comments the youth makes about others.

In each of these situations, a contract could be used to monitor and record the progress a youth makes toward a goal.

Here's how a contract might work with Jaydon, a thirteen-year-old boy who consistently bullies other children to get things he wants from them.

Jaydon's Contract

I, Jaydon, agree not to tease or bully other kids. That means I will not yell, verbally threaten, curse, hit, or punch others. I have to do this for two weeks in a row before I earn a later bedtime on the weekends. If I do bully and tease other kids during this time, I will have to go to bed one-half hour earlier the following two weekends. This contract starts today.

We (caregivers) agree to let Jaydon stay up until 11:30 p.m. on Friday and Saturday nights when he doesn't bully or tease other kids for two weeks in a row. We will mark the calendar each day that Jaydon doesn't bully or tease other kids. This will continue for two weeks or until the contract is renegotiated.

_____   _____
(Jaydon's signature)   (Date)

_____
(Caregivers' signature)

Mia's Contract

I, Mia, will help other kids or adults at least two times each day for the next ten days before I am able to rent a movie. This means that I will help others with their chores or homework, make positive and encouraging statements, find tasks to be done (like taking out the trash) without being asked, and help my caregivers with other tasks when they ask me without complaining or arguing. I understand that if I don't do this, I don't get to rent a movie.

We (caregivers) will let Mia rent a movie when she completes the agreement that is discussed here. We will go over Mia's helping behavior(s) each night. We will continue this contract for ten days.

_____   _____

(Mia's signature)   (Date)

_____

(Caregivers' signature)

Tips for Successful Contracts

> **State the goal positively.** Say "When you finish your homework, you can watch TV" instead of, "If you don't finish your homework, you won't get to watch TV." Both of these statements can be true, but it's easier to reach a goal if you're working toward something positive.

> **Follow through on the agreement.** Be sure to review your child's progress each day and provide encouragement to keep going. When a child reaches the goal, give what you promised. And pile on the praise!

> **Make the goals specific and measurable.** A goal of "completing homework each night" is easier to measure than a goal of "doing better in school." Likewise, it's easier to measure whether a child is "offering to help others once a day" than to measure whether he or she is "being more responsible." Being specific and clear helps you to know when your child has reached the goal.

> **Keep the goals reasonable.** Setting reachable goals is especially important when you are first introducing the idea of a contract.

> **Make it fun.** Using contracts to help kids reach goals and experience success is more enjoyable if it's fun for you and the child. Make a big deal out of each day's progress and use lots of praise as the child works toward the goal.

Contracts are a great way to help kids see the successes they achieve. They also open lines of communication so caregivers and children can work toward goals together. Identifying goals and planning requires conversation between the caregiver and child. For both to be winners, negotiation is necessary. The time spent setting up contracts shows kids that you care and are interested in helping them succeed.

Before kids get to do what they want, they have to keep their end of the bargain. Contracts are simple, straightforward, and geared toward helping caregivers and children make improvements and get things accomplished.

Other-Centered Rationales

Rationales are reasons that let youth know why they should use a particular skill or behavior. Rationales are important components of all the Boys Town Teaching Interactions because youngsters are much more likely to engage in positive behavior if they understand why it is important.

When you first begin working with aggressive youth, you will likely use rationales that let them know how they will personally benefit from using a skill or behavior correctly, or what negative consequences they might receive if they do not use the skill or behavior correctly. With proactive aggressive youth, it is essential to eventually move beyond using these two kinds of rationales and begin using other-centered rationales.

Other-centered rationales focus on how a youngster's behavior affects others. Using them creates great opportunities for developing morals and positive values in youth. Research shows that one of the best ways to teach morals and positive values is by using other-centered rationales. Saying things like, "When you hit someone, it hurts them," or "When you yell and curse at me, it hurts my feelings," are easy ways to let kids know that their aggressive behavior is harmful and that they need to be sensitive to others. Even though research shows that children don't develop moral reasoning until they are about seven years old (Piaget, 1932), they still benefit from hearing these rationales when they are very young. Frequently using other-centered rationales with proactive aggressive youth helps to create an atmosphere that teaches kids how valuable morals and high standards for behavior are. Kids must learn these important lessons in order to become respected and valued members of society.

Sample Treatment Plans

Now let's pull all this together. This section contains sample Treatment Plans for two proactive aggressive kids who are being treated in different settings. The first example takes place in a school setting; the second is in a residential group home environment. The two examples present a short summary of each youngster's behavioral and family history, and a completed Treatment Plan.

The information contained in each summary has been compiled through a comprehensive and careful evaluation process. Treatment strategies appear in bold type and specific social skills that are targeted for teaching appear in bold italic type so that you can see how they can be incorporated into a Treatment Plan.

Example 1

Robert is a twelve-year-old boy who lives at home with his mother and fifteen-year-old brother. Robert's father is currently in jail for assaulting a police officer. On numerous occasions when he was drunk, Robert's father beat Robert and his older brother. After one particularly severe beating, Robert was hospitalized for a week for treatment of three broken ribs.

After being evaluated by a mental health professional at the school's insistence, Robert was diagnosed with Attention-Deficit/Hyperactivity Disorder. He currently takes medication on a daily basis for this disorder. In situations that involve groups in school, Robert is easily distracted and overstimulated. He frequently does not pay attention during class activities and assignments, and repeatedly interrupts his teacher. Robert is fairly well-liked by other students, but has tremendous difficulty in his relationships with adults and in responding to their feedback or criticism. He also engages in activities without asking permission, which results in his teachers giving feedback and correction that is difficult for him to accept. When Robert's teachers correct him for his misbehavior or tell him "No," Robert regularly becomes verbally and physically aggressive. Typically, when Robert loses self-control in school, he immediately begins to argue loudly, swear, and throw his school supplies and books. On more than one occasion, these items have hit teachers, resulting in minor injuries. Robert's teachers have reported on several occasions that they have observed Robert smirking and laughing to himself on his way to the office after a situation where he lost self-control. In addition, Robert has been overheard telling other students things like, "Teachers are afraid of me" and "I've got these stupid teachers in my hip pocket."

Finally, Robert's teachers report that he "teases and bullies" other students – especially younger or smaller kids – when they have something he wants. Recently, Robert punched a younger boy in the face, breaking the boy's glasses and injuring his eye. Robert wanted the candy sale money the young boy had collected for the school's annual fund-raiser. Robert's Treatment Plan at school follows.

IEP Conference Form

DATE OF MEETING	1/1/20XX	SPECIAL EDUCATION VERIFICATION	OHI/ADHD	LAST MDT DATE	9/15/20XX

STUDENTS NAME	Robert Jones		DATE OF BIRTH	4/1/20XX	GRADE	6

PARENT / GUARDIAN	John and Jane Jones	PARENT / GUARDIAN PHONE	123-456-7890

THE INDIVIDUAL EDUCATION TEAM INCLUDED THE FOLLOWING PARTICIPANTS IN ATTENDANCE:

Signature	Position / Relationship to Student	Date

☒ **YES** ☐ **NO**   The school district has taken necessary action to insure that I understand the proceedings of this IEP Conference (including arrangement for an interpreter, if appropriate).

☒ **YES** ☐ **NO**   I will receive a copy of the IEP.

_____   _____

PARENT SIGNATURE   DATE OF RECEIPT

Present Level of Educational Performance

Includes how the child's disability affects the child's involvement in and progress in the general curriculum or child's participation in appropriate activities.

ACADEMIC: Robert is currently enrolled in the 6th grade. According to the most current, testing Robert is functioning at grade level in all academic areas and, when his behavior is stable, he can participate in the general curriculum and general education classroom.

BEHAVIORAL: Robert has been diagnosed with Attention Deficit-Hyperactivity Disorder and qualifies as a student with an Other Health Impairment. Robert currently is taking the medication Adderall for this condition. Robert is easily distracted and over-stimulated in the educational environment. He frequently is off-task during classroom lectures and when asked to do independent assignments. Robert also frequently interrupts the teacher. He struggles with developing relationships with adults and often does not accept feedback and/or behavioral and academic correction. When frustrated Robert regularly becomes verbally and physically aggressive by swearing and throwing textbooks and other school supplies within his reach. These items on occasion have hit teachers.

X	Student's Strengths	Enjoys helping out in the classroom; is good with animals; is athletic; is motivated by point card
X	Parental information, including concerns for enhancing child's education	Parents are concerned with amount of time spent out of the classroom and possible escalation in assaultive behaviors
X	Results of initial or recent evaluation(s) (this should include not only a report of test scores, but an explanation of results).	
	If behavior impedes learning, consideration of appropriate behavioral strategies/LRE (Least Restrictive Environment)	LRE was reviewed and determined that Robert can continue in the regular education classroom with appropriate modifications and behavior interventions
X	If limited English proficient, consideration of language needs	N/A

	If blind or visually impaired, the IEP shall provide Braille instruction and the use of Braille, unless after an evaluation is determined the Braille, and the use of Braille is not appropriate for the child.	
	Considerations of the child's communication needs.	N/A
	For the children who are deaf or hard of hearing we have considered the following: *Child's language and communication needs.*	N/A
	Opportunities for direct communication with peers and professionals in the child's language and communication mode.	N/A
	Academic levels and opportunities for direct instruction in the child's language and communication mode.	N/A
	Consideration of the child's need for assistive technology service or device	N/A

An additional page should be used for each goal, and goals for transition services can be recorded on this page.

Baseline: Currently Robert is earning on average of 6 concerns per week in the area of *accepting feedback* from adults

Measurable Annual Goal: Robert will earn on average of 3 concerns per week in the area of *accepting feedback* in a 36-week period

Short-Term Objectives or Benchmarks (Each objective or benchmark should be related to enabling the youth to be involved in or progress in the general curriculum, and should be related to meeting each of the youth's other needs.)

1. Will use the skills steps of *Accepting Feedback* by looking at the person, saying "Okay," and not arguing.

2. Will use the skill of *Disagreeing Appropriately* when needing to disagree about a teacher or adult decision.

Progress Report

Schedule	(I) Evaluation Procedures	(II) Progress (date of review)				(III) Is Progress Sufficient to Achieve Annual Goal?			
4 times	A, C, I	INITIALS	INITIALS	INITIALS	INITIALS	INITIALS	INITIALS	INITIALS	INITIALS
		DATE	DATE	DATE	DATE	DATE	DATE	DATE	DATE
		CODE	CODE	CODE	CODE	CODE	CODE	CODE	CODE
Person responsible for reporting progress		Student, Classroom Teacher, Special Education Teacher							
Comments on student progress in meeting the goals or objectives/benchmarks									
Statement of how student's progress will be reported to parents: (i.e., progress reports, letters, phone calls, etc.)									

(I) Evaluation Procedures / Instruments
- A. Teacher Observation
- B. Written Performance
- C. Oral Performance
- D. Criterion Reference Test
- E. Guardian
- F. Parent Report
- G. Time Sample
- H. Report Card
- I. Point Card
- J. Other

(II) Progress Measurement
- A. Goal Met
- B. Progress Made, Goal Not Met
- C. Little or No Progress
- D. Other, Specify

(III) Is Progress Sufficient to Achieve Annual Goal?
- A. Yes
- B. No

Baseline: As measured by a time sample, Robert is currently on task in the classroom approximately 60% of the time.

Measurable Annual Goal: Robert will increase his time on task in the classroom to at least 75% in a 36-week period.

Short-Term Objectives or Benchmarks (Each objective or benchmark should be related to enabling the youth to be involved in or progress in the general curriculum, and should be related to meeting each of the youth's other needs.)

1. Robert will begin his assignment within five minutes after receiving the assignment.

2. Robert will remain on task for short intervals with small breaks between. He will work for 10 minutes and then receive a 5-minute break.

3. Robert will ask for help when he does not understand the expectations or assignment.

4. Robert will use the skill of *Getting Teacher's Attention* by: Looking at the person, raising hand, waiting to be called on, and using a pleasant voice tone.

Progress Report

Schedule	(I) Evaluation Procedures	(II) Progress (date of review)				(III) Is Progress Sufficient to Achieve Annual Goal?			
4 times yearly	A, G	INITIALS	INITIALS	INITIALS	INITIALS	INITIALS	INITIALS	INITIALS	INITIALS
		DATE	DATE	DATE	DATE	DATE	DATE	DATE	DATE
		CODE	CODE	CODE	CODE	CODE	CODE	CODE	CODE
Person responsible for reporting progress		Student, Classroom Teacher, Special Education Teacher							
Comments on student progress in meeting the goals or objectives/benchmarks									
Statement of how student's progress will be reported to parents: (i.e., progress reports, letters, phone calls, etc.)									

(I) Evaluation Procedures / Instruments
- A. Teacher Observation
- B. Written Performance
- C. Oral Performance
- D. Criterion Reference Test
- E. Guardian
- F. Parent Report
- G. Time Sample
- H. Report Card
- I. Point Card
- J. Other

(II) Progress Measurement
- A. Goal Met
- B. Progress Made, Goal Not Met
- C. Little or No Progress
- D. Other, Specify

(III) Is Progress Sufficient to Achieve Annual Goal?
- A. Yes
- B. No

Baseline: Robert has been referred to the office on average 6 times a quarter during the past school year.

Measurable Annual Goal: Robert will decrease his office referrals to on average 3 per quarter during the next school year.

Short-Term Objectives or Benchmarks (Each objective or benchmark should be related to enabling the youth to be involved in or progress in the general curriculum, and should be related to meeting each of the youth's other needs.)

1. Robert will use a *self-control strategy* in the classroom when frustrated (visual imagery, counting, deep breaths).

2. Robert will meet with the school social worker weekly.

3. Robert will use appropriate boundaries with peers and adults.

Progress Report

Schedule	(I) Evaluation Procedures	(II) Progress (date of review)				(III) Is Progress Sufficient to Achieve Annual Goal?			
4 times yearly	A, I	INITIALS	INITIALS	INITIALS	INITIALS	INITIALS	INITIALS	INITIALS	INITIALS
		DATE	DATE	DATE	DATE	DATE	DATE	DATE	DATE
		CODE	CODE	CODE	CODE	CODE	CODE	CODE	CODE
Person responsible for reporting progress		Student, Classroom Teacher, Special Education Teacher							
Comments on student progress in meeting the goals or objectives/benchmarks									
Statement of how student's progress will be reported to parents: (i.e., progress reports, letters, phone calls, etc.)									

(I) Evaluation Procedures / Instruments
- A. Teacher Observation
- B. Written Performance
- C. Oral Performance
- D. Criterion Reference Test
- E. Guardian
- F. Parent Report
- G. Time Sample
- H. Report Card
- I. Point Card
- J. Other

(II) Progress Measurement
- A. Goal Met
- B. Progress Made, Goal Not Met
- C. Little or No Progress
- D. Other, Specify

(III) Is Progress Sufficient to Achieve Annual Goal?
- A. Yes
- B. No

Transition

| Transition needs were considered but not needed due to student's age. |

___ Beginning at age 14 (or younger, if appropriate), updated annually, a statement of the child's transition services, focusing on his/her course of study.

_____

_____

___ Beginning at age 16 (or younger, if appropriate), updated annually, a statement of needed transition services (indicate the strengths and/or needs for each area):

Instruction: _____

_____

Related Services: _____

_____

Community Experiences: _____

_____

Development of Employment and Other Post-School Options:

_____

_____

*Daily Living Skills:*_____

_____

Functional Vocational Evaluation: _____

_____

Interagency Linkages and Responsibilities: _____

_____

Transition Activities	Agency Responsible	Date

Anticipated graduation date: _____
(must be provided at least 18 months prior to graduation)

Notice of transfer of rights provided: _____

Transfer of rights will occur at age _____. Date:_____

Services	Duration (starting and ending dates)	Location (regular class, resource room, etc.)	Frequency (times per day, days per week)	School Calendar Does service follow the school calendar?
Special Education	1/1/20XX- 1/1/20XX	95%	5 days per week	yes
Related Services ☐ Speech Therapy ☐ Reading Specialist ☒ Other	1/1/20XX- 1/1/20XX	School Counseling Areas	1 time per week for 45 min	yes
Assistive Technology				
Other, describe:				

**Program Modifications or Instructional Accommodations
(Please include assessment accommodations):**

Learning Environment	Methods and Materials	Assessment Accommodations
Learning Environment	**Methods and Materials**	**Assessment Accommodations**
☐ Use study carrels or proximity seating	☐ Use mnemonic devices	☒ Extended time
☐ Provide guidance and assistance on tasks	☐ Use visual and graphic representations	☐ Use of magnifying equipment
☒ Use small group instruction	☒ Provide written notes and outlines	☐ Give response orally
☐ Provide peer tutoring	☐ Highlight important concepts	☐ Mark in test booklet
☒ Use specialized behavior management procedures	☒ Repeat key material	☐ Large-print edition
☒ Use checklists, notebooks, or other on-task aide	☐ Increase hands-on concrete learning experiences	☐ Oral reading of directions
☐ Modify the physical setting	☐ Use alternative methods of providing information	☐ Clarification of directions
☐ Use study carrels or proximity seating	☒ Break lesson into smaller segments	☐ Point to response
☐ Test individually	☐ Allowing use of tape recorders or devices	☐ Other:
☐ Other	☐ Other	

Transportation:

Child qualifies for special education transportation: ☐ YES ☐ NO

If child qualifies, why:

- ☐   Child is below age five

- ☐   Child is required to attend a facility other than normal attendance facility

- ☐   Nature of the child's disability is such that special education transportation is required

If the child qualifies for special education transportation, please describe the plan for transportation, including any special conditions necessary for safe transport

Assessment	

☐ The child will participate in district-wide assessments
 	
  ☐ without accommodations
 	
  ☐ with accommodations, as specified	

☐ The child will not participate in the regular district-wide assessment for the following reasons:	
☐ The child will participate in the following alternate assessment:	

Extend School Year Special Education Services: ☒ YES ☐ NO

194

Example 2

Marie is a fifteen-year-old girl who has been in four out-of-home placements in four years. Currently, she is receiving treatment in a residential group home program. Marie has a history of being sexually abused by her natural father (who later committed suicide), and also by her stepfather. At age eleven, Marie became sexually active with older boys and currently displays an extremely advanced knowledge of sexual issues for her age. In social situations with adults and other kids, Marie demonstrates many pseudo-mature and overly sophisticated behaviors (e.g., too much make-up, making and laughing at sexual innuendoes and jokes, and others). In fact, Marie tends to treat adults as peers and is overly affectionate with them. Her male teachers at school have repeatedly expressed concerns about having Marie in class.

When confronted about these behaviors – as well as other problem behaviors like dishonesty, manipulation, and stealing – by her Family-Teachers in the group home, Marie becomes verbally and physically aggressive. Typically, she starts screaming and crying. But her Family-Teachers have observed that she can "turn the tears on and off like a faucet." Once Marie recognized that screaming and crying wouldn't help her to escape the consequences of her negative behaviors, she began threatening to kill herself by swallowing pills or drinking cleaning supplies. These self-harm threats have twice resulted in short stays at a secure inpatient psychiatric facility. Marie said she "hated being locked up," and didn't exhibit any aggressive or self-harm behavior while at the inpatient program. Marie's treatment team has concluded that in order to adequately help Marie with her sexual abuse issues, they must first address her self-harm issues and her aggression problem. Here we will deal with only her aggression issues.

Treatment Plan – Group Home Program

Name: Marie   **Motivation System:** Daily   **Date:** 4/1/20XX

Diagnostic/Referral Problem: Aggression

Target Skill #1: *Accepting Consequences*

Baseline: Percent of teaching to target skill per week = 12%

Frequency of problem behavior per week = 13 incidents

Percent of positive displayed skill per week = 15%

Problem Definition:

When given a consequence, Marie screams, curses, and begins to cry. She blames others for her behavior. Often, she becomes verbally abusive; this is more prevalent when she is not expecting a consequence (e.g., phone call from school about her negative behavior). Lately, she has begun making self-harm statements. These behaviors happen regardless of who gives the consequence or the amount of the consequence.

Long-Term Goal: Percent of teaching to target skill per week = 25%

Frequency of problem behavior per week = 0-1 incidents

Percent of positive displayed skill per week = 80%

Treatment Strategies:

Social Skill Teaching: 1) Quiz Marie on the components of *Accepting Consequences* two times per day; 2) **Proactive Teaching** session one time per day; 3) **Preventively prompt** before each consequence; 4) Spontaneously use Teaching Interactions for positive and negative behavior; 5) During Family Meeting, *Accepting Consequences* will be taught and reviewed a minimum of one time per week using the **SODAS** problem-solving method; 6) A **contract** will be drafted that specifically states that when Marie reduces the frequency of her problem behavior by one-half during any week, she will earn a predetermined "special."

Therapy: Marie will attend **individual therapy** with Dr. Smith once a week for one-half hour.

Medications: None at this time.

_____   _____
Youth   Family-Teacher

_____
Consultant

Treatment Plan – Group Home Program

Name: Marie   **Motivation System:** Daily   **Date:** 4/1/20XX

Diagnostic/Referral Problem: Aggression

Target Skill #2: *Accepting Decisions of Authority*

Baseline: Percent of teaching to target skill per week = 13%

Frequency of problem behavior per week = 23 incidents

Percent of positive displayed skill per week = 4%

Problem Definition:

When Marie is approached by an authority figure (e.g., parents, Family-Teachers, schoolteachers, youth managers, etc.) regarding a task to be done, a rule she broke, or an incident she was involved in, Marie frequently loses self-control. She begins by arguing; when she realizes she will not get her way, she escalates into shouting and cursing, and often becomes verbally aggressive. Lately, she has begun making self-harm statements.

Long-Term Goal: Percent of teaching to target skill per week = 25%

Frequency of problem behavior per week = 0-1 incidents

Percent of positive displayed skill per week = 80%

Treatment Strategies:

Social Skill Teaching: 1) Quiz Marie on the components of *Accepting Adult Authority* two times per day; 2) **Proactive Teaching** session one time per day; 3) **Preventively prompt** as situation demands; 4) Spontaneously use **Teaching Interactions** for positive and negative behavior; 5) During Family Meeting, *Accepting Adult Authority* will be taught and reviewed a minimum of one time per week using the **SODAS** method of problem-solving; 6) A **contract** will be drafted that specifically states that when Marie reduces the frequency of her problem behavior by one-half during any week, she will earn a predetermined "special." 7) A **work chore** jar will be used as a consequence for the times that Marie has problems in this targeted area.

Therapy: Marie will attend **individual therapy** with Dr. Smith once a week for one-half hour.

Medications: None at this time.

_____   _____
Youth   Family-Teacher

_____
Consultant

Treatment Plan – Group Home Program

Name: Marie   **Motivation System:** Daily   **Date:** 4/1/20XX

Diagnostic/Referral Problem: Aggression

Target Skill #3: *Expressing Feelings Appropriately*

Baseline: Percent of teaching to target skill per week = 7%

Frequency of problem behavior per week = 19 incidents

Percent of positive displayed skill per week = 4%

Problem Definition:

When confronted with situations that frustrate or upset her, Marie often loses self-control. She expresses how she feels by arguing and yelling. Frequently, she escalates her behavior to cursing and often becomes verbally abusive and verbally aggressive. Lately, she has made statements that she is going to hurt herself.

Long-Term Goal: Percent of teaching to target skill per week = 25%

Frequency of problem behavior per week = 0-1 incidents

Percent of positive displayed skill per week = 80%

Treatment Strategies:

Social Skill Teaching: 1) Quiz Marie on the components of *Expressing Feelings Appropriately* two times per day; 2) **Proactive Teaching** session one time per day; 3) **Preventively prompt** as situation demands; 4) Spontaneously use **Teaching Interactions** for positive and negative behavior; 5) During Family Meeting, *Expressing Feelings Appropriately* will be taught and reviewed a minimum of one time per week using the **SODAS** method of problem-solving; 6) **Other-centered rationales** will be used in the Teaching Interactions; 7) One day each month, Marie will participate in a **"good deed day"** with the other kids in the group home. This will involve activities like serving dinner at a homeless shelter, helping in a neighborhood cleanup, and so on.

Therapy: Marie will attend **individual therapy** with Dr. Smith once a week for one-half hour. Marie will keep a **"feelings log"** and share it with her Family-Teachers (and therapist) each night.

Medications: None at this time.

_____   _____
Youth   Family-Teacher

_____
Consultant

Summary

Individualizing treatment for every youngster in your care is essential if kids are to overcome their problems. The first step to individualizing treatment is to carefully and thoroughly complete an evaluation of a youngster's problem. Once this is done, a Treatment Plan can be tailored to match the needs of each child. Proactive aggressive children and adolescents have a unique set of issues and problems that require special attention and treatment. Some strategies that have proven effective for these kids include social skill instruction, work chores, the SODAS method of problem-solving, contracts, the use of other-centered rationales, and others. The appropriate use of several of these interventions is what helps make treatment effective and successful.

CHAPTER 12

Social Skills for Aggressive Youth

The charts in this chapter list social skills that can be taught as part of treatment for kids who tend to use either reactive aggressive behaviors or proactive aggressive behaviors. (For complete step-by-step breakdowns of these skills, please refer to *Teaching Social Skills to Youth: A Step-by-Step Guide to 182 Basic to Complex Skills Plus Helpful Teaching Techniques,* Dowd & Tierney, 2005.) There are two charts; one is labeled "Social Skills for Proactive Aggression" and the other is labeled "Social Skills for Reactive Aggression." As we've discussed throughout this book, once a caregiver evaluates and determines the type of aggressive behavior a child tends to display, he or she is better equipped to develop an effective, therapeutic, and successful Treatment Plan and to identify the social skills that will help the child move toward prosocial, appropriate behaviors.

The two charts are intended to be a resource and a guide for caregivers who are in the process of selecting and assigning appropriate social skills for teaching. Many of the social skills included in each chart overlap and can be used with proactive aggressive kids or reactive aggressive kids. However, many skills pertain specifically to behaviors typically exhibited by one type of youth or the other. Keep in mind that once you assess and diagnose a child's problem as either proactive or reactive aggression, and begin to utilize social skill instruction as a treatment strategy, any skill that needs to be taught should be taught, regardless of what chart it is in.

In the charts, skills are classified as basic, intermediate, advanced, or complex. Generally speaking, when caregivers first begin working with an aggressive youngster, the youth will need to learn the basic skills first. The basic skills are necessary building blocks; they provide a foundation for the other higher-level skills. Mastery of the basic skills improves the child's chances for successfully learning intermediate, advanced, and complex skills.

Social Skills for Proactive Aggression

Basic Skills Group

Accepting Criticism or a Consequence

Accepting "No" for an Answer

Disagreeing Appropriately

Following Instructions

Showing Respect

Showing Sensitivity to Others

Talking to Others

Intermediate Skills Group

Accepting Apologies from Others

Accepting Compliments

Accepting Consequences

Accepting Decisions of Authority

Asking for Clarification

Asking for Help

Checking In (or Checking Back)

Choosing Appropriate Words to Say

Complying with Reasonable Requests

Correcting Another Person (or Giving Criticism)

Following Rules

Getting Another Person's Attention

Getting the Teacher's Attention

Giving Compliments

Interrupting Appropriately

Listening to Others

Making an Apology

Making a Request (Asking a Favor)

Making Positive Statements about Others

Offering Assistance or Help

Participating in Activities

Reporting Other Youths' Behavior (Peer Reporting)

Resisting Peer Pressure

Saying "No" Assertively

Seeking Positive Attention

Showing Appreciation

Showing Interest

Using Appropriate Voice Tone

Structured Problem-Solving (SODAS)

Volunteering

Waiting Your Turn

Advanced Skills Group

Accepting Defeat or Loss

Accepting Help or Assistance

Accepting Winning Appropriately

Analyzing Skills Needed for Different Situations

Analyzing Social Situations

Borrowing from Others

Caring for Others' Property

Choosing Appropriate Friends

Communicating Honestly

Compromising with Others

Controlling Sexually Abusive Impulses toward Others

Controlling the Impulse to Lie

Controlling the Impulse to Steal

Cooperating with Others

Coping with Anger and Aggression from Others

Coping with Conflict

Dealing with Accusation

Dealing with Boredom

Dealing with Contradictory Messages

Dealing with Embarrassing Situations

Dealing with Failure

Dealing with Frustration

Dealing with Group Pressure

Dealing with Rejection

Delaying Gratification

Expressing Feelings Appropriately

Following Through on Agreement and Contracts

Giving Instructions

Giving Rationales

Interacting Appropriately with Members of the Opposite Sex

Keeping Property in Its Place

Making Decisions

Making New Friends

Making Restitution (Compensating)

Negotiating with Others

Persevering on Tasks and Projects

Preparing for a Stressful Conversation

Preventing Trouble with Others

Problem-Solving a Disagreement

Responding to Complaints

Responding to Others' Feelings

Responding to Teasing

Self-Correcting Own Behaviors

Self-Reporting Own Behaviors

Setting Appropriate Boundaries

Using Appropriate Humor

Using Appropriate Language

Using Relaxation Strategies

Using Self-Talk or Self-Instruction

Using Spontaneous Problem-Solving

Complex Skills Group

Altering One's Environment

Asking for Advice

Assessing Own Abilities

Being Assertive

Being Patient

Displaying Appropriate Control

Expressing Empathy and Understanding for Others

Formulating Strategies

Gathering Information

Laughing at Oneself

Maintaining Relationships

Making an Appropriate Complaint

Making Moral and Spiritual Decisions

Managing Stress

Planning Ahead

Recognizing Moods of Others

Resolving Conflicts

Stopping Negative or Harmful Thoughts

Tolerating Differences

Using Self-Monitoring and Self-Reflection

Social Skills for Reactive Aggression

Basic Skills Group

Accepting Criticism or a Consequence

Accepting "No" for an Answer

Following Instructions

Disagreeing Appropriately

Talking to Others

Showing Sensitivity to Others

Intermediate Skills Group

Accepting Compliments

Accepting Decisions of Authority

Asking for Clarification

Asking for Help

Choosing Appropriate Words to Say

Correcting Another Person (or Giving Criticism)

Following Rules

Getting Another Person's Attention

Getting the Teacher's Attention

Ignoring Distractions by Others

Interrupting Appropriately

Listening to Others

Making an Apology

Making a Request (Asking a Favor)

Making Positive Self-Statements

Reporting Other Youths' Behavior (or Peer Reporting)

Resisting Peer Pressure

Saying "No" Assertively

Seeking Positive Attention

Using Appropriate Voice Tone

Using Anger Control Strategies

Using Structured Problem-Solving (SODAS)

Waiting Your Turn

Advanced Skills Group

Accepting Defeat or Loss

Accepting Help or Assistance

Advocating for Oneself

Analyzing Skills Needed for Different Situations

Analyzing Social Situations

Choosing Appropriate Friends

Communicating Honestly

Compromising with Others

Controlling Emotions

Cooperating with Others

Coping with Anger and Aggression from Others

Coping with Change

Coping with Conflict

Coping with Sad Feelings (or Depression)

Dealing with an Accusation

Dealing with Being Left Out

Dealing with Contradictory Messages

Dealing with Embarrassing Situations

Dealing with Failure

Dealing with Fear

Dealing with Frustration

Dealing with Group Pressure

Dealing with Rejection

Delaying Gratification

Expressing Appropriate Affection

Expressing Feelings Appropriately

Expressing Pride in Accomplishments

Making Decisions

Making New Friends

Making Restitution (Compensating)

Negotiating with Others

Persevering on Tasks and Projects

Preparing for a Stressful Conversation

Preventing Trouble with Others

Problem-Solving a Disagreement

Responding to Complaints

Responding to Others' Feelings

Responding to Others' Humor

Responding to Teasing

Self-Correcting Own Behaviors

Setting Appropriate Boundaries

Sharing Attention with Others

Using Appropriate Language
Using Relaxation Strategies
Using Self-Talk or Self-Instruction
Using Spontaneous Problem-Solving

Complex Skills Group

Accepting Self
Altering One's Environment
Asking for Advice
Assessing Own Abilities
Being Assertive
Being Patient
Displaying Appropriate Control
Expressing Empathy and Understanding for Others
Expressing Grief
Formulating Strategies
Gathering Information
Identifying Own Feelings
Laughing at Oneself
Maintaining Relationships
Making an Appropriate Complaint
Making Moral and Spiritual Decisions
Managing Stress
Planning Ahead
Recognizing Moods of Others
Resolving Conflicts
Rewarding Yourself
Setting Goals
Stopping Negative or Harmful Thoughts
Using Self-Monitoring and Self-Reflection

LIMERICK
COUNTY LIBRARY

References

Ackerson, L. (1931). **Children's behavior problems** (Vol. 1). Chicago: University of Chicago Press.

Aten, J.D., & Leach, M.M. (2009). A primer on spirituality and mental health. In J.D. Aten & M.M. Leach (Eds.), **Spirituality and the therapeutic process: A comprehensive resource from intake to termination** (p. 12). Washington, DC: American Psychological Association.

Baer, D., Wolf, M., & Risley, T. (1968). Some current dimensions of applied behavior analysis. **Journal of Applied Behavior Analysis**, 1, 91-98.

Bedlington, M.M., Solnick, J.R., Braukmann, C.J., Kirigin, K.A., & Wolf, M.M. (1979, August). The correlation between some parenting behaviors, delinquency and youth satisfaction in Teaching-Family group homes. In J.R. Solnick (Chair), **Family interaction and deviant behavior.** Symposium conducted at the 87th Annual Convention of the American Psychological Association, New York.

Behar, D., & Stewart, M.A. (1982). Aggressive conduct disorder in children. **Acta Psychiatric Scandinavia, 65,** 210-220.

Blonigen, D.M., & Krueger, R.F. (2006). Human quantitative genetics of aggression. In R.J. Nelson (Ed.), **Biology of aggression** (pp. 20-37). New York, NY: Oxford University Press.

Bolton, J., & Graeve, S. (2005) **No Room for bullies: From the classroom to cyberspace.** Boys Town, NE: Boys Town Press.

Borum, R., & Verhaagen, D. (2006). **Assessing and managing violence risk in juveniles.** New York, NY: Guilford Press

Boys Town National Research Institute for Child and Family Studies. (2006a, April). **Boys Town residential data summary** (Tech, Rep. No. 011-06). Boys Town, NE: Author.

Boys Town National Research Institute for Child and Family Studies. (2006b). **Lasting results: Five-year follow-up study** (Brochure). Boys Town, NE: Author.

Braukmann, C.J., Kirigin, K.A., & Wolf, M.M. (1976). **Achievement place: The researcher's perspective.** Paper presented at the 84th Annual Convention of the American Psychological Association, Washington, DC.

Brown, G.L., Ebert, M.H., Goyer, P.F., Jimerson, D.C., Klein, W.J., Bunney, W.E., & Goodwin, F.K. (1982). Aggression, suicide and serotonin: Relationships to CSF amine metabolites. **American Journal of Psychiatry,** 139, 741-745.

Butts, J.A., Snyder, H.N., Finnegan, T.A., Augenbaugh, A.L., & Poole, R.S. (1996). **Juvenile court statistics 1994**. Washington, DC: Office of Juvenile Justice and Delinquency Prevention, U.S. Department of Justice.

Cadoret, R.J. (1978). Psychopathology in adopted-away offspring of biological parents with antisocial behavior. **Archives of General Psychiatry, 35,** 176-184.

Centers for Disease Control and Prevention. (2009). **Facts at a glance, Youth violence, Summer (On-line).** Available: http://www.cdc.gov/violenceprevention/pdf/YV-DataSheet-a.pdf.

Christiansen, K.O. (1974). Seriousness of criminality and concordance among Danish twins. In R. Hood (Ed.), **Crime, criminology and public policy** (pp. 63-67). London: Heinemann.

Cloninger, C.R., Reich, T., & Guze, S.B. (1978). Genetic-environmental interactions and antisocial behaviour. In R.D. Hare & D. Schalling (Eds.), **Psychopathic behaviour: Approaches to research** (pp. 225-237). Chichester, England: John Wiley & Sons.

Combs, M.L., & Slaby, D.A. (1977). Social skills training with children. In B.B. Lahey & A.E. Kazdin (Eds.), **Advances in clinical child psychology** (pp. 161-201). New York: Plenum Press.

Commission on Children At Risk (2003). **Hardwired to connect: The new scientific case for authoritative communities.** New York: Institute for American Values.

Crow, R. (1974). An adoption study of antisocial personality. **Archives of General Psychiatry, 31,** 785-791.

Dinkes, R., Kemp, J., & Baum, K. (2009). **Indicators of School Crime and Safety: 2008** (NCES 2009–022/NCJ 226343). National Center for Education Statistics, Institute of Education Sciences, U.S. Department of Education, and Bureau of Justice Statistics, Office of Justice Programs, U.S. Department of Justice. Washington, DC.

Dishion, T.J., & Dodge, K. A. (2005). Peer contagion in interventions for children and adolescents: Moving towards an understanding of the ecology and dynamics of change. **Journal of Abnormal Child Psychology, 33(3),** 395-400.

Dishion, T.J., Loeber, R., Stouthamer-Loeber, M., & Patterson, G.R. (1984). Skill deficits and male adolescent delinquency. **Journal of Abnormal Child Psychology, 12,** 37-54.

Dishion, T.J., & Patterson, G.R. (2006). The development and ecology of antisocial behavior. In D. Cicchetti & D. Cohen (Eds.), **Developmental psychopathology. Vol. 3: Risk, disorder, and adaptation** (Revised ed., pp. 503-541). New York: Wiley & Sons.

Dodge, K.A. (1991). The structure and function of reactive and proactive aggression. In D.J. Pepler and K.H. Rubin (Eds.), **The development and treatment of childhood aggression** (pp. 201-218). Hillsdale, NJ: Lawrence Erlbaum Associates, Inc.

Dowd, T., & Tierney, J. (2005). **Teaching social skills to youth: A step-by-step guide to 182 basic to complex skills plus helpful teaching techniques.** Boys Town, NE: Boys Town Press.

Edelbrock, C. (1983). **The antecedents of antisocial behavior: A cross-sectional analysis.** Unpublished manuscript, University of Pittsburgh School of Medicine.

Farrington, D.P. (1978). The family background of aggressive youths. In L.A. Hersov, M. Berger, & D. Schaffer (Eds.), **Aggressive and antisocial behavior in childhood and adolescence** (pp. 73-94). Oxford, England: Pergamon Press.

Federal Bureau of Investigation. (1996). **Crime in the United States 1995.** Washington, DC: Government Printing Office.

Fixsen, D.L., Blasé, K.A., Timbers, G.D., & Wolf, M.M. (2001). In search of program implementation: 792 replications of the Teaching Family Model. In G.A. Bernfeld, D.P. Farrington, & A.W. Leschied (Eds.), **Offender rehabilitation in practice: Implementing and evaluating effective programs** (pp. 149-166). New York: John Wiley & Sons Ltd.

Forgatch, D.P. (1988, February). **A social learning approach to family therapy.** Paper presented at the Taboroff Child and Adolescent Psychiatry Conference on Conduct Disorders in Children and Adolescents, Snowbird, UT.

Freedman, B.J., Rosenthal, L., Donahue, L.P. Jr., Schlundt, D.G., & McFall, R.M. (1978). A social-behavioral analysis of skill deficits in delinquent and nondelinquent adolescent boys. **Journal of Consulting and Clinical Psychology, 46,** 1448-1462.

Friman, P.C., Handwerk, M.L., Smith, G., Larzelere, R., Lucas, C.P., & Shaffer, D. (1998). **Clinical validity of the Diagnostic Interview Schedule for Children-Child (DISC:C): Determined conduct and oppositional defiant disorders.** Manuscript submitted to the **Psychological Assessment.**

Gilbert, G.M. (1957). A survey of "referral problems" in metropolitan child guidance centers. **Journal of Clinical Psychology, 13,** 37-42.

Glueck, S., & Glueck, E.T. (1950). **Unravelling juvenile delinquency.** Cambridge, MA: Harvard University Press.

Glueck, S., & Glueck, E.T. (1968). **Delinquents and nondelinquents in perspective.** Cambridge, MA: Harvard University Press.

Goldstein, A.P., & Keller, H. (1989). **Aggressive behavior: Assessment and intervention.** New York: Pergamon.

Goldstein, A.P., Sprafkin, R.R., Gershaw, N.J., & Klien, P. (1980). **Skillstreaming the adolescent: A structured learning approach to teaching prosocial skills.** Champaign, IL: Research Press.

Griffith, A.K. (in press). The use of behavioral parent training program for parents of adolescents. **Journal of At-Risk Issues.**

Grisso, T. (1996). Introduction: An interdisciplinary approach to understanding aggressive behavior in children. In C.F. Ferris & T. Grisso (Eds.), **Understanding aggressive behavior in children.** New York: The New York Academy of Sciences.

Handwerk, M.L., Smith, G.L., Thompson, R., Chmelka, M.B., Howard, B.K., & Daly, D.L. (2008). Psychotropic medication utilization at a group home residential care facility. In C. Newman, C.J. Liberton, K. Kutash, & R.M. Friedman (Eds.), **Proceedings of the 20th Annual Florida Mental Health Institute Research Conference. A system of care for children's mental health: Expanding the research base** (pp. 297-300). Tampa: University of South Florida.

Hardy, R. (1988). **Behavior analysis: A computer-based tutorial** (computer program). DePere, WI: St. Norbert College.

Hetherington, E.M., & Martin, B. (1979). Family interaction. In H.C. Quay & J.S. Werry (Eds.), **Psychopathological disorders of childhood,** 2nd ed., 247-302. New York: John Wiley & Sons.

Hirschi, T. (1969). **Causes of delinquency.** Berkeley: University of California Press.

Hirschi, T., & Hindeland, M.J. (1977). Intelligence and delinquency: A revisionist's review. **American Sociological Review, 42,** 571-587.

Horne, A.M., Raczynski, K., & Orpinas, P. (2008). A clinical laboratory approach to reducing bullying and aggression in schools and families. In L. L'Abate (Ed.), **Toward a science of clinical psychology: Laboratory evaluations and interventions** (pp. 117-131). New York: Nova Science Publishers, Inc.

Huefner, J.C., Handwerk, M.L., Ringle, J.L., & Field, C.E. (2009). Conduct disordered youth in group care: An examination of negative peer influence. **Journal of Child and Family Studies, 18(6),** 719-730.

Huefner, J.C., Ringle, J.L., Chmelka, M.B., & Ingram, S.D. (2007). Breaking the cycle of intergenerational abuse: The long-term impact of a residential care program. **Child Abuse & Neglect, 31,** 187-199.

Huefner, J.C., Spellman, D.F., & Thompson, R.W. (2009, August). Psychotropic medication utilization in two intensive residential programs. **Poster presented at the American Psychological Association Annual Convention,** Toronto, Ontario, Canada.

Kanfer, F.H., & Saslow, S. (1969). Behavioral diagnosis. In C.M. Franks (Ed.), **Behavior therapy: Appraisal and status** (pp. 417-444). New York: McGraw-Hill.

Kazdin, A.E. (1985). **Treatment of antisocial behavior in children and adolescents.** Homewood, IL: The Dorsey Press.

Kazdin, A.E. (1987). Treatment of antisocial behavior in children: Current status and future directions. **Psychological Bulletin, 102,** 187-203.

Klein, N.C., Alexander, J.F., & Parsons, B.Y. (1977). Impact of family system interventions on recidivism and sibling delinquency: A model of primary prevention and program evaluation. **Journal of Consulting and Clinical Psychology, 45,** 469-474.

Koenig, H.G. (2004). Religion, spirituality, and medicine: Research findings and implications for clinical practice. **Southern Medical Journal, 97,** 1194-1200.

Lange, A.J., & Jakubowski, P. (1976). **Responsible assertive behavior: Cognitive/behavioral procedures for trainers.** Champaign, IL: Research Press.

Larzelere, R.E., Daly, D.L., Davis, J.L., Chemelka, M.B., & Handwerk, M.L. (2004). Outcome evaluation of Boys Town's family home program. **Education and Treatment of Children, 27(2),** 130-149.

Ledingham, J.E., & Schwartzman, A.E. (1984). A 3-year follow-up of aggressive and withdrawn behavior in childhood: Preliminary findings. **Journal of Abnormal Child Psychology, 12,** 157-168.

Lesser, G.S. (1959). The relationships between various forms of aggression and popularity among lower-class children. **Journal of Educational Psychology, 50,** 20-25.

Loeber, R., & Hay, D. (1997). Key issues in the development of aggression and violence from childhood to early adulthood. **Annual Review in Psychology, 48,** 371-410.

Loeber, R. & Pardini, D. (2008). Neurobiology and the development of violence: common assumptions and controversies. **Philosophical Transactions of the Royal Society B, 363,** 2491-2503.

MacFarlane, J.W., Allen, L., & Honzik, M.P. (1954). **A developmental study of the behavior problems of normal children 21 months and 14 years.** Berkeley: University of California Press.

Maerov, S.L., Brummett, B., Patterson, G.R., & Reid, J.B. (1978). Coding of family interactions. In J.B. Reid (Ed.), **A social learning approach to family intervention** (pp. 21-37). Eugene, OR: Castalia.

Mattsson, A., Schalling, D., Olweus, D., Low, H., & Svensson, J. (1980). Plasma testosterone, aggressive behavior, and personality dimensions in young male delinquents. **Journal of the American Academy of Child Psychiatry, 19,** 476-490.

McCord, W., McCord, J., & Zola, J.K. (1959). **Origins of crime.** New York: Columbia University Press.

Mednick, S.A. (1978). You don't need a weatherman! In L. Otten (Ed.), **Colloquim on the correlates of crime and the determinants of criminal behavior** (pp. 133-151). Arlington, VA: MITRE.

Mednick, S.A., & Hutchings, B. (1978). Genetic and psychophysiological factors in asocial behaviour. In R.D. Hare & D. Schalling (Eds.), **Psychopathic behaviour: Approaches to research** (pp. 239-253). Chichester, England: John Wiley & Sons.

Murray-Close, D., & Ostrov, J.M. (2009). A longitudinal study of the forms and functions of aggressive behavior in early childhood. **Child Development, 80 (3),** 828-842.

Nye, F.I. (1958). **Family relationships and delinquent behavior.** New York: John Wiley & Sons.

Olweus, D. (1996). Bullying at school: Knowledge base and an effective intervention program. In C.F. Ferris & T. Grisso (Eds.), **Understanding aggressive behavior in children** (pp. 265-276). New York: The New York Academy of Sciences.

Patterson, G.R. (1971). **Applications of social learning to family life.** Champaign, IL: Research Press.

Patterson, G.R. (1982). **Coercive family process.** Eugene, OR: Castalia.

Patterson, G.R. (Ed.) (1990). **Depression and aggression in family interaction.** Hillsdale, NJ: Erlbaum.

Patterson, G.R., DeBaryshe, B.D., & Ramsey, E. (1989). A developmental perspective on antisocial behavior. **American Psychologist,** February, 329-335.

Patterson, G.R., Dishion, T.J., & Bank, L. (1984). Family interaction: A process model of deviancy training. **Aggressive Behavior, 10,** 253-267.

Patterson, G.R., Dishion, T.J., & Reid, J.B. (1989). **A social learning approach: Volume 4, a coercion model.** Eugene, OR: Castalia.

Patterson, G.R., & Forgatch, M. (1987). **Parents and adolescents: 1. Living together.** Eugene, OR: Castalia.

Patterson, G.R., Forgatch, M.S., Yoerger, K., & Stoolmiller, M. (1998). Variables that initiate and maintain an early-onset trajectory for juvenile offending. **Development and Psychopathology, 10,** 531-547.

Patterson, G.R., Shaw, D., Snyder, J., & Yoerger, K. (2005). Maternal ratings of growth in children's overt and covert antisocial behavior. **Aggressive Behavior, 31,** 473-484.

Patterson, G.R., & Stouthamer-Loeber, M. (1984). The correlation of family management practices and delinquency. **Child Development, 55,** 1299-1307.

Peter, V.J. (1999). **What makes Boys Town successful.** Boys Town, NE: Boys Town Press.

Piaget, J. (1932). **The moral judgment of the child.** New York: Harcourt Brace Jovanovich.

214

Puzzanchera, C. (2009). Juvenile Arrests 2007. **OJJDP Juvenile Justice Bulletin** (April). Available from URL: http://www.ncjrs.gov/pdffiles1/ojjdp/225344.pdf.

Raz, E. (1977). **The relationship of youth ratings and future delinquent behavior.** Unpublished master's thesis. Lawrence, KS: University of Kansas.

Reiss, A.J., & Roth, J.A. (Eds.). (1993). **Understanding and preventing violence.** Washington, DC: National Academy Press.

Ringle, J.L., Chmelka, B., Ingram, S., & Huefner, J. (2006, February) **The sixteen-year post-discharge Boys Town study: Positive outcomes for behaviorally and emotionally troubled youth.** Poster presented at the Midwest Symposium for Leadership in Behavior Disorders, Kansas City, MO.

Ringle, J.L., Kingsley, D., Ingram, S., Chmelka, B., & Thompson, R.W. (2007, November). **Using Cox Regression Modeling to predict recidivism for youth departing out-of-home care: Implications for program evaluation and treatment of at-risk youth.** Paper presented at the American Evaluation Conference, Baltimore, MD.

Risley, T.R. (2005). Montrose M. Wolf (1935-2004). **Journal of Applied Behavior Analysis, 38(2),** 279-287.

Robins, L.N. (1966). **Deviant children grown up.** Baltimore: Williams & Wilkins.

Robins, L.N. (1978). Sturdy childhood predictors of adult antisocial behavior: Replications from longitudinal studies. **Psychological Medicine, 8,** 611-622.

Roosa, J.B. (1973). **SOCS: Situations, options, consequences, simulation: A technique for teaching social interactions.** Unpublished paper presented to the American Psychological Association, Montreal.

Ruma, P.R., Burke, R.V., & Thompson, R.W. (1996). **Group parent training: Is it effective for children of all ages?** Behavior Therapy, 27, 159-169.

Rutter, M., & Giller, H. (1983). **Juvenile delinquency: Trends and perspectives.** New York: Penguin Books.

Rutter, M., Tizard, J., & Whitmore, K. (Eds.) (1970). **Education, health and behavior.** London: Longmans.

Sheard, M.H. (1975). Lithium in the treatment of aggression. **Journal of Nervous and Mental Disease, 160,** 108-118.

Sickmund, M., Snyder, H.N., & Poe-Yamagata, E. (1997). **Juvenile offenders and victims: 1997 update on violence.** Washington, DC: Office of Juvenile Justice and Delinquency Prevention.

Snyder, J., Dishion, T.J., & Patterson, G.R. (1986). Determinants and consequences of associating with deviant peers during preadolescence and adolescence. **Journal of Early Adolescence, 6,** 29-43.

Stumphauzer, J.S. (1986). **Helping delinquents change: A treatment manual of social learning approaches.** New York: Haworth Press.

Sturge, C. (1982). Reading retardation and antisocial behavior. **Journal of Child Psychology and Psychiatry, 23,** 21-31.

Thompson, R.W., Ruma, P.R., Brewster, A.L., Besetsney, L.K., & Burke, R.V. (1997). Evaluation of an Air Force Physical Abuse Prevention Project using the reliable change index. **Journal of Child and Family Studies,** 6, 421-434.

Thompson, R.W., Ruma, P.R., Schuchmann, L.P., & Burke, R.V. (1996). A cost-effectiveness evaluation of parent training. **Journal of Child and Family Studies,** 5, 415-429.

Thompson, R.W., & Teare, J.F. (1997, June). **Measuring outcomes across a continuum of programs in the managed care environment.** Paper presented at the Professional Child Care Conference, Boys Town, NE.

Thompson, R.W., Ringle, J.L., & Kingsley, D. (2007, November). **Applying Cox Regression to evaluation of post-treatment studies of the teaching family model.** Paper presented at the Teaching-Family Association 30th Annual Conference, Washington, D.C.

Thompson, R.W., Smith, G.L., Osgood, D.W., Dowd, T.P., Friman, P.C., & Daly, D.L. (1996). Residential care: A study of short- and long-term educational effects. **Children and Youth Services Review, 18,** 221-242.

U.S. Department of Health and Human Services. (2001) **Youth violence: A report of the Surgeon General.** This report was retrieved from http://www.surgeon-general.gov/library/youthviolence/toc.html.

U.S. Department of Health and Human Services. (2007). **Youth violence: A report of the Surgeon General.** The information was retrieved from http://www.surgeongeneral.gov/library/youthviolence/messages.htm.

Wadsworth, M. (1979). **Roots of delinquency: Infancy, adolescence and crime.** New York: Barnes & Noble.

Werry, J.S., & Quay, H.C. (1971). The prevalence of behavior symptoms in younger elementary school children. **American Journal of Orthopsychiatry, 41,** 136-143.

West, D.J. (1982). **Delinquency: Its roots, careers and prospects.** Cambridge, MA: Harvard University Press.

Willner, A.G., Braukmann, C.J., Kirigin, K.A., Fixsen, D.L., Phillips, E.L., & Wolf, M.M. (1975, September). Training and validation: Youth preferred social behavior with child care personnel. In C.J. Braukmann (chair), **New directions in behavioral group home research.** Symposium conducted at the 83rd Annual Convention of the American Psychological Association, Chicago.

Wolf, M.M., Kirigin, K.A., Fixsen, D.L., Blasé, K.A., & Braukmann, C.J. (1995). The teaching-family model: A case study in data-based program development and refinement (and dragon wrestling). **Journal of Organizational Behavior Management, 15(1/2),** 11-68.

Wolfgang, M.E., Figlio, R., & Sellin, T. (1972). **Delinquency in a birth cohort.** Chicago: University of Chicago Press.

Wood, M.M., & Long, N.J. (1991). **Life space intervention.** Austin, TX: PRO-ED, Inc.

Index

220